RYAN **PARROTT** • FRANCESCO **MORTARINO** • MARCO **RENNA**
RAÚL **ANGULO** • SARA **ANTONELLINI**

# POWER RANGERS

## VOLUME FOUR

Published by

SERIES DESIGNER
**MADISON GOYETTE**

COLLECTION DESIGNER
**VERONICA GUTIERREZ**

ASSISTANT EDITOR
**GWEN WALLER**

EDITOR
**DAFNA PLEBAN**

HASBRO SPECIAL THANKS
**ED LANE**, **TAYLA REO**,
AND **MICHAEL KELLY**

**Ross Richie** Chairman & Founder
**Jen Harned** CFO
**Matt Gagnon** Editor-in-Chief
**Filip Sablik** President, Publishing & Marketing
**Stephen Christy** President, Development
**Lance Kreiter** Vice President, Licensing & Merchandising
**Bryce Carlson** Vice President, Editorial & Creative Strategy
**Hunter Gorinson** Vice President, Business Development
**Josh Hayes** Vice President, Sales
**Ryan Matsunaga** Director, Marketing
**Stephanie Lazarski** Director, Operations
**Elyse Strandberg** Manager, Finance
**Michelle Ankley** Manager, Production Design
**Cheryl Parker** Manager, Human Resources
**Sierra Hahn** Executive Editor
**Eric Harburn** Executive Editor
**Dafna Pleban** Senior Editor
**Elizabeth Brei** Editor
**Kathleen Wisneski** Editor
**Sophie Philips-Roberts** Editor
**Allyson Gronowitz** Associate Editor
**Gavin Gronenthal** Assistant Editor
**Gwen Waller** Assistant Editor
**Ramiro Portnoy** Assistant Editor
**Kenzie Rzonca** Assistant Editor
**Rey Netschke** Editorial Assistant
**Marie Krupina** Design Lead
**Crystal White** Design Lead
**Grace Park** Design Coordinator
**Madison Goyette** Production Designer
**Veronica Gutierrez** Production Designer
**Jessy Gould** Production Designer
**Nancy Mojica** Production Designer
**Samantha Knapp** Production Design Assistant
**Esther Kim** Marketing Lead
**Breanna Sarpy** Marketing Lead, Digital
**Amanda Lawson** Marketing Coordinator
**Alex Lorenzen** Marketing Coordinator, Copywriter
**Grecia Martinez** Marketing Assistant, Digital
**José Meza** Consumer Sales Lead
**Ashley Troub** Consumer Sales Coordinator
**Morgan Perry** Retail Sales Lead
**Harley Salbacka** Sales Coordinator
**Megan Christopher** Operations Lead
**Rodrigo Hernandez** Operations Coordinator
**Jason Lee** Senior Accountant
**Sabrina Lesin** Accounting Assistant

Licensed by:

WRITTEN BY
**RYAN PARROTT**

ILLUSTRATED BY
**FRANCESCO MORTARINO**
WITH INK ASSISTANCE BY **CHRISTIAN PRUNESTI**
**MARCO RENNA** (CHAPTER 15)

COLORS BY
**RAÚL ANGULO**
**& SARA ANTONELLINI** (CHAPTER 15)

LETTERS BY
**ED DUKESHIRE**

COVER BY
**GERALD PAREL**

FERAL DRAKKON, EMPYREALS, & ELTARIAN
CHARACTER DESIGNS BY
**DAN MORA**

# CHAPTER THIRTEEN

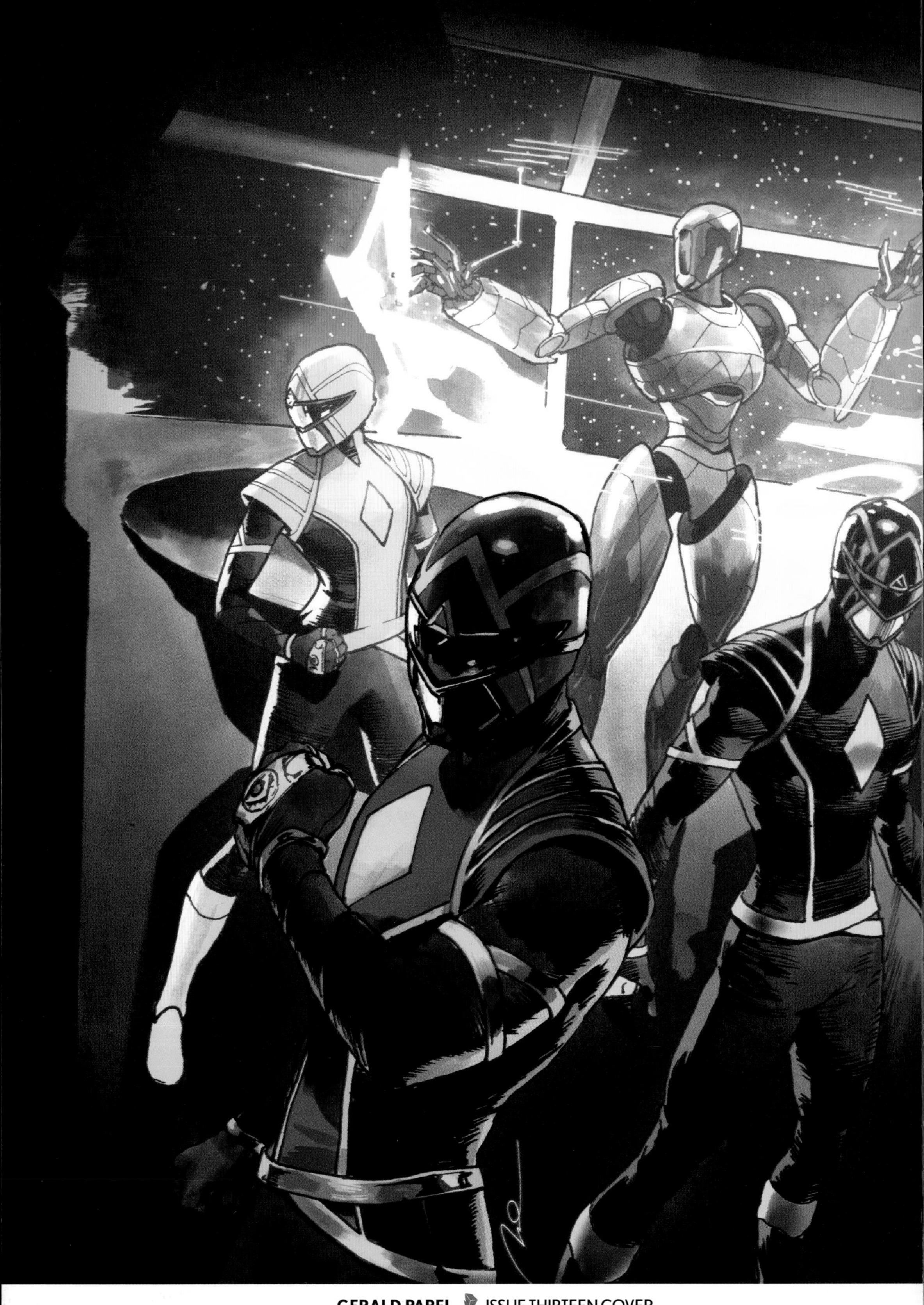

GERALD PAREL | ISSUE THIRTEEN COVER

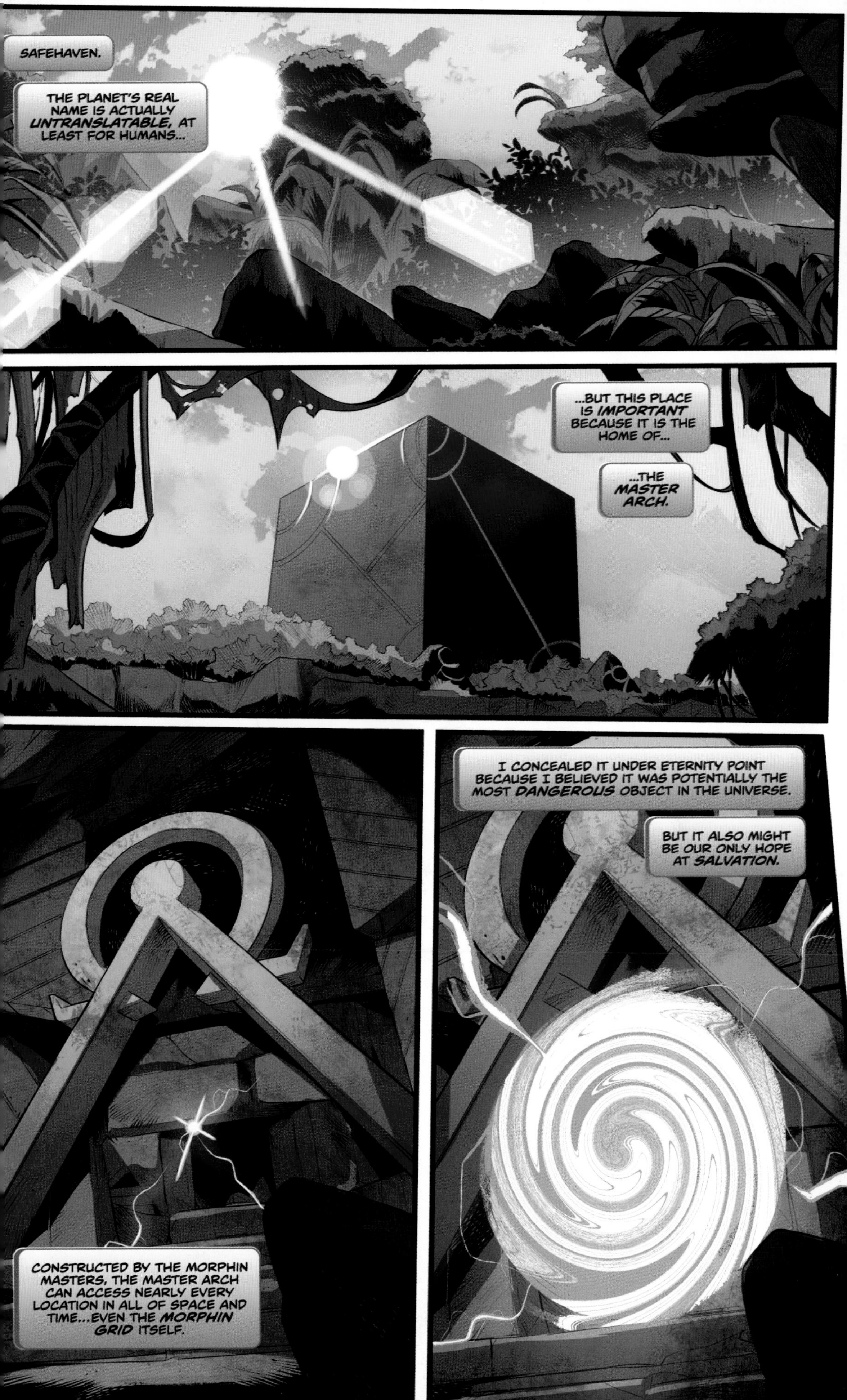
SAFEHAVEN.
THE PLANET'S REAL NAME IS ACTUALLY UNTRANSLATABLE, AT LEAST FOR HUMANS...
...BUT THIS PLACE IS IMPORTANT BECAUSE IT IS THE HOME OF...
...THE MASTER ARCH.
CONSTRUCTED BY THE MORPHIN MASTERS, THE MASTER ARCH CAN ACCESS NEARLY EVERY LOCATION IN ALL OF SPACE AND TIME...EVEN THE MORPHIN GRID ITSELF.
I CONCEALED IT UNDER ETERNITY POINT BECAUSE I BELIEVED IT WAS POTENTIALLY THE MOST DANGEROUS OBJECT IN THE UNIVERSE.
BUT IT ALSO MIGHT BE OUR ONLY HOPE AT SALVATION.

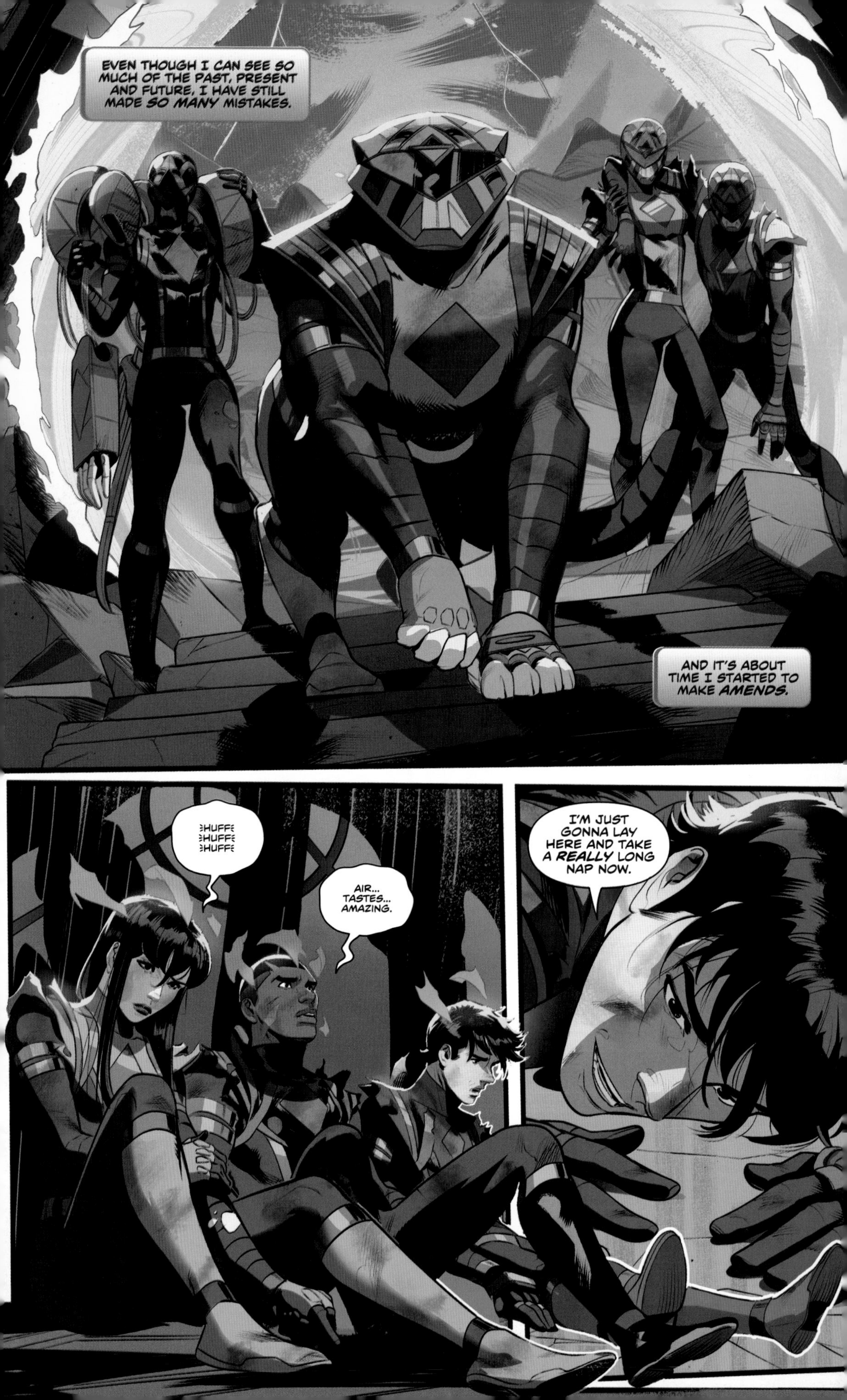
EVEN THOUGH I CAN SEE SO MUCH OF THE PAST, PRESENT AND FUTURE, I HAVE STILL MADE SO MANY MISTAKES.
AND IT'S ABOUT TIME I STARTED TO MAKE AMENDS.
HUFF HUFF HUFF
AIR... TASTES... AMAZING.
I'M JUST GONNA LAY HERE AND TAKE A REALLY LONG NAP NOW.

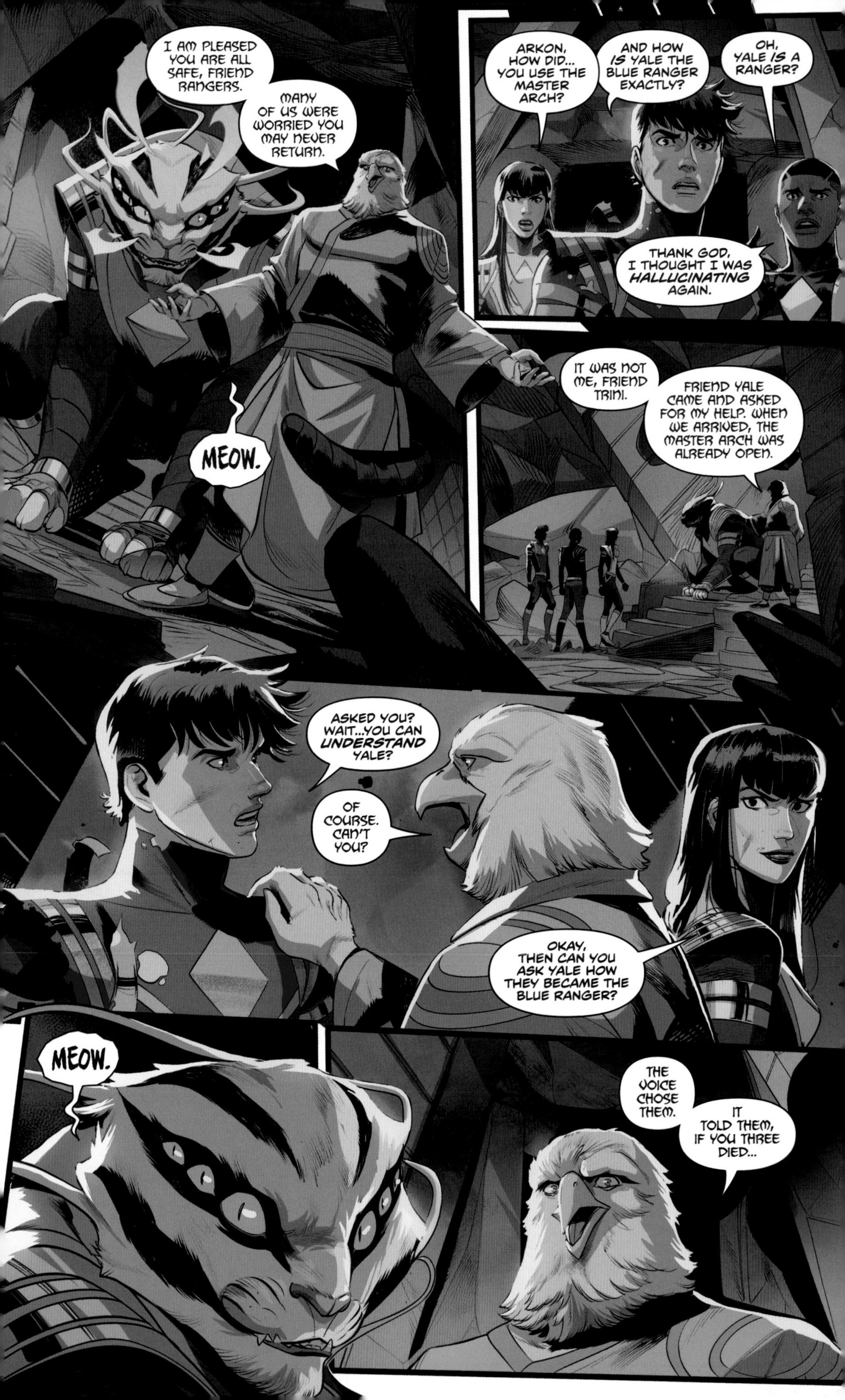
I AM PLEASED YOU ARE ALL SAFE, FRIEND RANGERS.
MANY OF US WERE WORRIED YOU MAY NEVER RETURN.
MEOW.
ARKON, HOW DID... YOU USE THE MASTER ARCH?
AND HOW *IS* YALE THE BLUE RANGER EXACTLY?
OH, YALE *IS* A RANGER?
THANK GOD, I THOUGHT I WAS ***HALLUCINATING*** AGAIN.
IT WAS NOT ME, FRIEND TRINI.
FRIEND YALE CAME AND ASKED FOR MY HELP. WHEN WE ARRIVED, THE MASTER ARCH WAS ALREADY OPEN.
ASKED YOU? WAIT...YOU CAN ***UNDERSTAND*** YALE?
OF COURSE. CAN'T YOU?
OKAY, THEN CAN YOU ASK YALE HOW THEY BECAME THE BLUE RANGER?
MEOW.
THE VOICE CHOSE THEM.
IT TOLD THEM, IF YOU THREE DIED...

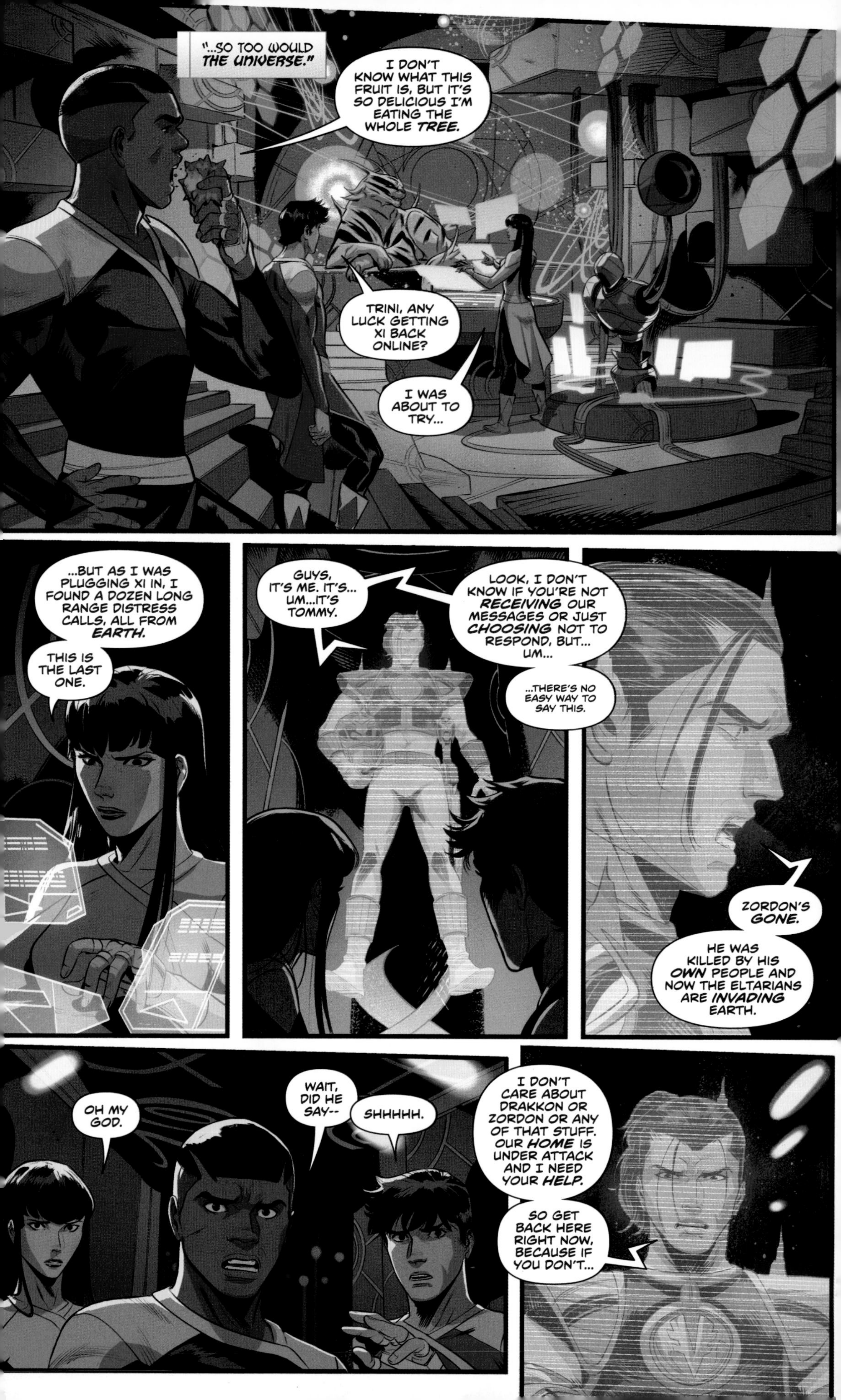
"...SO TOO WOULD THE UNIVERSE."
I DON'T KNOW WHAT THIS FRUIT IS, BUT IT'S SO DELICIOUS I'M EATING THE WHOLE TREE.
TRINI, ANY LUCK GETTING XI BACK ONLINE?
I WAS ABOUT TO TRY...
...BUT AS I WAS PLUGGING XI IN, I FOUND A DOZEN LONG RANGE DISTRESS CALLS, ALL FROM EARTH.
THIS IS THE LAST ONE.
GUYS, IT'S ME. IT'S... UM...IT'S TOMMY.
LOOK, I DON'T KNOW IF YOU'RE NOT RECEIVING OUR MESSAGES OR JUST CHOOSING NOT TO RESPOND, BUT... UM...
...THERE'S NO EASY WAY TO SAY THIS.
ZORDON'S GONE.
HE WAS KILLED BY HIS OWN PEOPLE AND NOW THE ELTARIANS ARE INVADING EARTH.
OH MY GOD.
WAIT, DID HE SAY--
SHHHHH.
I DON'T CARE ABOUT DRAKKON OR ZORDON OR ANY OF THAT STUFF. OUR HOME IS UNDER ATTACK AND I NEED YOUR HELP.
SO GET BACK HERE RIGHT NOW, BECAUSE IF YOU DON'T...

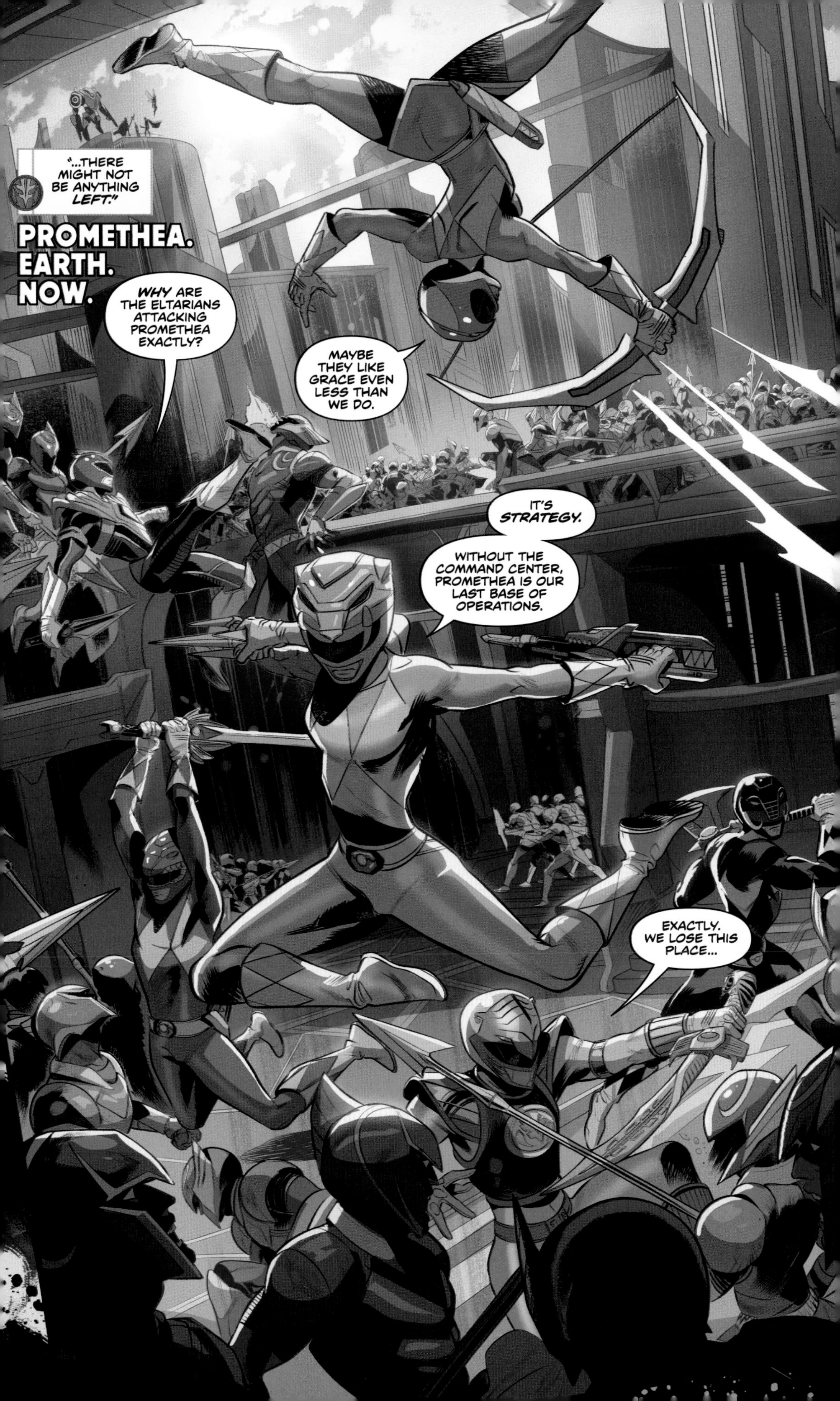
"...THERE MIGHT NOT BE ANYTHING *LEFT*."
PROMETHEA. EARTH. NOW.
*WHY* ARE THE ELTARIANS ATTACKING PROMETHEA EXACTLY?
MAYBE THEY LIKE GRACE EVEN LESS THAN WE DO.
IT'S *STRATEGY*.
WITHOUT THE COMMAND CENTER, PROMETHEA IS OUR LAST BASE OF OPERATIONS.
EXACTLY. WE LOSE THIS PLACE...

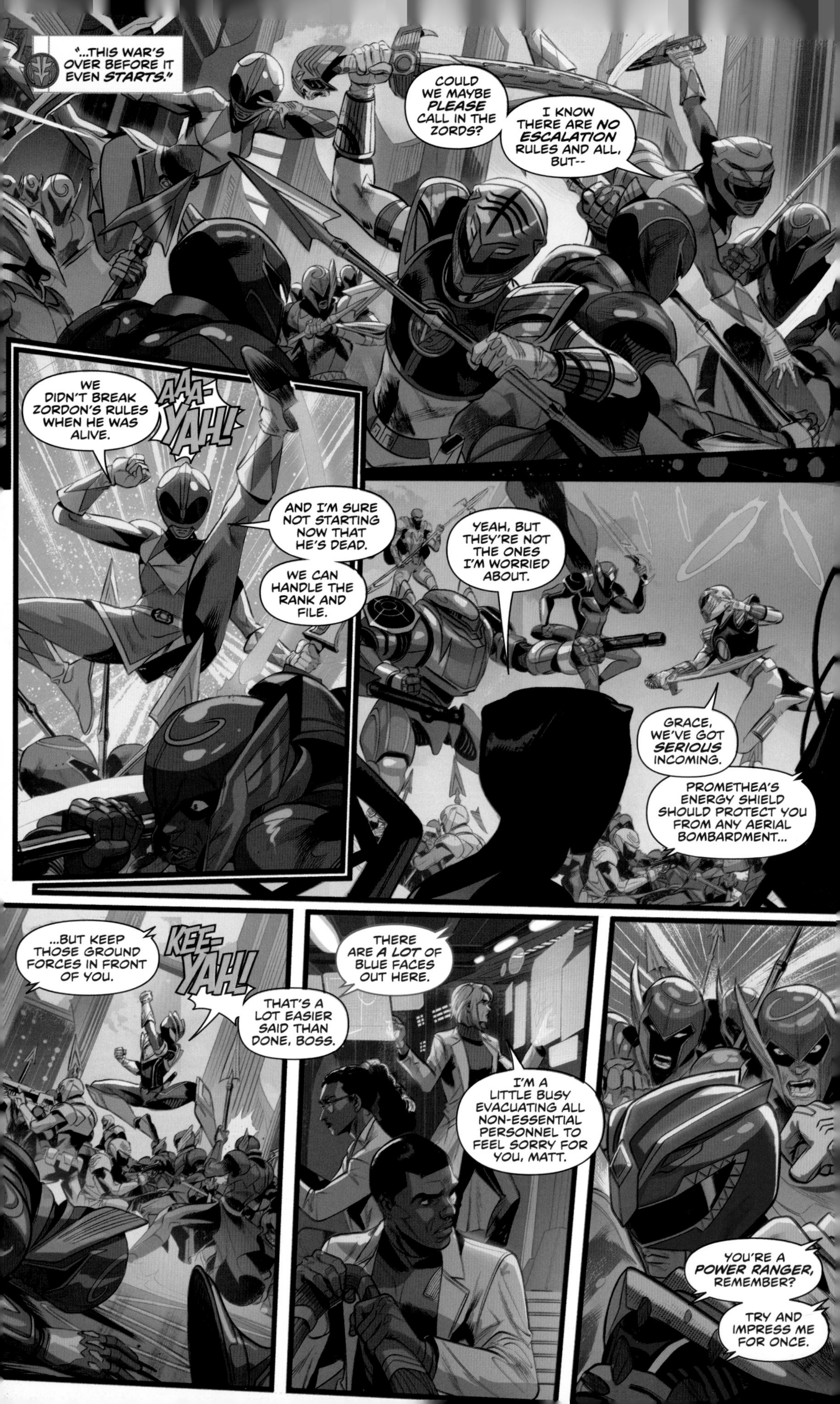

"...THIS WAR'S OVER BEFORE IT EVEN *STARTS.*"
COULD WE MAYBE *PLEASE* CALL IN THE ZORDS?
I KNOW THERE ARE *NO ESCALATION* RULES AND ALL, BUT--
WE DIDN'T BREAK ZORDON'S RULES WHEN HE WAS ALIVE.
AAA-YAH!
AND I'M SURE NOT STARTING NOW THAT HE'S DEAD.
WE CAN HANDLE THE RANK AND FILE.
YEAH, BUT THEY'RE NOT THE ONES I'M WORRIED ABOUT.
GRACE, WE'VE GOT *SERIOUS* INCOMING.
PROMETHEA'S ENERGY SHIELD SHOULD PROTECT YOU FROM ANY AERIAL BOMBARDMENT...
...BUT KEEP THOSE GROUND FORCES IN FRONT OF YOU.
KEE-YAH!
THAT'S A LOT EASIER SAID THAN DONE, BOSS.
THERE ARE *A LOT* OF BLUE FACES OUT HERE.
I'M A LITTLE BUSY EVACUATING ALL NON-ESSENTIAL PERSONNEL TO FEEL SORRY FOR YOU, MATT.
YOU'RE A *POWER RANGER,* REMEMBER?
TRY AND IMPRESS ME FOR ONCE.

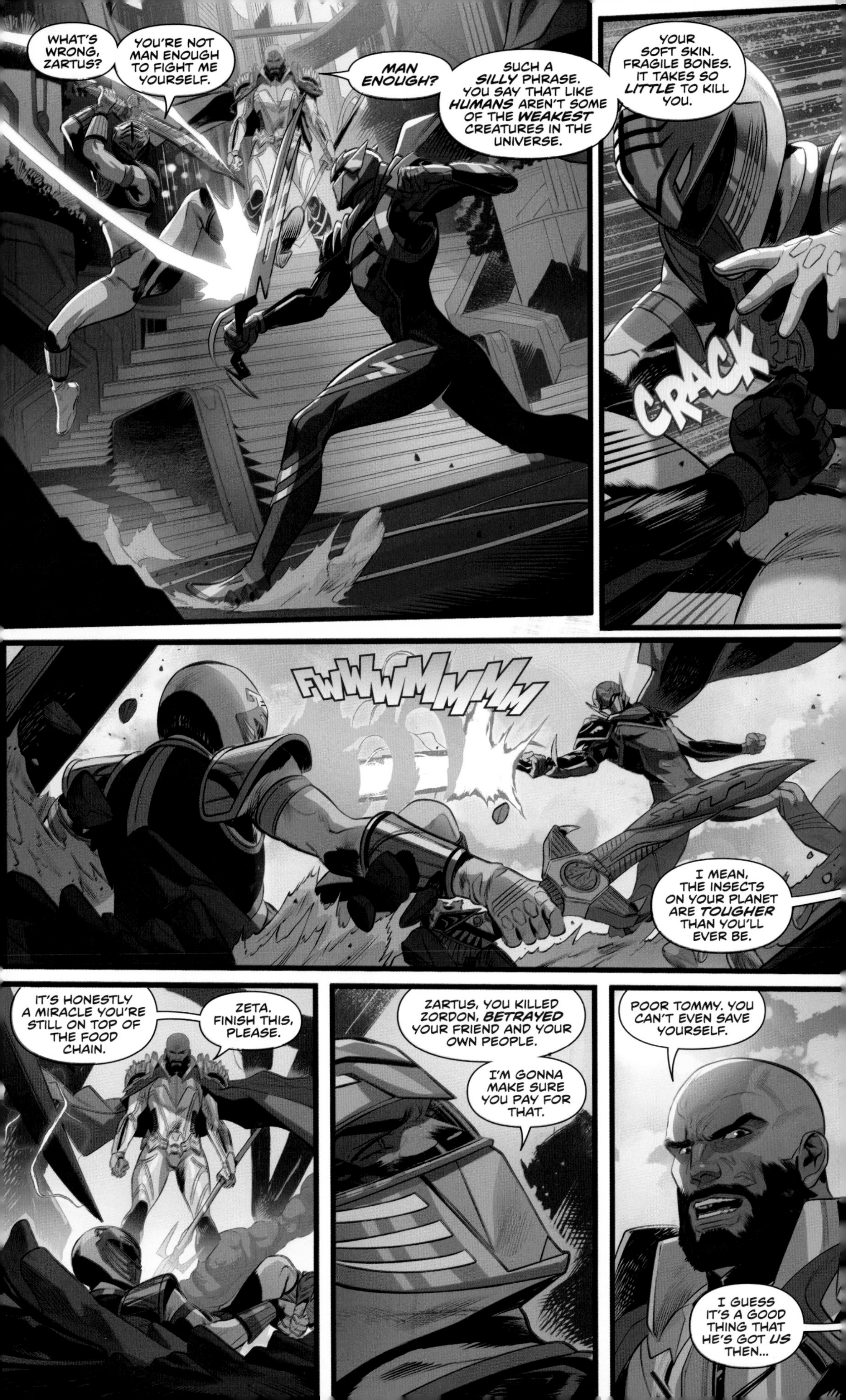
WHAT'S WRONG, ZARTUS?
YOU'RE NOT MAN ENOUGH TO FIGHT ME YOURSELF.
MAN ENOUGH?
SUCH A SILLY PHRASE. YOU SAY THAT LIKE HUMANS AREN'T SOME OF THE WEAKEST CREATURES IN THE UNIVERSE.
YOUR SOFT SKIN. FRAGILE BONES. IT TAKES SO LITTLE TO KILL YOU.
CRACK
FWWWMMMM
I MEAN, THE INSECTS ON YOUR PLANET ARE TOUGHER THAN YOU'LL EVER BE.
IT'S HONESTLY A MIRACLE YOU'RE STILL ON TOP OF THE FOOD CHAIN.
ZETA. FINISH THIS, PLEASE.
ZARTUS, YOU KILLED ZORDON, BETRAYED YOUR FRIEND AND YOUR OWN PEOPLE.
I'M GONNA MAKE SURE YOU PAY FOR THAT.
POOR TOMMY. YOU CAN'T EVEN SAVE YOURSELF.
I GUESS IT'S A GOOD THING THAT HE'S GOT US THEN...

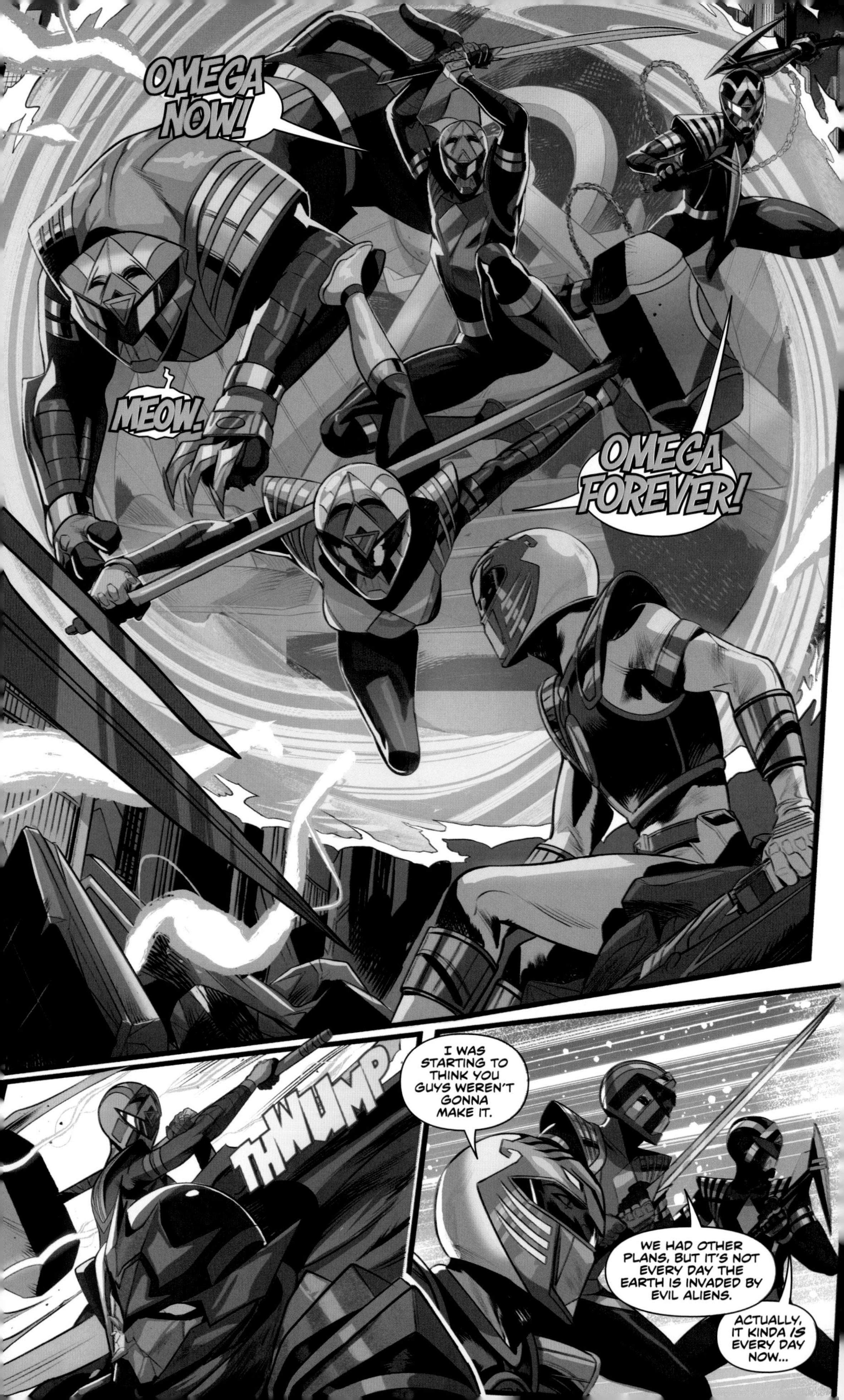
OMEGA NOW!
MEOW.
OMEGA FOREVER!
THWUMP!
I WAS STARTING TO THINK YOU GUYS WEREN'T GONNA MAKE IT.
WE HAD OTHER PLANS, BUT IT'S NOT EVERY DAY THE EARTH IS INVADED BY EVIL ALIENS.
ACTUALLY, IT KINDA *IS* EVERY DAY NOW...

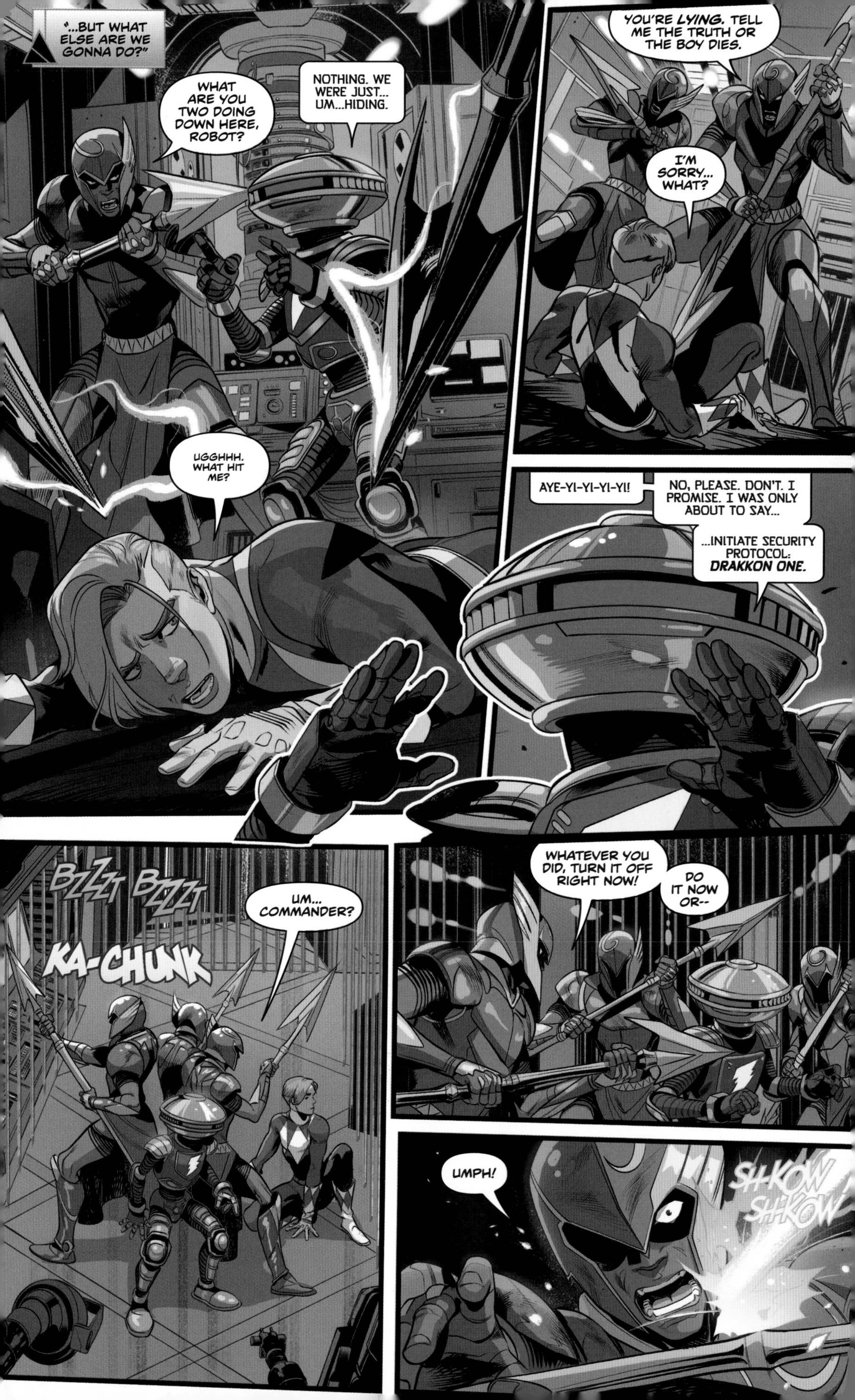
"...BUT WHAT ELSE ARE WE GONNA DO?"
WHAT ARE YOU TWO DOING DOWN HERE, ROBOT?
NOTHING. WE WERE JUST... UM...HIDING.
UGGHHH. WHAT HIT ME?
YOU'RE *LYING*. TELL ME THE TRUTH OR THE BOY DIES.
I'M SORRY... WHAT?
AYE-YI-YI-YI-YI!
NO, PLEASE. DON'T. I PROMISE. I WAS ONLY ABOUT TO SAY...
...INITIATE SECURITY PROTOCOL: **DRAKKON ONE.**
BZZZT BZZZT
KA-CHUNK
UM... COMMANDER?
WHATEVER YOU DID, TURN IT OFF RIGHT NOW!
DO IT NOW OR--
UMPH!
SH-KOW SH-KOW

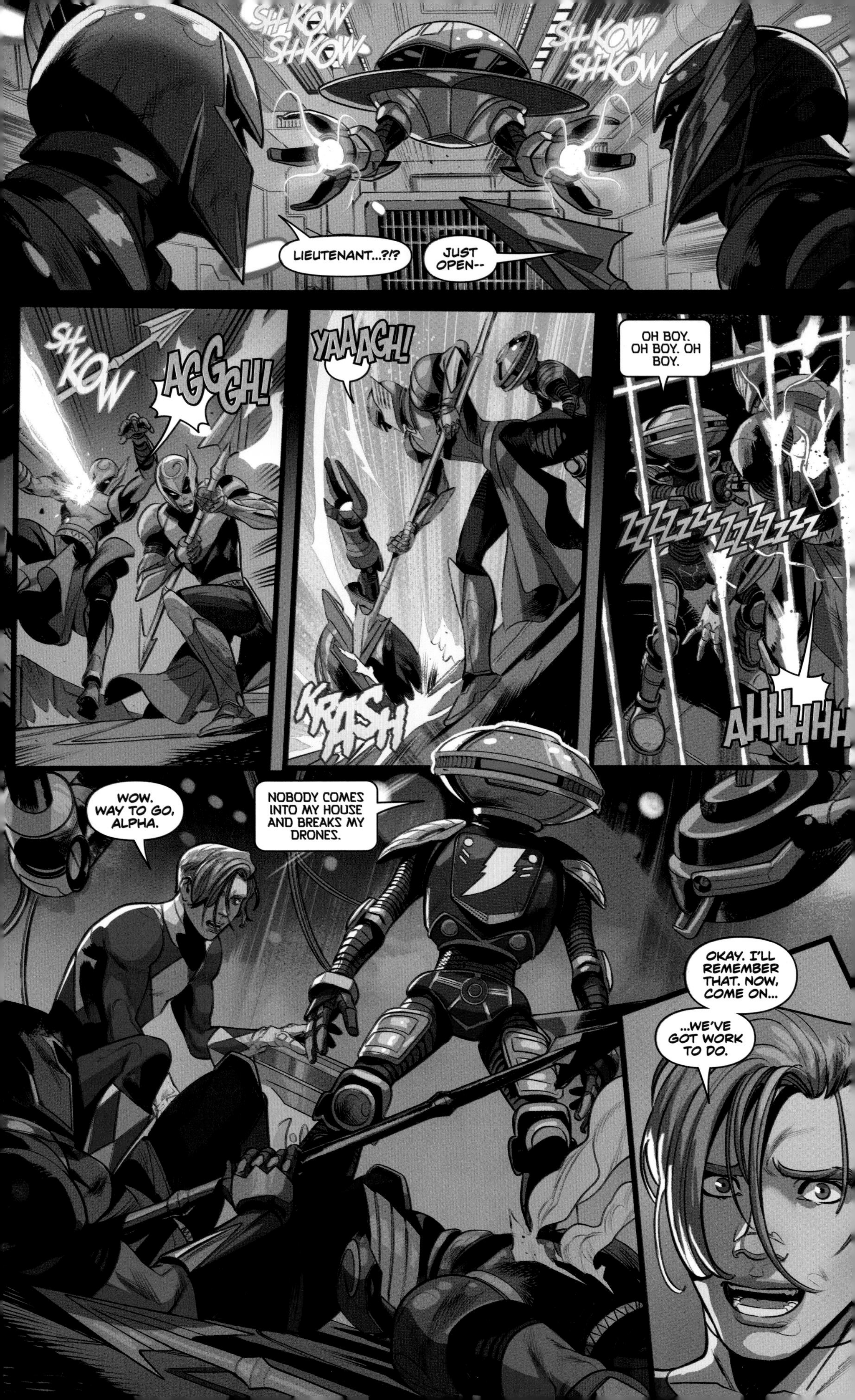
SH-KOW SH-KOW
SH-KOW SH-KOW
LIEUTENANT...?!?
JUST OPEN--
SH-KOW
AGGGH!
YAAAGH!
KRASH!
OH BOY. OH BOY. OH BOY.
ZZZZZZZZZZZZZZZ
AHHHHHH
WOW. WAY TO GO, ALPHA.
NOBODY COMES INTO MY HOUSE AND BREAKS MY DRONES.
OKAY. I'LL REMEMBER THAT. NOW, COME ON...
...WE'VE GOT WORK TO DO.

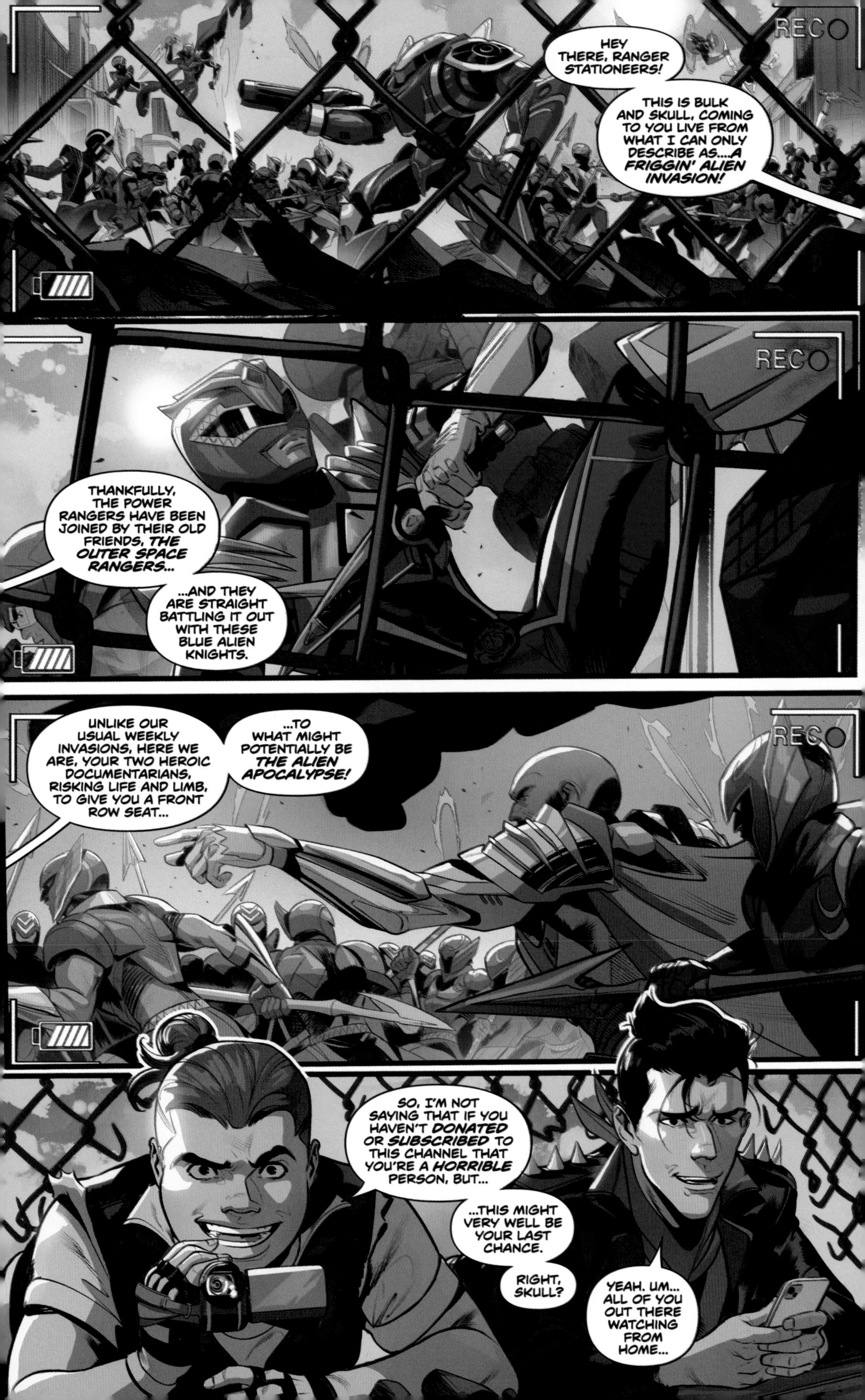
REC
HEY THERE, RANGER STATIONEERS!
THIS IS BULK AND SKULL, COMING TO YOU LIVE FROM WHAT I CAN ONLY DESCRIBE AS....A FRIGGIN' ALIEN INVASION!
REC
THANKFULLY, THE POWER RANGERS HAVE BEEN JOINED BY THEIR OLD FRIENDS, THE OUTER SPACE RANGERS...
...AND THEY ARE STRAIGHT BATTLING IT OUT WITH THESE BLUE ALIEN KNIGHTS.
REC
UNLIKE OUR USUAL WEEKLY INVASIONS, HERE WE ARE, YOUR TWO HEROIC DOCUMENTARIANS, RISKING LIFE AND LIMB, TO GIVE YOU A FRONT ROW SEAT...
...TO WHAT MIGHT POTENTIALLY BE THE ALIEN APOCALYPSE!
SO, I'M NOT SAYING THAT IF YOU HAVEN'T DONATED OR SUBSCRIBED TO THIS CHANNEL THAT YOU'RE A HORRIBLE PERSON, BUT...
...THIS MIGHT VERY WELL BE YOUR LAST CHANCE.
RIGHT, SKULL?
YEAH. UM... ALL OF YOU OUT THERE WATCHING FROM HOME...

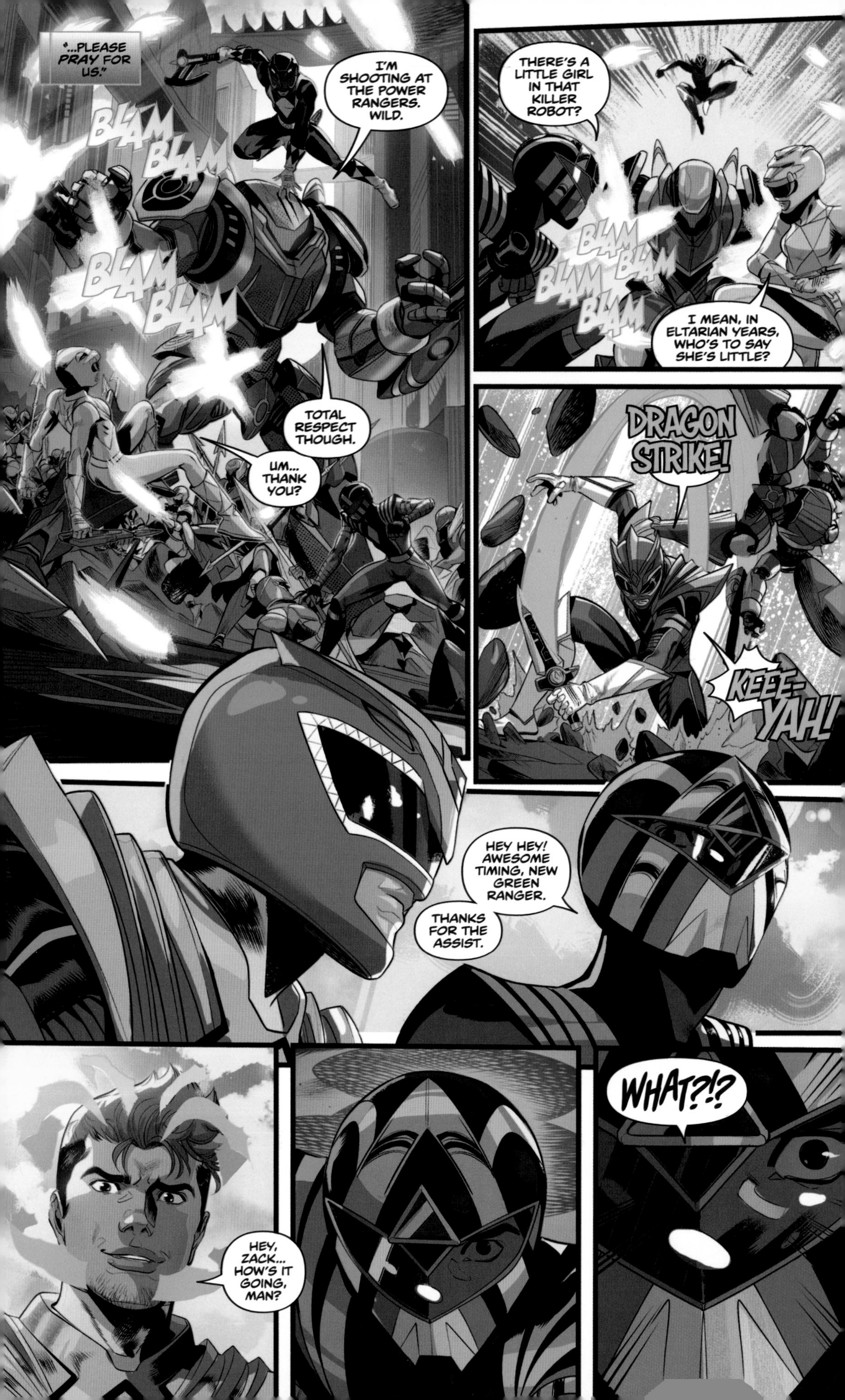
"...PLEASE PRAY FOR US."
BLAM BLAM
I'M SHOOTING AT THE POWER RANGERS. WILD.
BLAM BLAM
TOTAL RESPECT THOUGH.
UM... THANK YOU?
THERE'S A LITTLE GIRL IN THAT KILLER ROBOT?
BLAM BLAM BLAM BLAM
I MEAN, IN ELTARIAN YEARS, WHO'S TO SAY SHE'S LITTLE?
DRAGON STRIKE!
KEEE-YAH!
HEY HEY! AWESOME TIMING, NEW GREEN RANGER.
THANKS FOR THE ASSIST.
HEY, ZACK... HOW'S IT GOING, MAN?
WHAT?!?

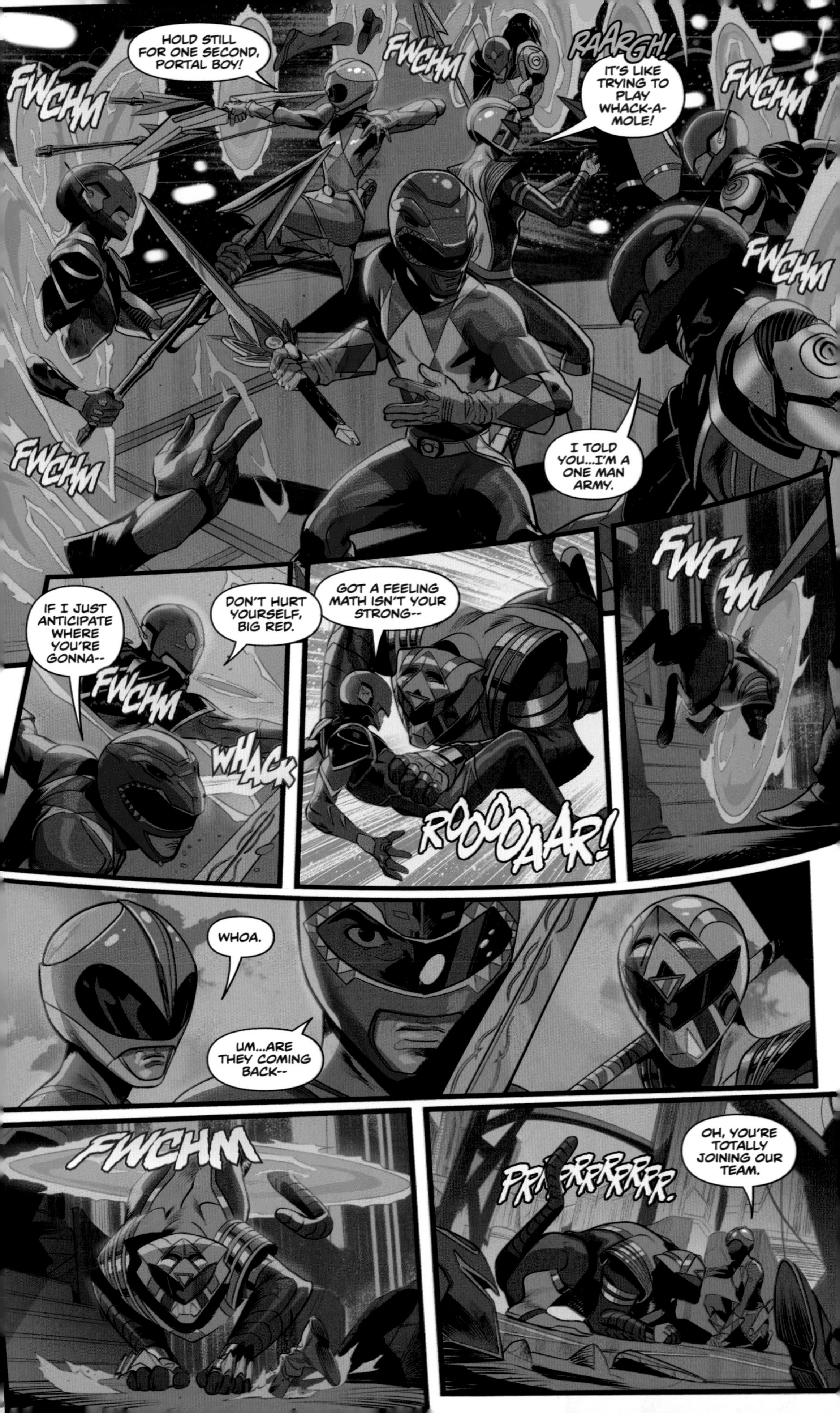
FWCHM
HOLD STILL FOR ONE SECOND, PORTAL BOY!
FWCHM
RAARGH!
IT'S LIKE TRYING TO PLAY WHACK-A-MOLE!
FWCHM
FWCHM
FWCHM
I TOLD YOU...I'M A ONE MAN ARMY.
IF I JUST ANTICIPATE WHERE YOU'RE GONNA--
DON'T HURT YOURSELF, BIG RED.
FWCHM
WHACK
GOT A FEELING MATH ISN'T YOUR STRONG--
ROOOOAAR!
FWCHM
WHOA.
UM...ARE THEY COMING BACK--
FWCHM
PRRRRRRRRRR.
OH, YOU'RE TOTALLY JOINING OUR TEAM.

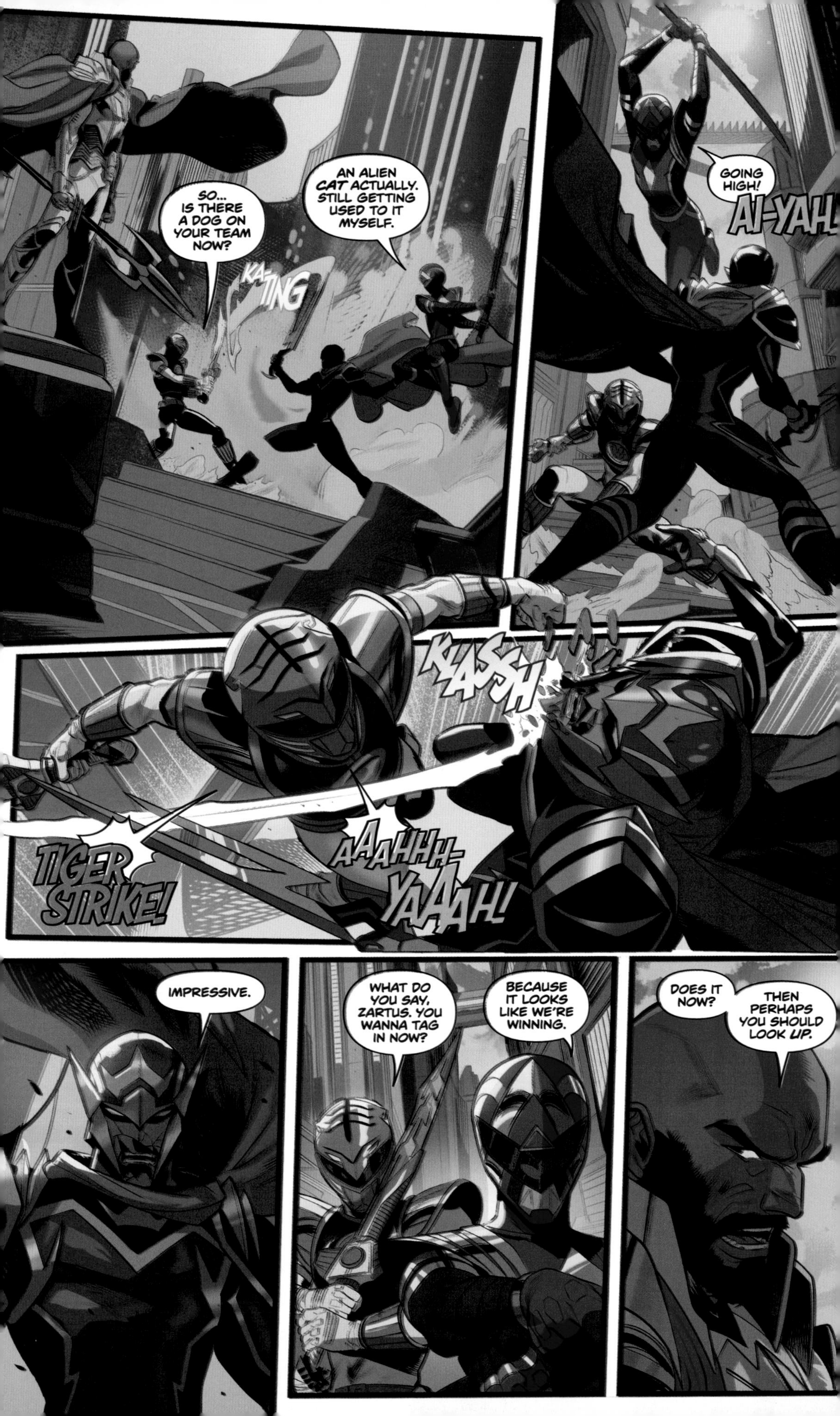
SO... IS THERE A DOG ON YOUR TEAM NOW?
AN ALIEN CAT ACTUALLY. STILL GETTING USED TO IT MYSELF.
KA-TING
GOING HIGH!
AI-YAH
KLASSH
TIGER STRIKE!
AAAHHH-YAAAH!
IMPRESSIVE.
WHAT DO YOU SAY, ZARTUS. YOU WANNA TAG IN NOW?
BECAUSE IT LOOKS LIKE WE'RE WINNING.
DOES IT NOW?
THEN PERHAPS YOU SHOULD LOOK UP.

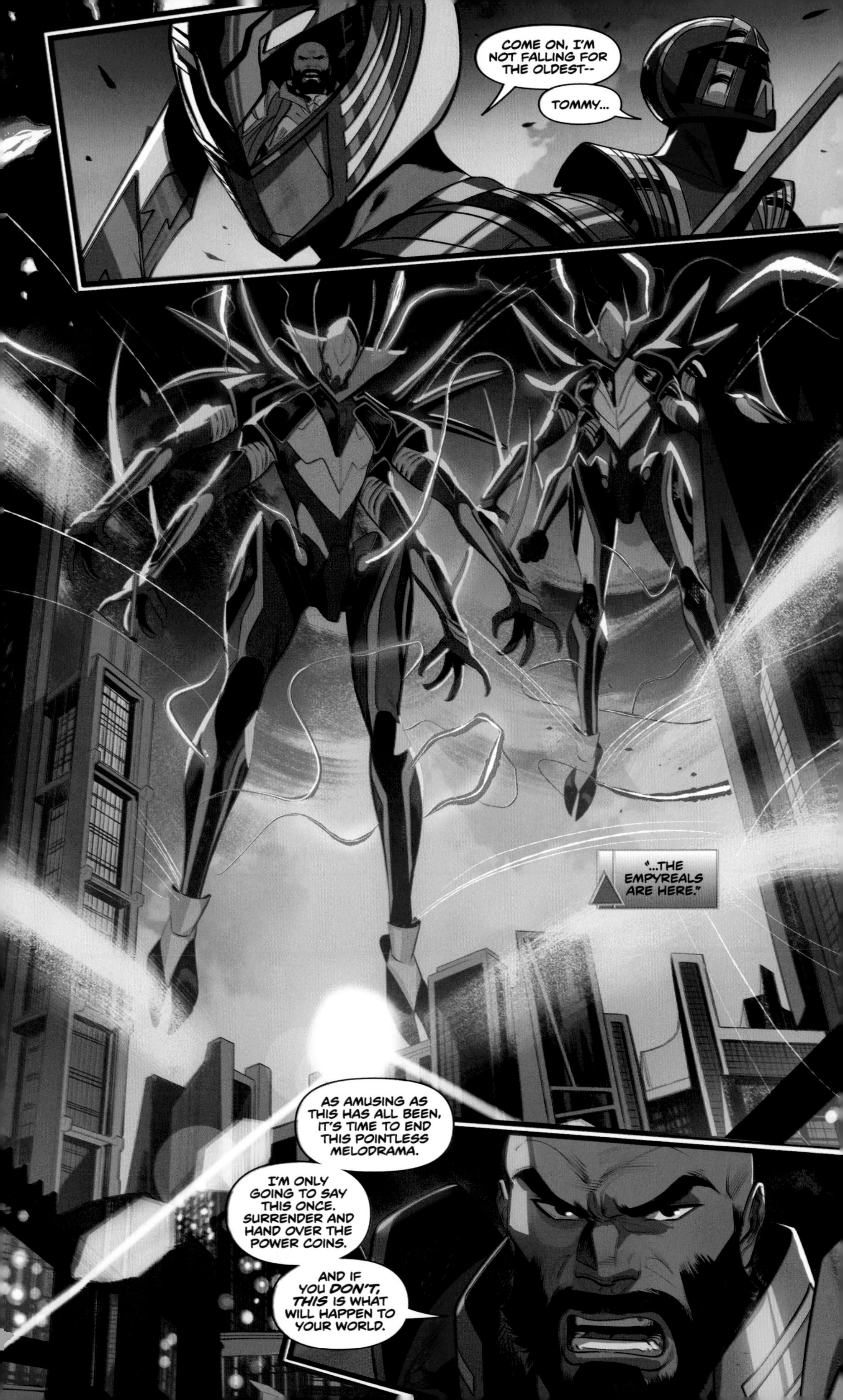
COME ON, I'M NOT FALLING FOR THE OLDEST--
TOMMY...
"...THE EMPYREALS ARE HERE."
AS AMUSING AS THIS HAS ALL BEEN, IT'S TIME TO END THIS POINTLESS MELODRAMA.
I'M ONLY GOING TO SAY THIS ONCE. SURRENDER AND HAND OVER THE POWER COINS.
AND IF YOU *DON'T*, *THIS* IS WHAT WILL HAPPEN TO YOUR WORLD.

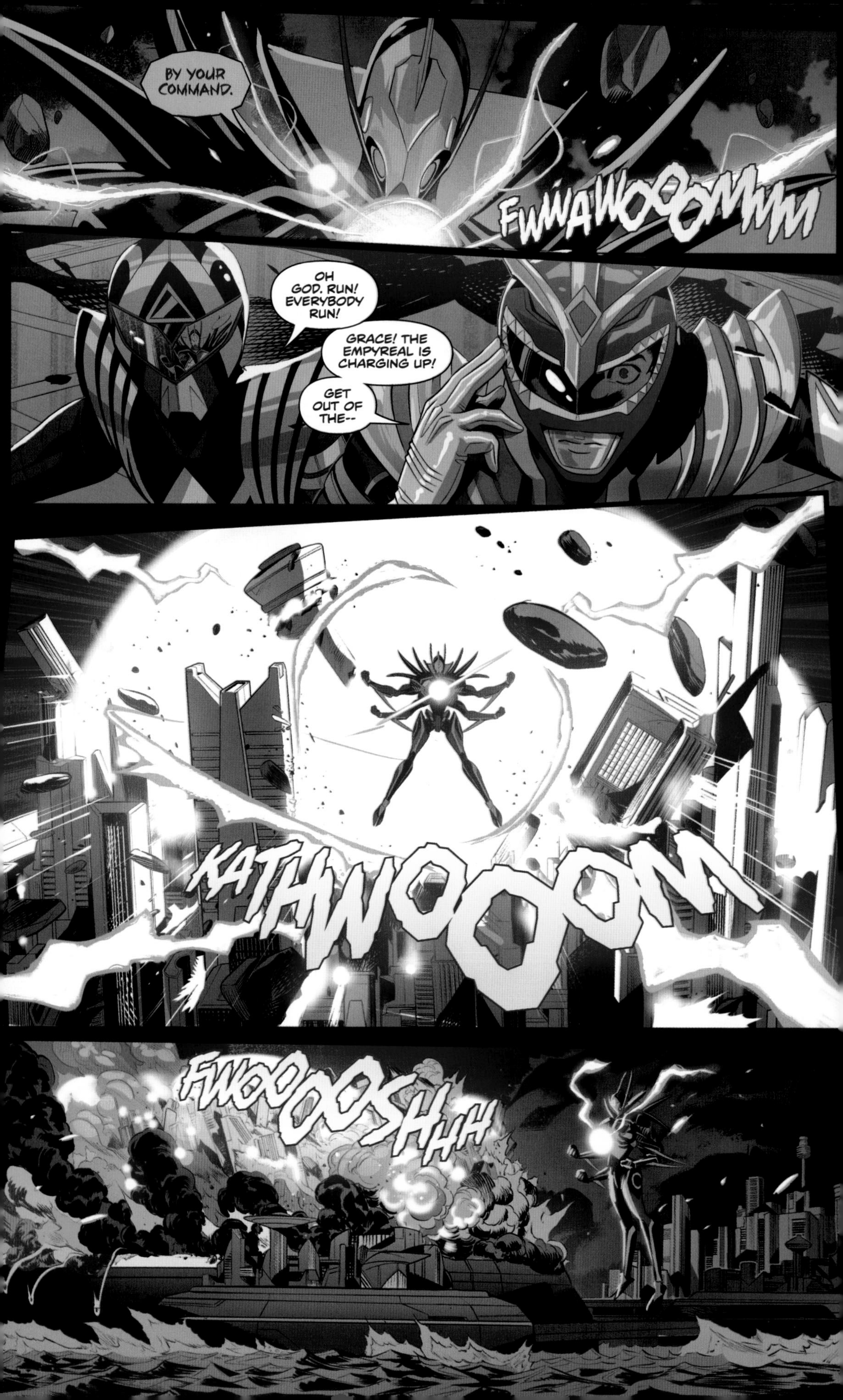
BY YOUR COMMAND.
FWWAWOOOMMM
OH GOD. RUN! EVERYBODY RUN!
GRACE! THE EMPYREAL IS CHARGING UP!
GET OUT OF THE--
KATHWOOOM
FWOOOOSHHH

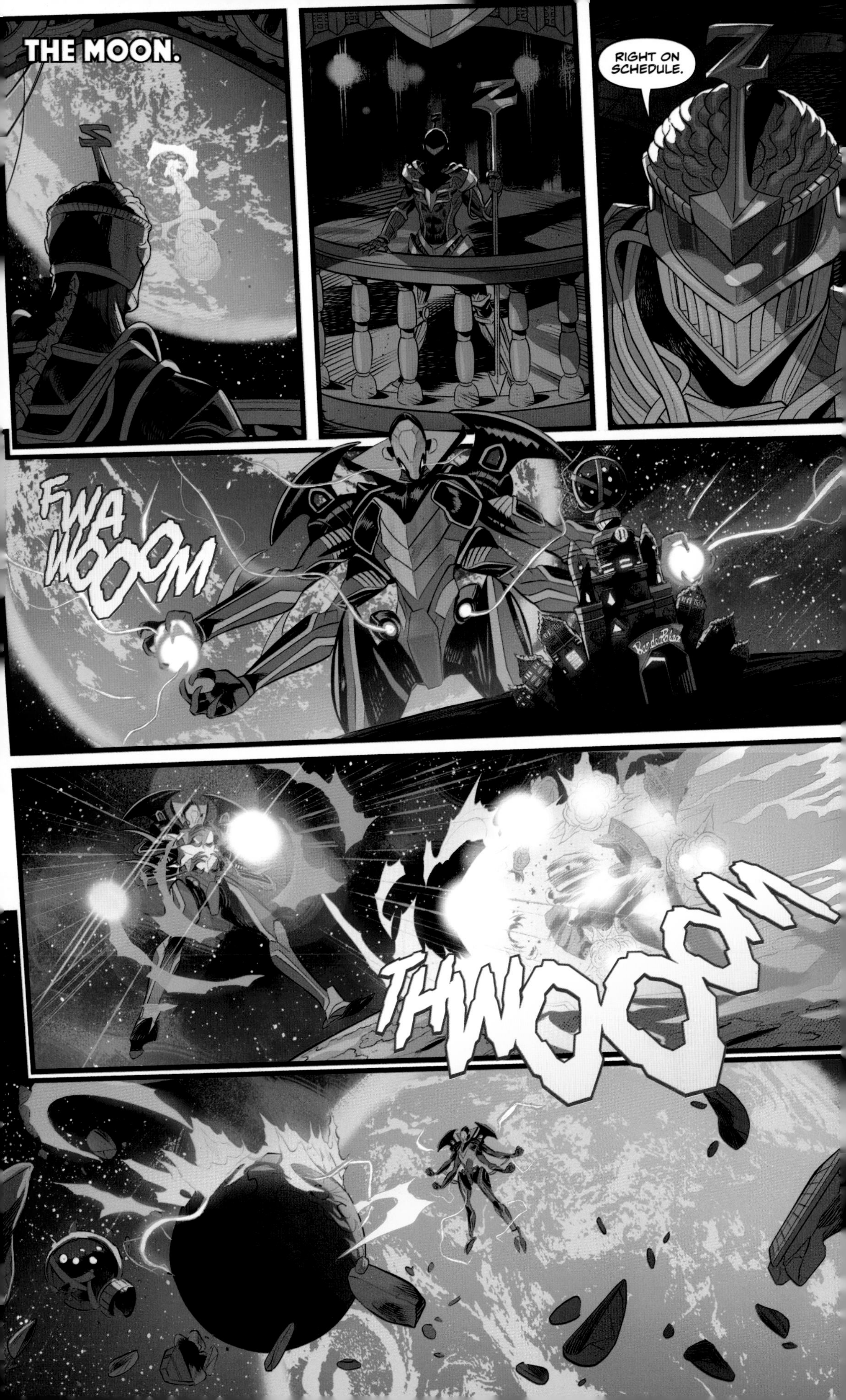
THE MOON.
RIGHT ON SCHEDULE.
FWA WOOOM
THWOOOM

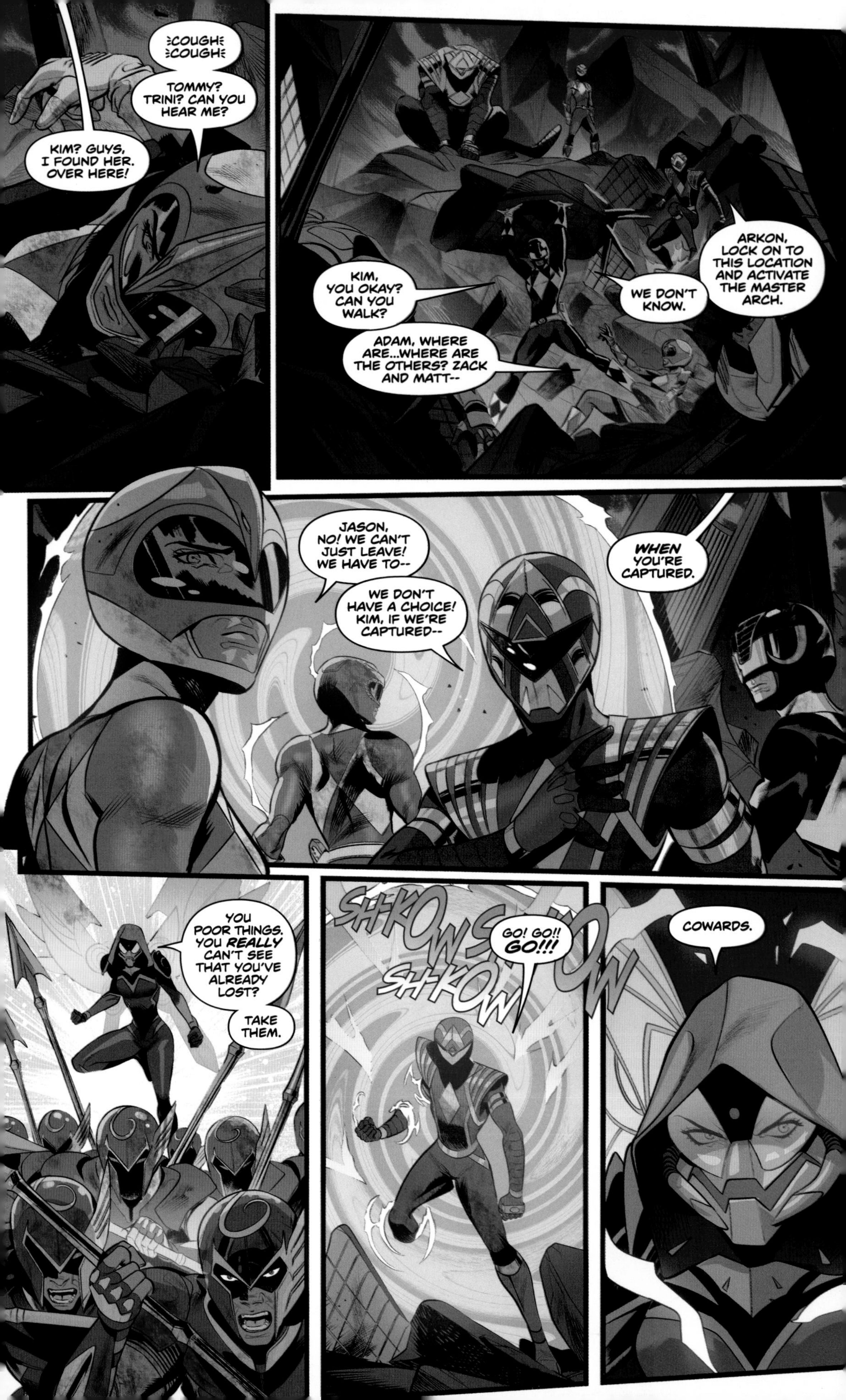

*COUGH*
*COUGH*
TOMMY? TRINI? CAN YOU HEAR ME?
KIM? GUYS, I FOUND HER. OVER HERE!
KIM, YOU OKAY? CAN YOU WALK?
ADAM, WHERE ARE...WHERE ARE THE OTHERS? ZACK AND MATT--
WE DON'T KNOW.
ARKON, LOCK ON TO THIS LOCATION AND ACTIVATE THE MASTER ARCH.
JASON, NO! WE CAN'T JUST LEAVE! WE HAVE TO--
WE DON'T HAVE A CHOICE! KIM, IF WE'RE CAPTURED--
*WHEN* YOU'RE CAPTURED.
YOU POOR THINGS. YOU *REALLY* CAN'T SEE THAT YOU'VE ALREADY LOST?
TAKE THEM.
SHKOW
SHKOW
GO! GO!! ***GO!!!***
COWARDS.

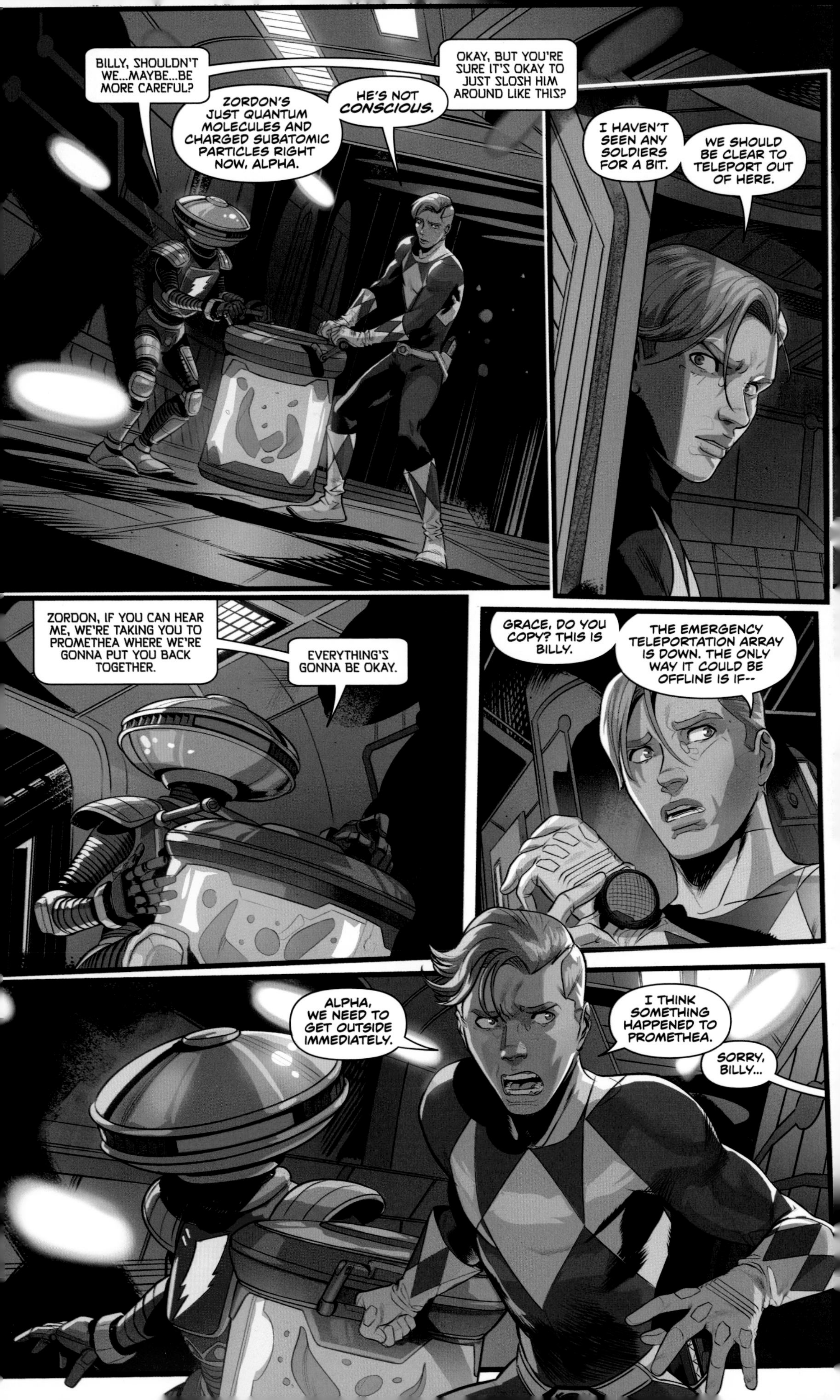

BILLY, SHOULDN'T WE...MAYBE...BE MORE CAREFUL?
ZORDON'S JUST QUANTUM MOLECULES AND CHARGED SUBATOMIC PARTICLES RIGHT NOW, ALPHA.
HE'S NOT CONSCIOUS.
OKAY, BUT YOU'RE SURE IT'S OKAY TO JUST SLOSH HIM AROUND LIKE THIS?
I HAVEN'T SEEN ANY SOLDIERS FOR A BIT.
WE SHOULD BE CLEAR TO TELEPORT OUT OF HERE.
ZORDON, IF YOU CAN HEAR ME, WE'RE TAKING YOU TO PROMETHEA WHERE WE'RE GONNA PUT YOU BACK TOGETHER.
EVERYTHING'S GONNA BE OKAY.
GRACE, DO YOU COPY? THIS IS BILLY.
THE EMERGENCY TELEPORTATION ARRAY IS DOWN. THE ONLY WAY IT COULD BE OFFLINE IS IF--
ALPHA, WE NEED TO GET OUTSIDE IMMEDIATELY.
I THINK SOMETHING HAPPENED TO PROMETHEA.
SORRY, BILLY...

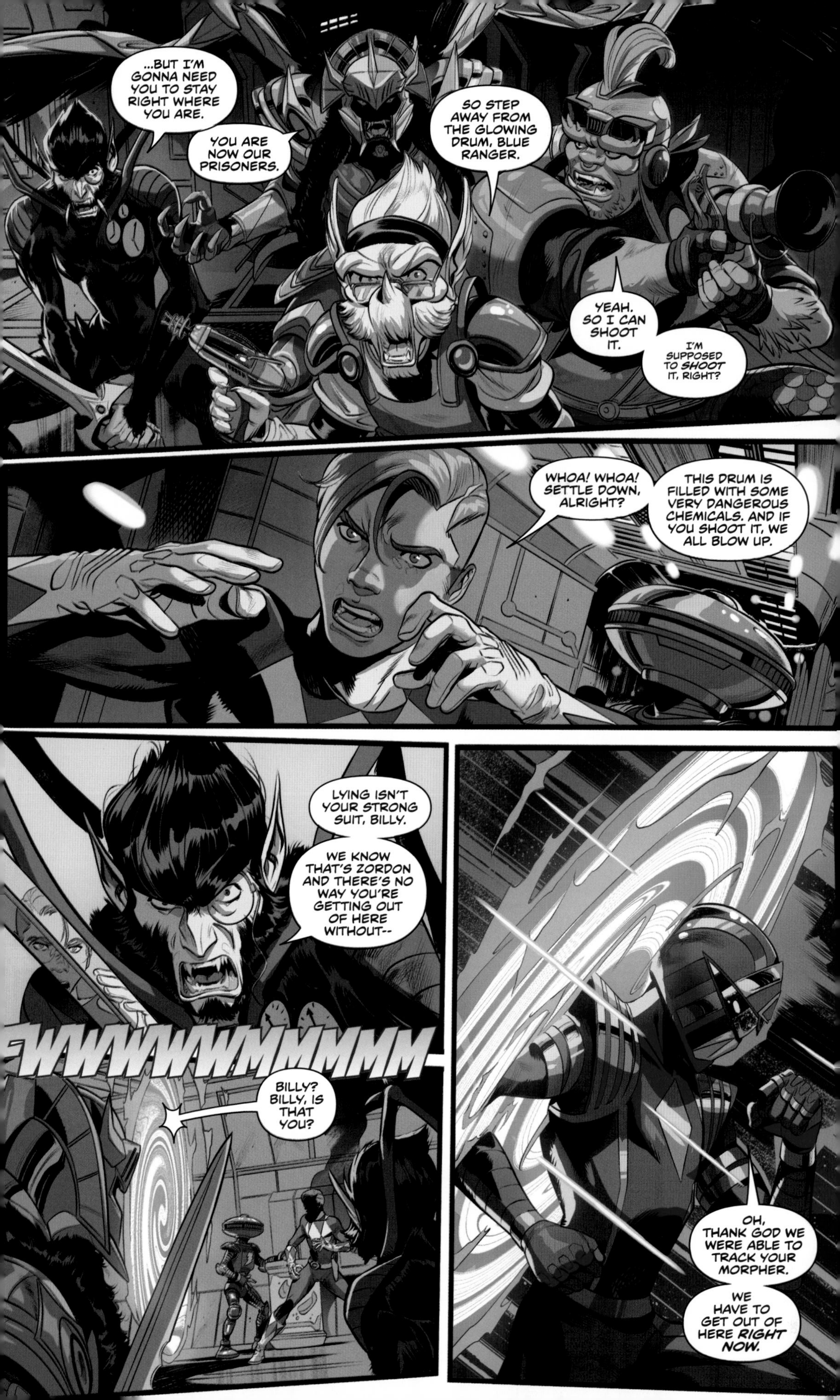
...BUT I'M GONNA NEED YOU TO STAY RIGHT WHERE YOU ARE.
YOU ARE NOW OUR PRISONERS.
SO STEP AWAY FROM THE GLOWING DRUM, BLUE RANGER.
YEAH. SO I CAN SHOOT IT.
I'M SUPPOSED TO SHOOT IT, RIGHT?
WHOA! WHOA! SETTLE DOWN, ALRIGHT?
THIS DRUM IS FILLED WITH SOME VERY DANGEROUS CHEMICALS. AND IF YOU SHOOT IT, WE ALL BLOW UP.
LYING ISN'T YOUR STRONG SUIT, BILLY.
WE KNOW THAT'S ZORDON AND THERE'S NO WAY YOU'RE GETTING OUT OF HERE WITHOUT--
WWWWWMMMMMM
BILLY? BILLY, IS THAT YOU?
OH, THANK GOD WE WERE ABLE TO TRACK YOUR MORPHER.
WE HAVE TO GET OUT OF HERE RIGHT NOW.

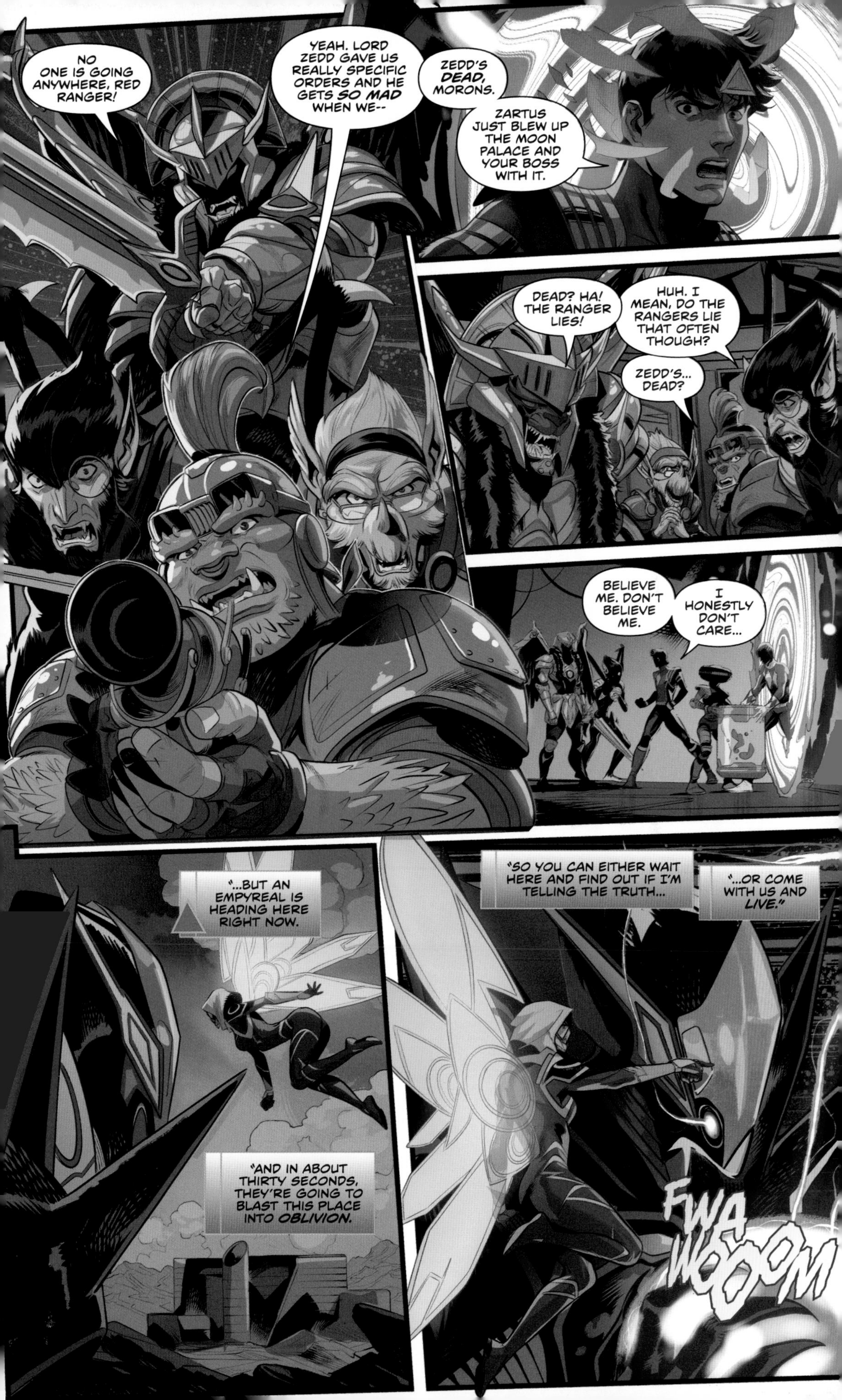
NO ONE IS GOING ANYWHERE, RED RANGER!
YEAH. LORD ZEDD GAVE US REALLY SPECIFIC ORDERS AND HE GETS *SO MAD* WHEN WE--
ZEDD'S *DEAD,* MORONS.
ZARTUS JUST BLEW UP THE MOON PALACE AND YOUR BOSS WITH IT.
DEAD? HA! THE RANGER LIES!
HUH. I MEAN, DO THE RANGERS LIE THAT OFTEN THOUGH?
ZEDD'S... DEAD?
BELIEVE ME. DON'T BELIEVE ME.
I HONESTLY DON'T CARE...
"...BUT AN EMPYREAL IS HEADING HERE RIGHT NOW.
"AND IN ABOUT THIRTY SECONDS, THEY'RE GOING TO BLAST THIS PLACE INTO *OBLIVION*.
"SO YOU CAN EITHER WAIT HERE AND FIND OUT IF I'M TELLING THE TRUTH...
"...OR COME WITH US AND *LIVE.*"
FWA WOOOM

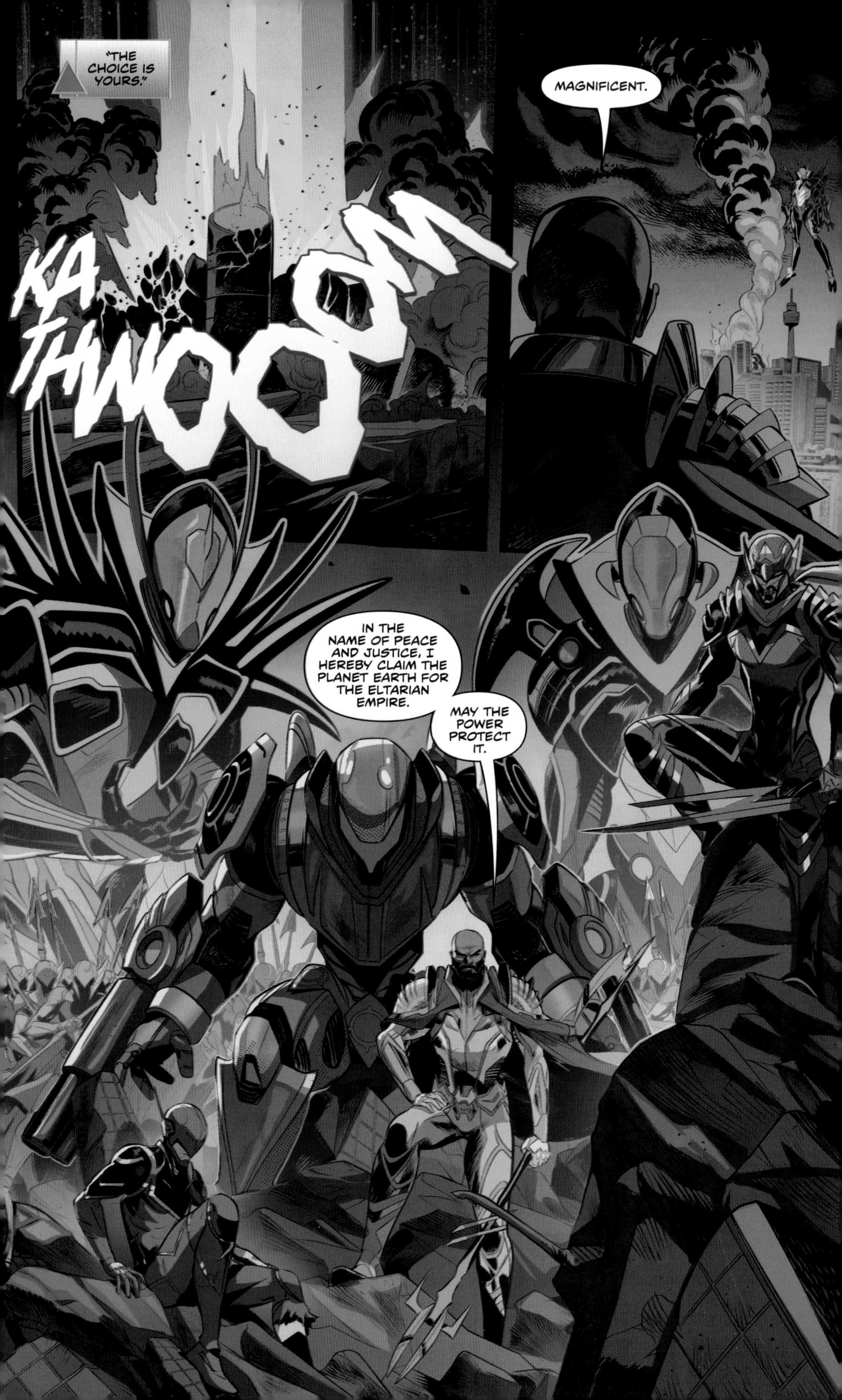
"THE CHOICE IS YOURS."
KA THWOOOM
MAGNIFICENT.
IN THE NAME OF PEACE AND JUSTICE, I HEREBY CLAIM THE PLANET EARTH FOR THE ELTARIAN EMPIRE.
MAY THE POWER PROTECT IT.

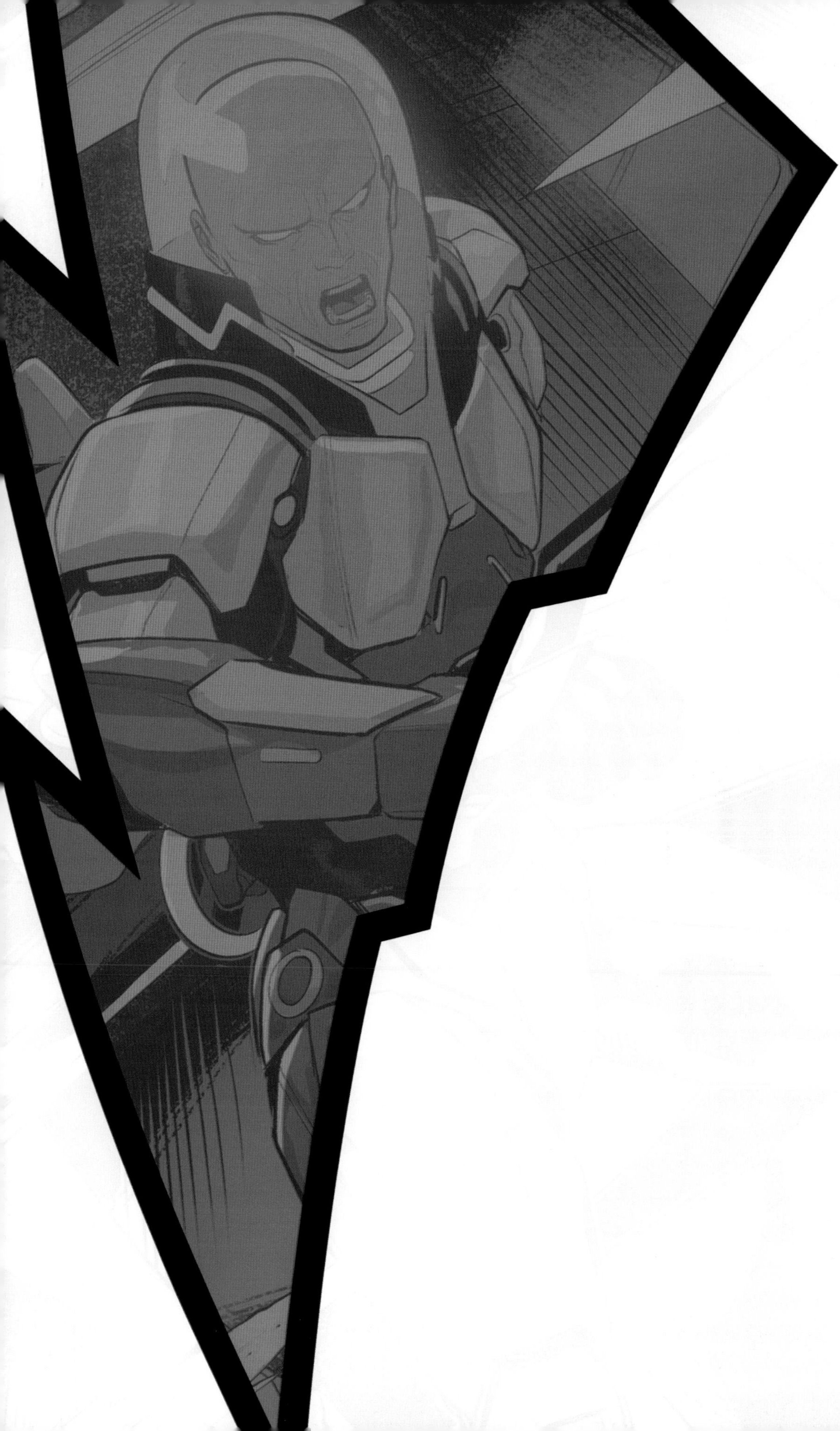

# CHAPTER FOURTEEN

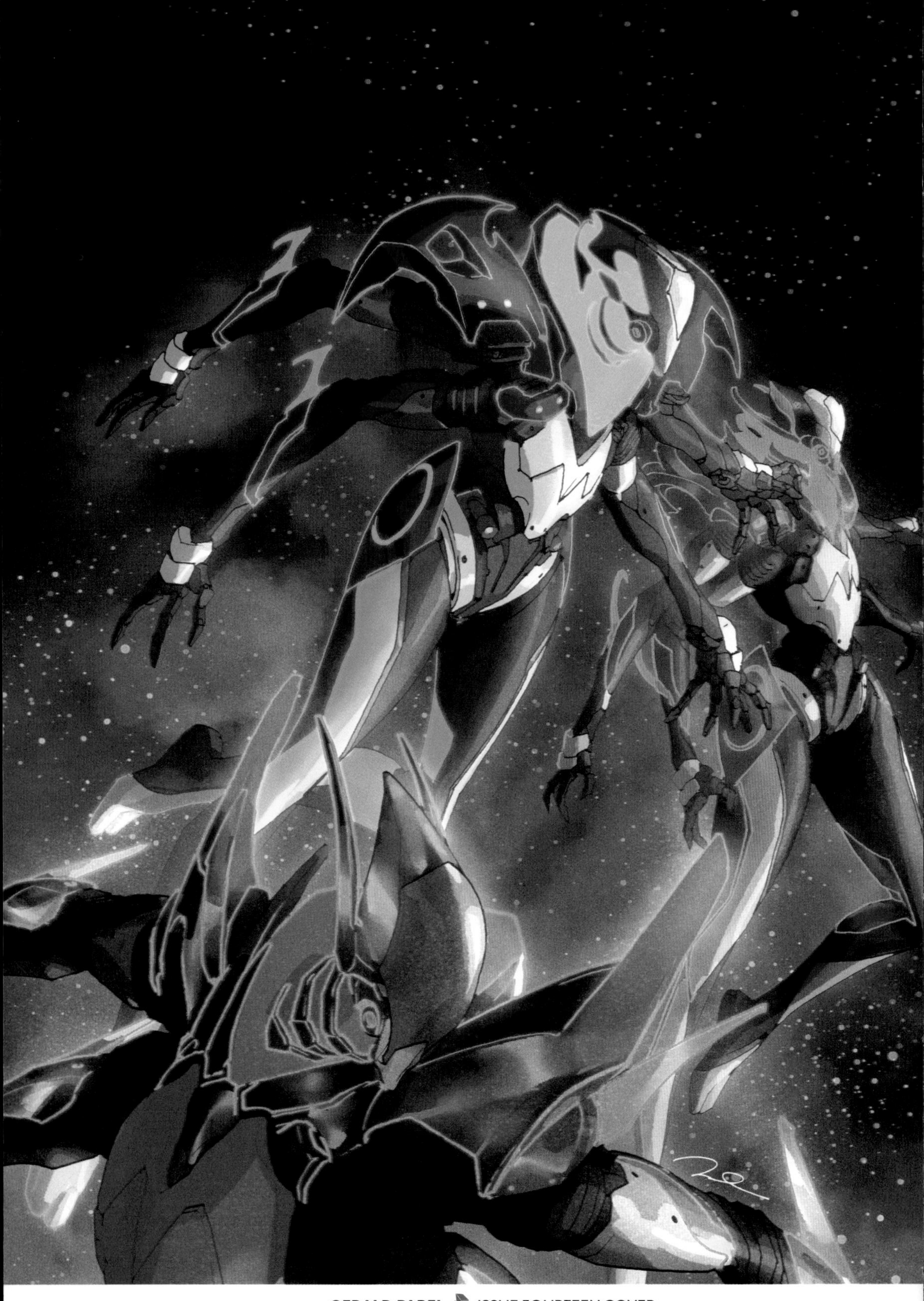

GERALD PAREL | ISSUE FOURTEEN COVER

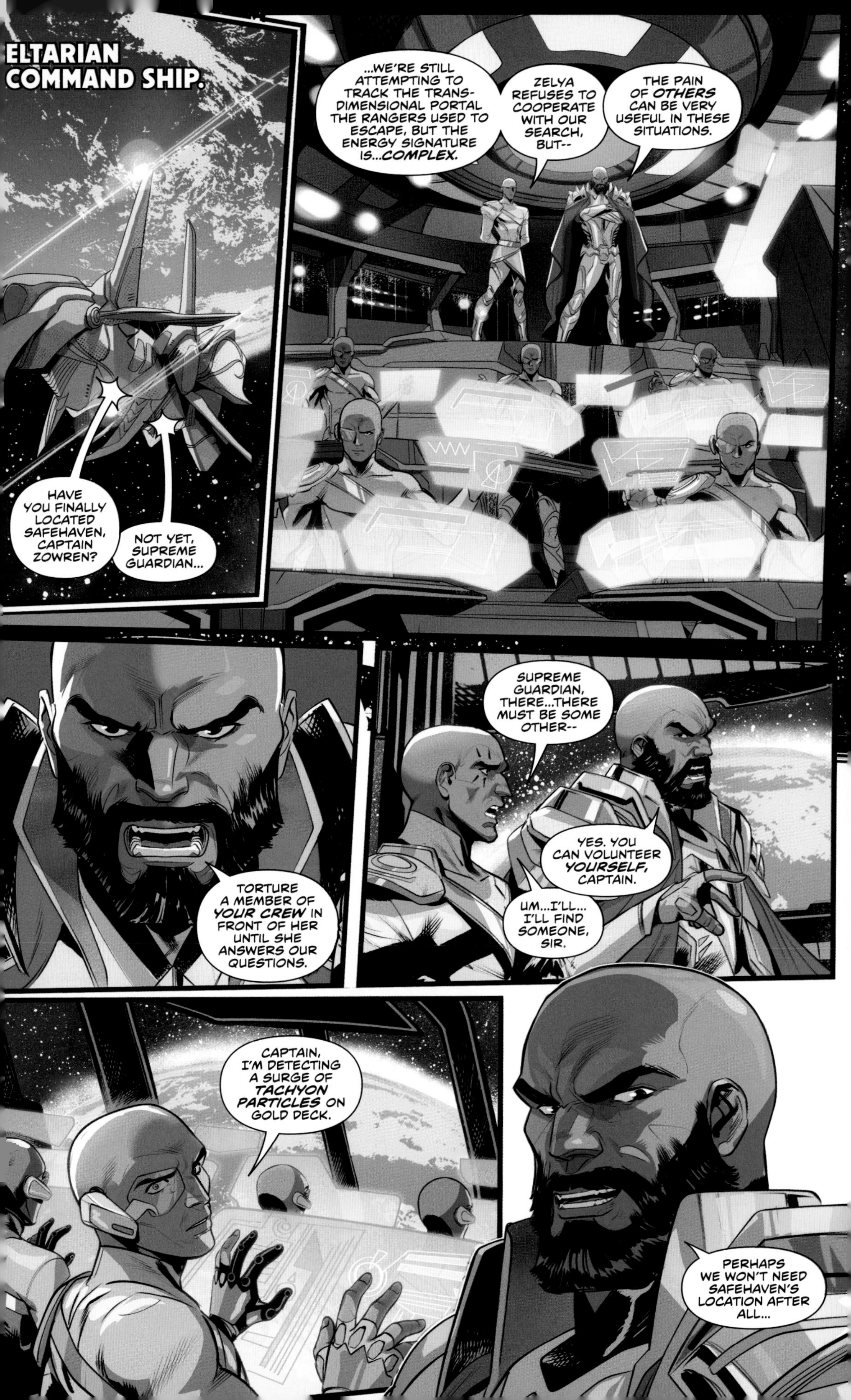
ELTARIAN COMMAND SHIP.
HAVE YOU FINALLY LOCATED SAFEHAVEN, CAPTAIN ZOWREN?
NOT YET, SUPREME GUARDIAN...
...WE'RE STILL ATTEMPTING TO TRACK THE TRANS-DIMENSIONAL PORTAL THE RANGERS USED TO ESCAPE, BUT THE ENERGY SIGNATURE IS...COMPLEX.
ZELYA REFUSES TO COOPERATE WITH OUR SEARCH, BUT--
THE PAIN OF OTHERS CAN BE VERY USEFUL IN THESE SITUATIONS.
TORTURE A MEMBER OF YOUR CREW IN FRONT OF HER UNTIL SHE ANSWERS OUR QUESTIONS.
SUPREME GUARDIAN, THERE...THERE MUST BE SOME OTHER--
YES. YOU CAN VOLUNTEER YOURSELF, CAPTAIN.
UM...I'LL... I'LL FIND SOMEONE, SIR.
CAPTAIN, I'M DETECTING A SURGE OF TACHYON PARTICLES ON GOLD DECK.
PERHAPS WE WON'T NEED SAFEHAVEN'S LOCATION AFTER ALL...

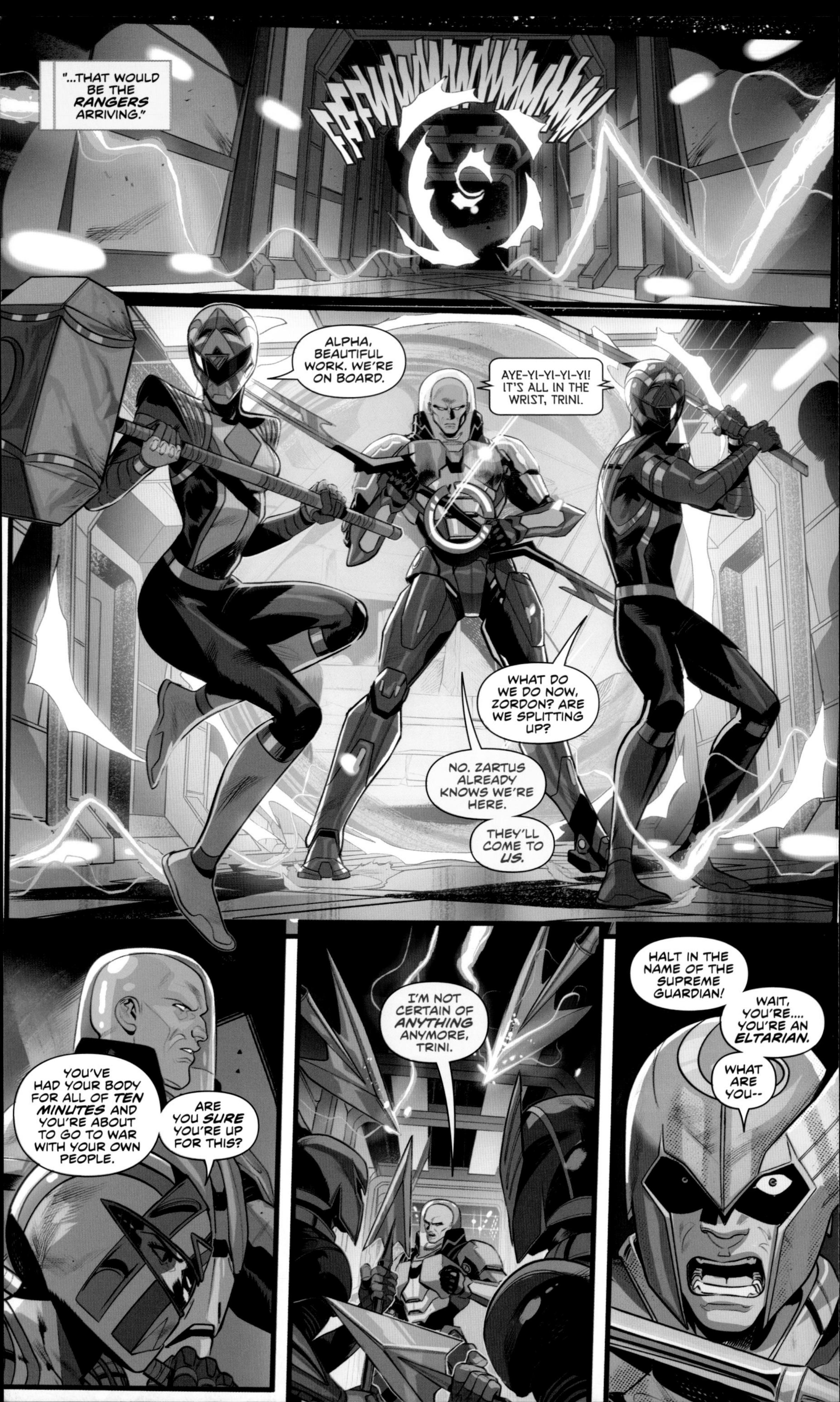
"...THAT WOULD BE THE *RANGERS* ARRIVING."
FFFWWAAAAWWWMMMMM
ALPHA, BEAUTIFUL WORK. WE'RE ON BOARD.
AYE-YI-YI-YI-YI! IT'S ALL IN THE WRIST, TRINI.
WHAT DO WE DO NOW, ZORDON? ARE WE SPLITTING UP?
NO. ZARTUS ALREADY KNOWS WE'RE HERE.
THEY'LL COME TO *US*.
YOU'VE HAD YOUR BODY FOR ALL OF *TEN MINUTES* AND YOU'RE ABOUT TO GO TO WAR WITH YOUR OWN PEOPLE.
ARE YOU *SURE* YOU'RE UP FOR THIS?
I'M NOT CERTAIN OF *ANYTHING* ANYMORE, TRINI.
HALT IN THE NAME OF THE SUPREME GUARDIAN!
WAIT, YOU'RE.... YOU'RE AN *ELTARIAN*.
WHAT ARE YOU--

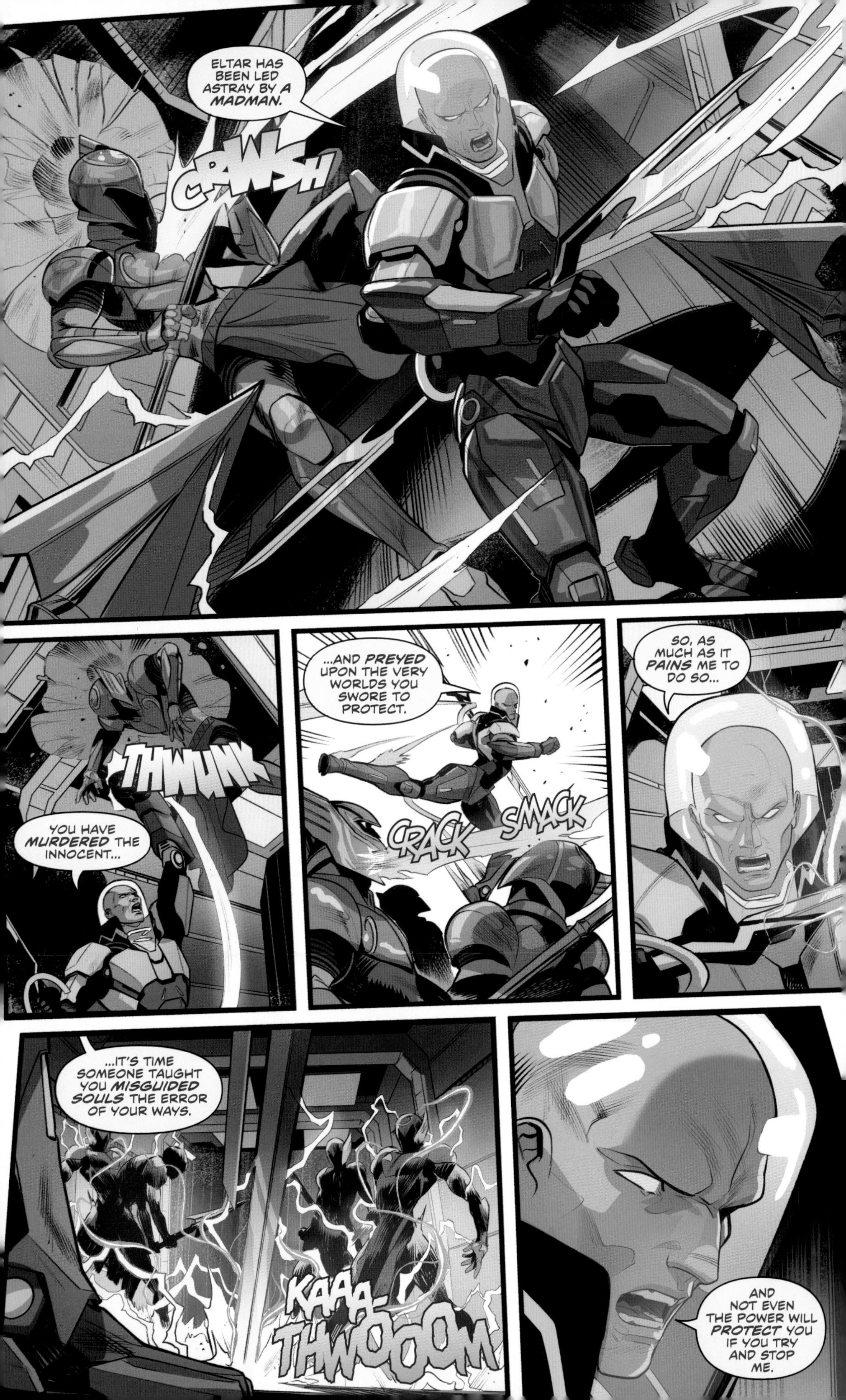
ELTAR HAS BEEN LED ASTRAY BY A MADMAN.
CRASH
THWUNK
YOU HAVE MURDERED THE INNOCENT...
...AND PREYED UPON THE VERY WORLDS YOU SWORE TO PROTECT.
CRACK
SMACK
SO, AS MUCH AS IT PAINS ME TO DO SO...
...IT'S TIME SOMEONE TAUGHT YOU MISGUIDED SOULS THE ERROR OF YOUR WAYS.
KAAA-THWOOOM
AND NOT EVEN THE POWER WILL PROTECT YOU IF YOU TRY AND STOP ME.

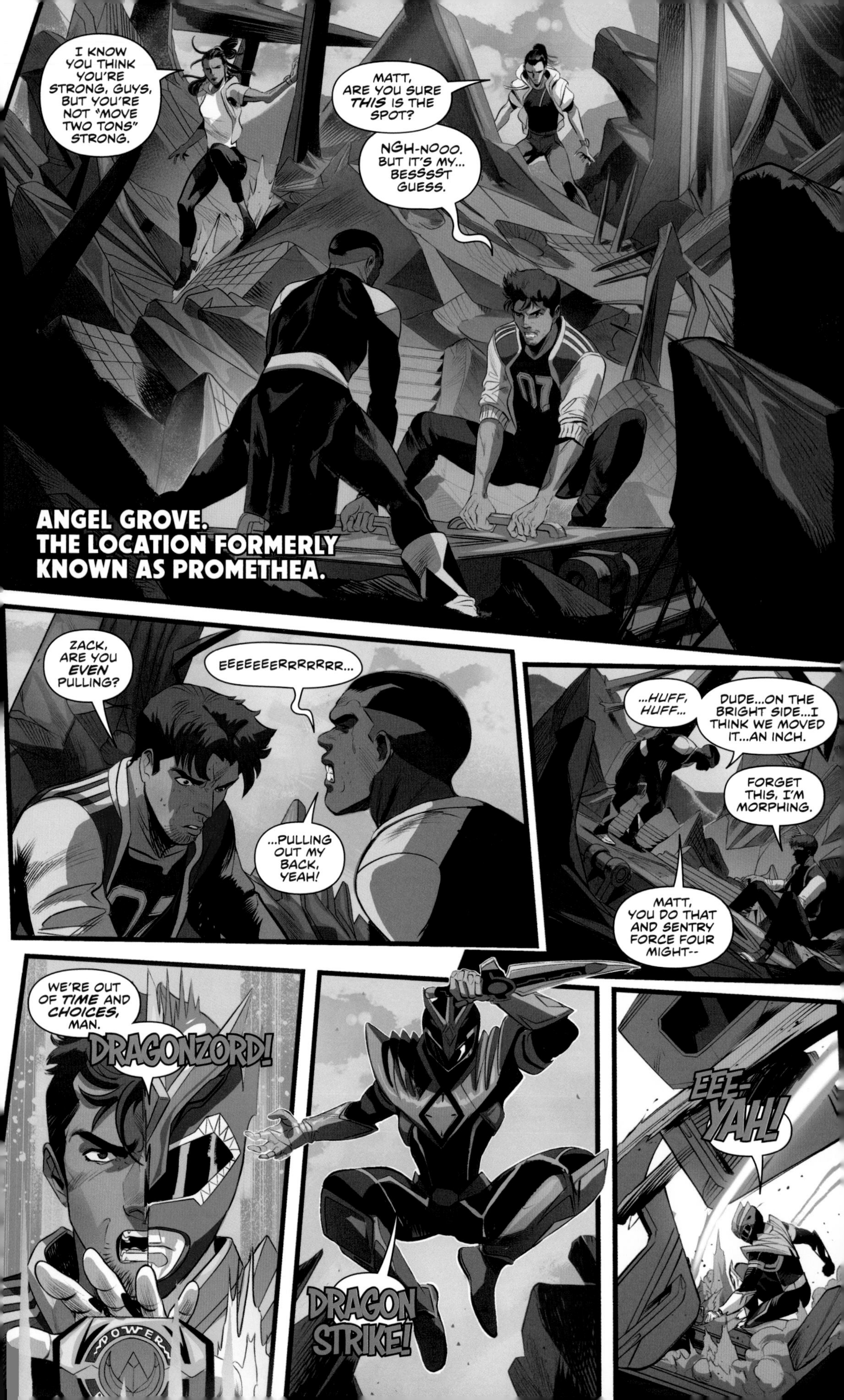
I KNOW YOU THINK YOU'RE STRONG, GUYS, BUT YOU'RE NOT "MOVE TWO TONS" STRONG.
MATT, ARE YOU SURE THIS IS THE SPOT?
NGH-NOOO. BUT IT'S MY... BESSSST GUESS.
ANGEL GROVE. THE LOCATION FORMERLY KNOWN AS PROMETHEA.
ZACK, ARE YOU EVEN PULLING?
EEEEEEERRRRRR...
...PULLING OUT MY BACK, YEAH!
...HUFF, HUFF...
DUDE...ON THE BRIGHT SIDE...I THINK WE MOVED IT...AN INCH.
FORGET THIS, I'M MORPHING.
MATT, YOU DO THAT AND SENTRY FORCE FOUR MIGHT--
WE'RE OUT OF TIME AND CHOICES, MAN.
DRAGONZORD!
POWER
DRAGON STRIKE!
EEE-YAH!

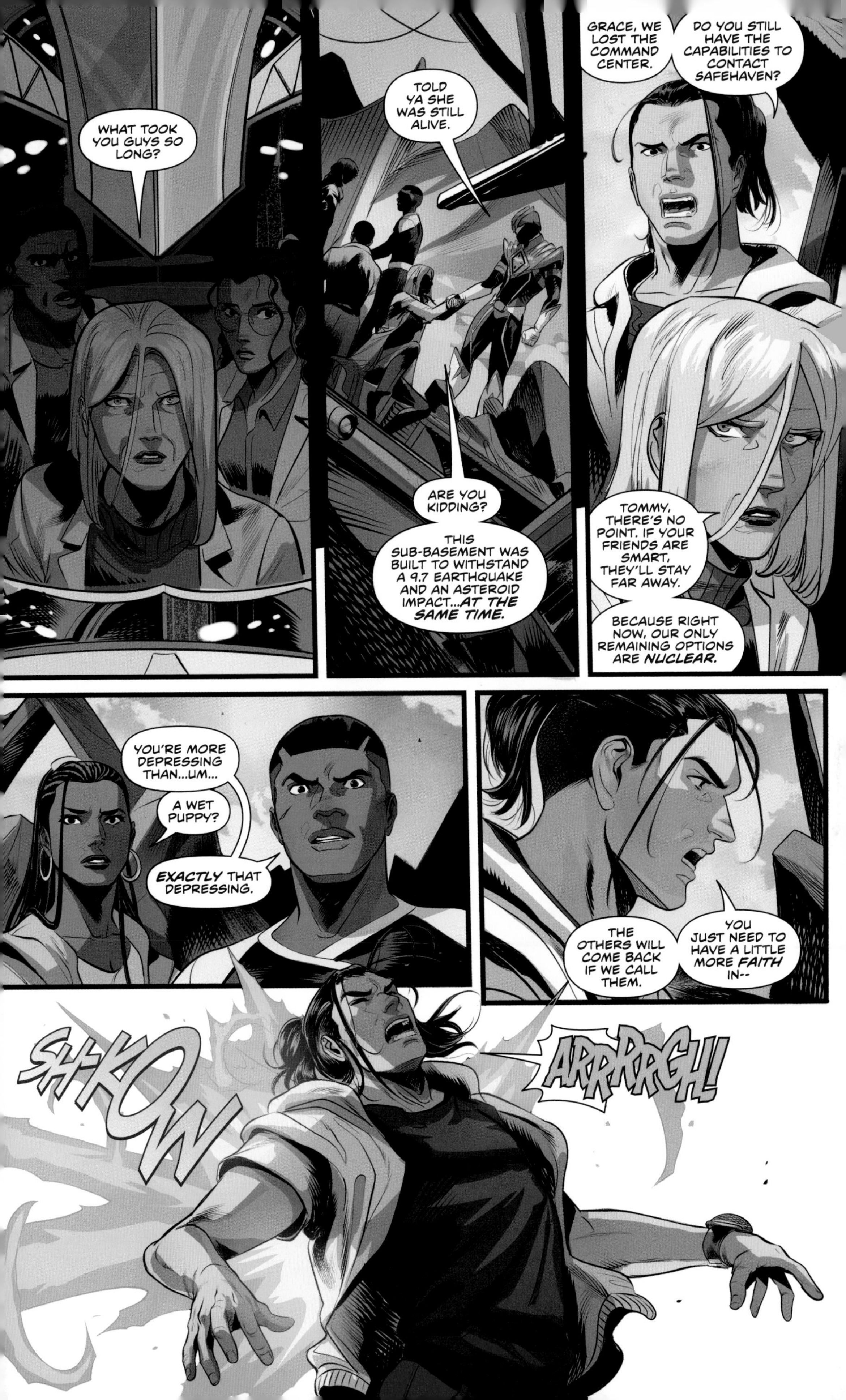
WHAT TOOK YOU GUYS SO LONG?
TOLD YA SHE WAS STILL ALIVE.
ARE YOU KIDDING?
THIS SUB-BASEMENT WAS BUILT TO WITHSTAND A 9.7 EARTHQUAKE AND AN ASTEROID IMPACT...AT THE SAME TIME.
GRACE, WE LOST THE COMMAND CENTER.
DO YOU STILL HAVE THE CAPABILITIES TO CONTACT SAFEHAVEN?
TOMMY, THERE'S NO POINT. IF YOUR FRIENDS ARE SMART, THEY'LL STAY FAR AWAY.
BECAUSE RIGHT NOW, OUR ONLY REMAINING OPTIONS ARE NUCLEAR.
YOU'RE MORE DEPRESSING THAN...UM...
A WET PUPPY?
EXACTLY THAT DEPRESSING.
THE OTHERS WILL COME BACK IF WE CALL THEM.
YOU JUST NEED TO HAVE A LITTLE MORE FAITH IN--
SH-KOW
ARRRRGH!

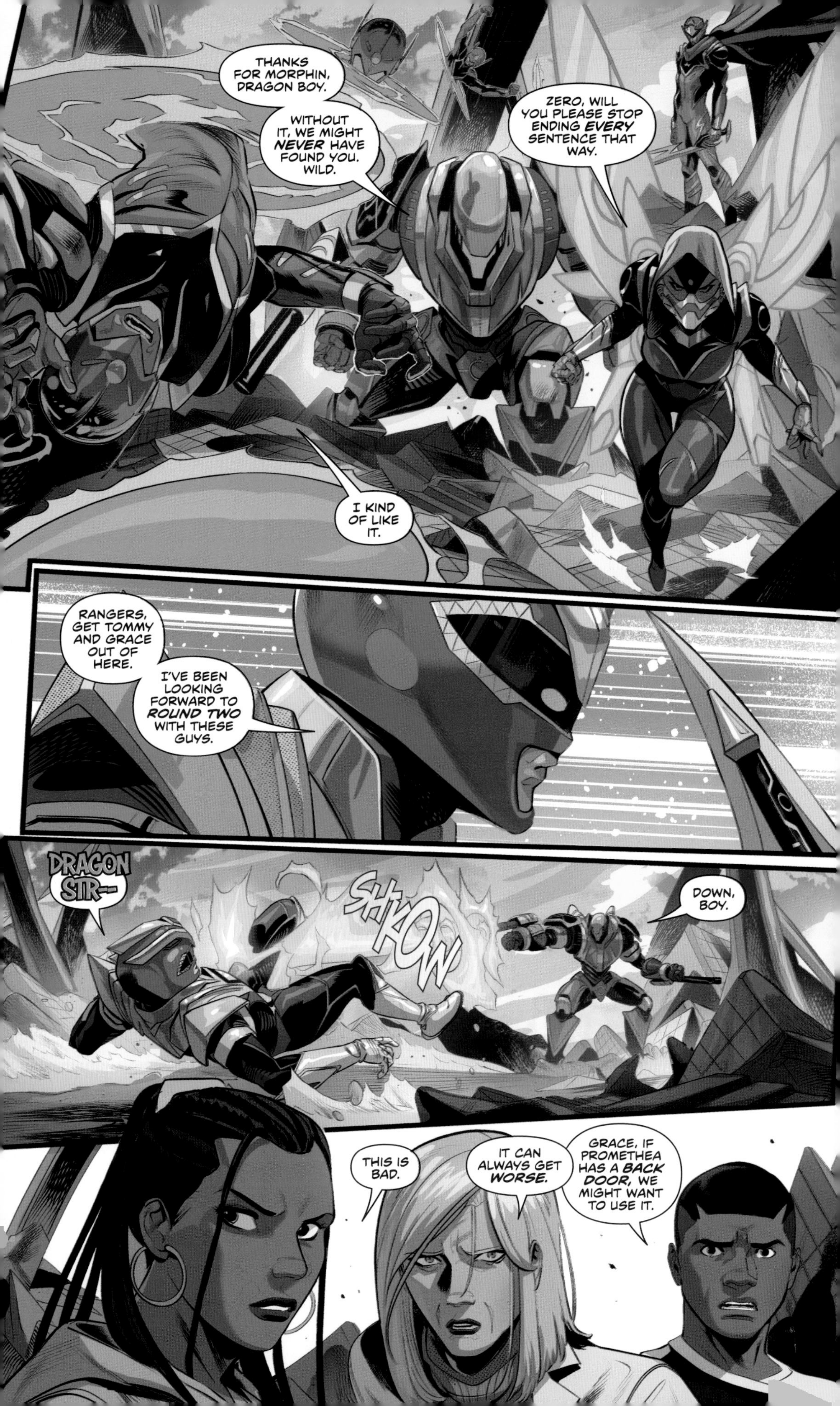
THANKS FOR MORPHIN, DRAGON BOY.
WITHOUT IT, WE MIGHT NEVER HAVE FOUND YOU. WILD.
ZERO, WILL YOU PLEASE STOP ENDING EVERY SENTENCE THAT WAY.
I KIND OF LIKE IT.
RANGERS, GET TOMMY AND GRACE OUT OF HERE.
I'VE BEEN LOOKING FORWARD TO ROUND TWO WITH THESE GUYS.
DRAGON STR--
SHKOW
DOWN, BOY.
THIS IS BAD.
IT CAN ALWAYS GET WORSE.
GRACE, IF PROMETHEA HAS A BACK DOOR, WE MIGHT WANT TO USE IT.

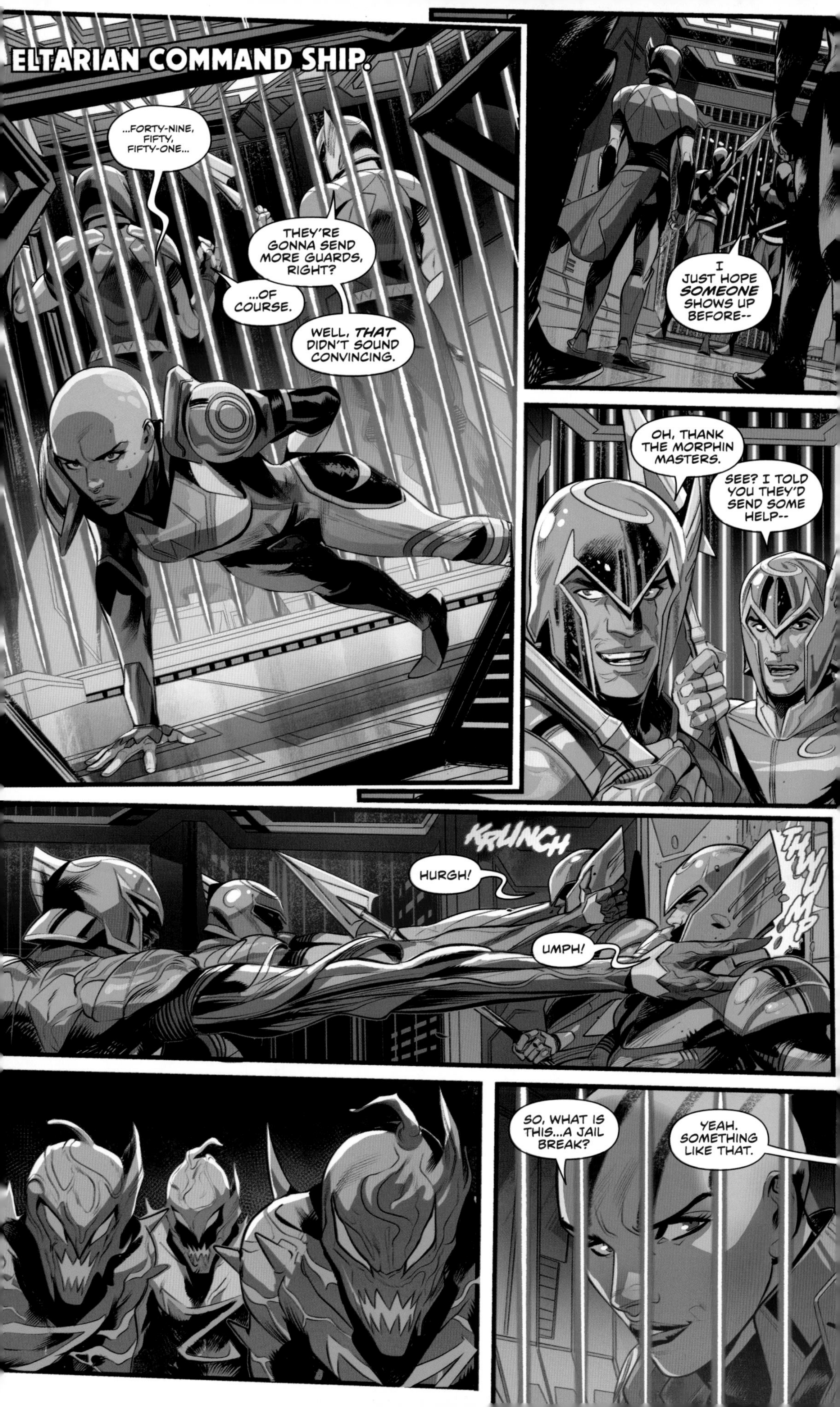
ELTARIAN COMMAND SHIP.
...FORTY-NINE, FIFTY, FIFTY-ONE...
THEY'RE GONNA SEND MORE GUARDS, RIGHT?
...OF COURSE.
WELL, *THAT* DIDN'T SOUND CONVINCING.
I JUST HOPE *SOMEONE* SHOWS UP BEFORE--
OH, THANK THE MORPHIN MASTERS.
SEE? I TOLD YOU THEY'D SEND SOME HELP--
KRUNCH
HURGH!
THWUMP
UMPH!
SO, WHAT IS THIS...A JAIL BREAK?
YEAH. SOMETHING LIKE THAT.

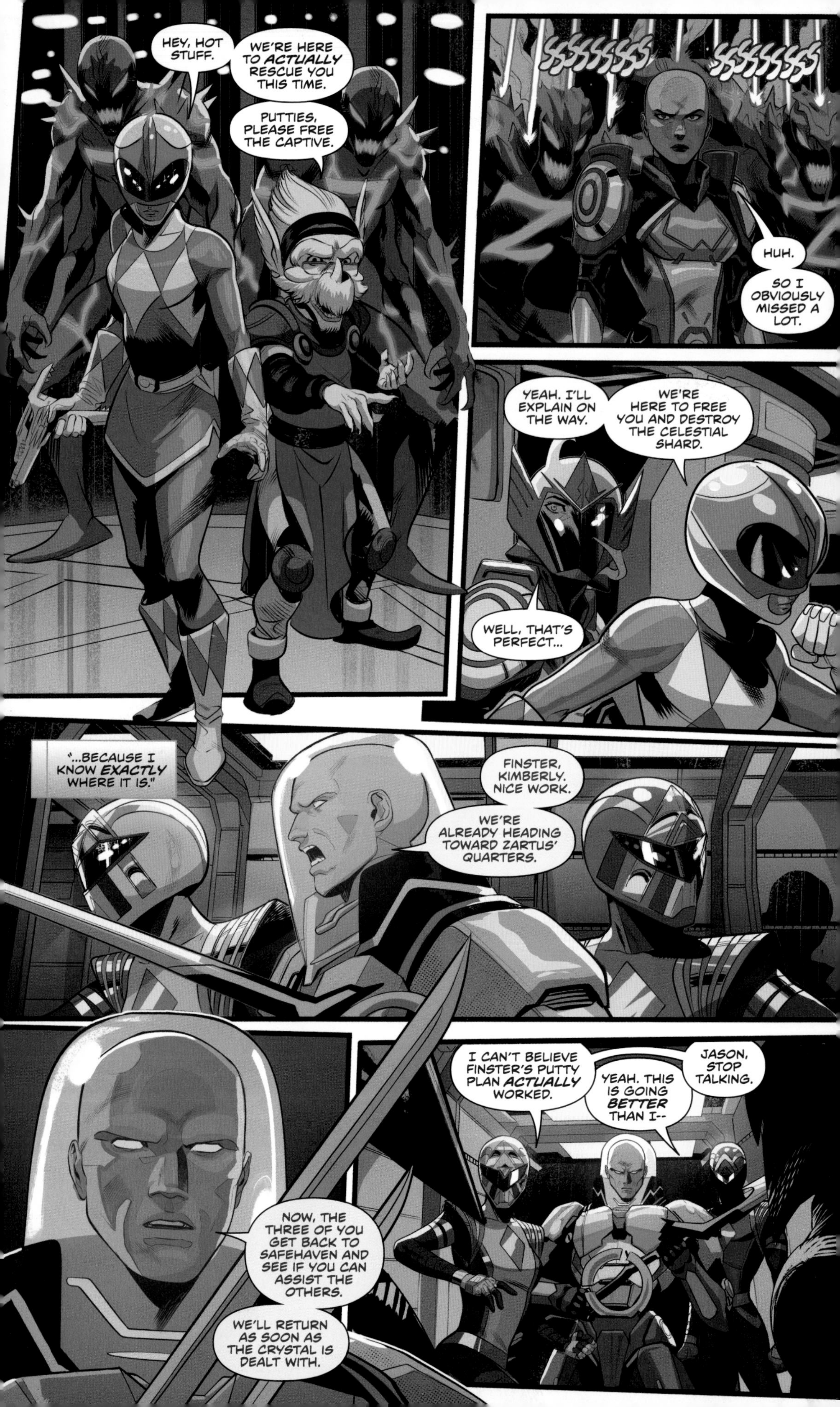
HEY, HOT STUFF.
WE'RE HERE TO ACTUALLY RESCUE YOU THIS TIME.
PUTTIES, PLEASE FREE THE CAPTIVE.
SSSSSSSSS
SSSSSSSSS
HUH.
SO I OBVIOUSLY MISSED A LOT.
YEAH. I'LL EXPLAIN ON THE WAY.
WE'RE HERE TO FREE YOU AND DESTROY THE CELESTIAL SHARD.
WELL, THAT'S PERFECT...
"...BECAUSE I KNOW EXACTLY WHERE IT IS."
FINSTER, KIMBERLY. NICE WORK.
WE'RE ALREADY HEADING TOWARD ZARTUS' QUARTERS.
NOW, THE THREE OF YOU GET BACK TO SAFEHAVEN AND SEE IF YOU CAN ASSIST THE OTHERS.
WE'LL RETURN AS SOON AS THE CRYSTAL IS DEALT WITH.
I CAN'T BELIEVE FINSTER'S PUTTY PLAN ACTUALLY WORKED.
YEAH. THIS IS GOING BETTER THAN I--
JASON, STOP TALKING.

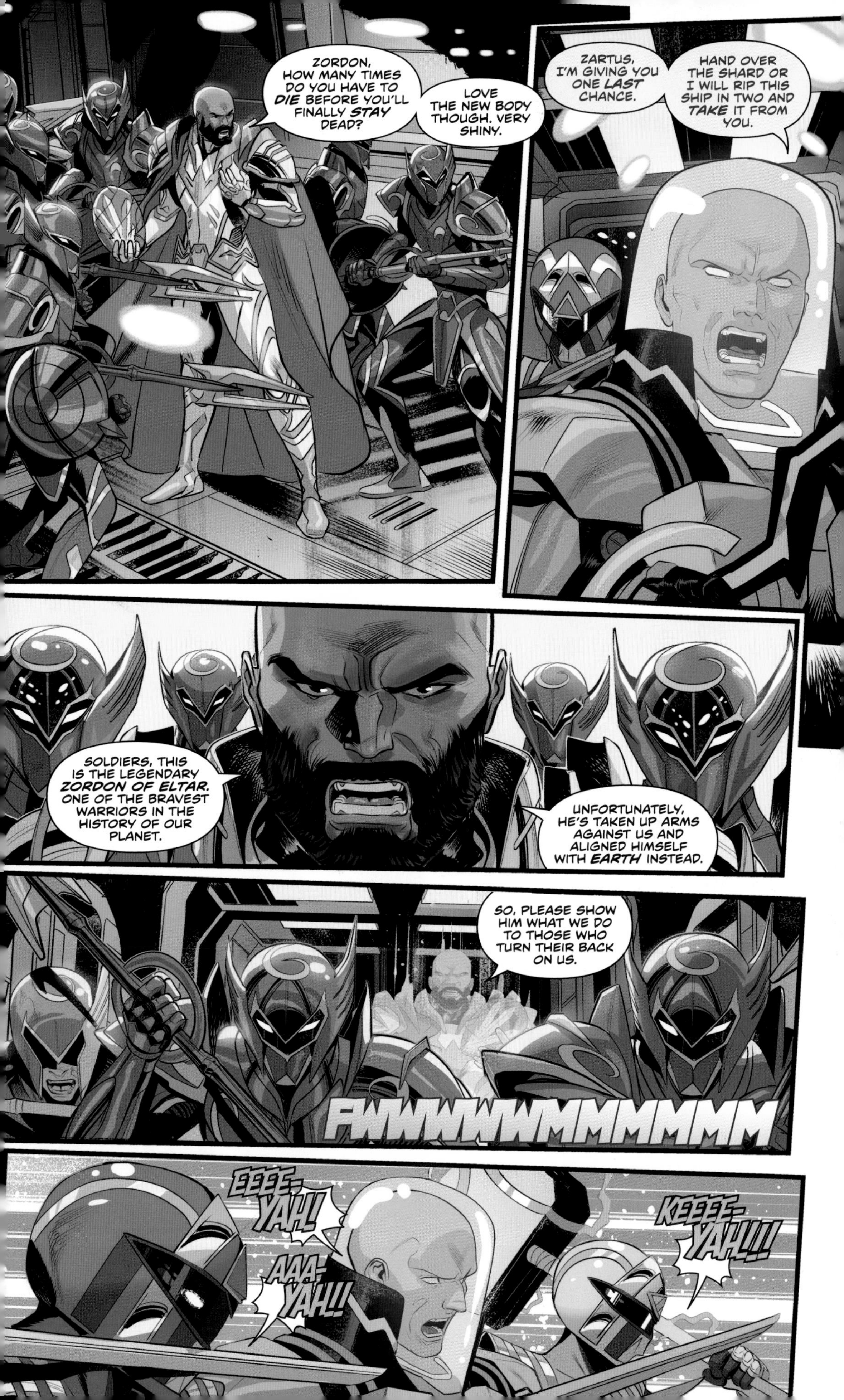
ZORDON, HOW MANY TIMES DO YOU HAVE TO DIE BEFORE YOU'LL FINALLY STAY DEAD?
LOVE THE NEW BODY THOUGH. VERY SHINY.
ZARTUS, I'M GIVING YOU ONE LAST CHANCE.
HAND OVER THE SHARD OR I WILL RIP THIS SHIP IN TWO AND TAKE IT FROM YOU.
SOLDIERS, THIS IS THE LEGENDARY ZORDON OF ELTAR. ONE OF THE BRAVEST WARRIORS IN THE HISTORY OF OUR PLANET.
UNFORTUNATELY, HE'S TAKEN UP ARMS AGAINST US AND ALIGNED HIMSELF WITH EARTH INSTEAD.
SO, PLEASE SHOW HIM WHAT WE DO TO THOSE WHO TURN THEIR BACK ON US.
FWWWWWMMMMMMM
EEEE-YAH!
AAA-YAH!!
KEEEE-YAH!!!

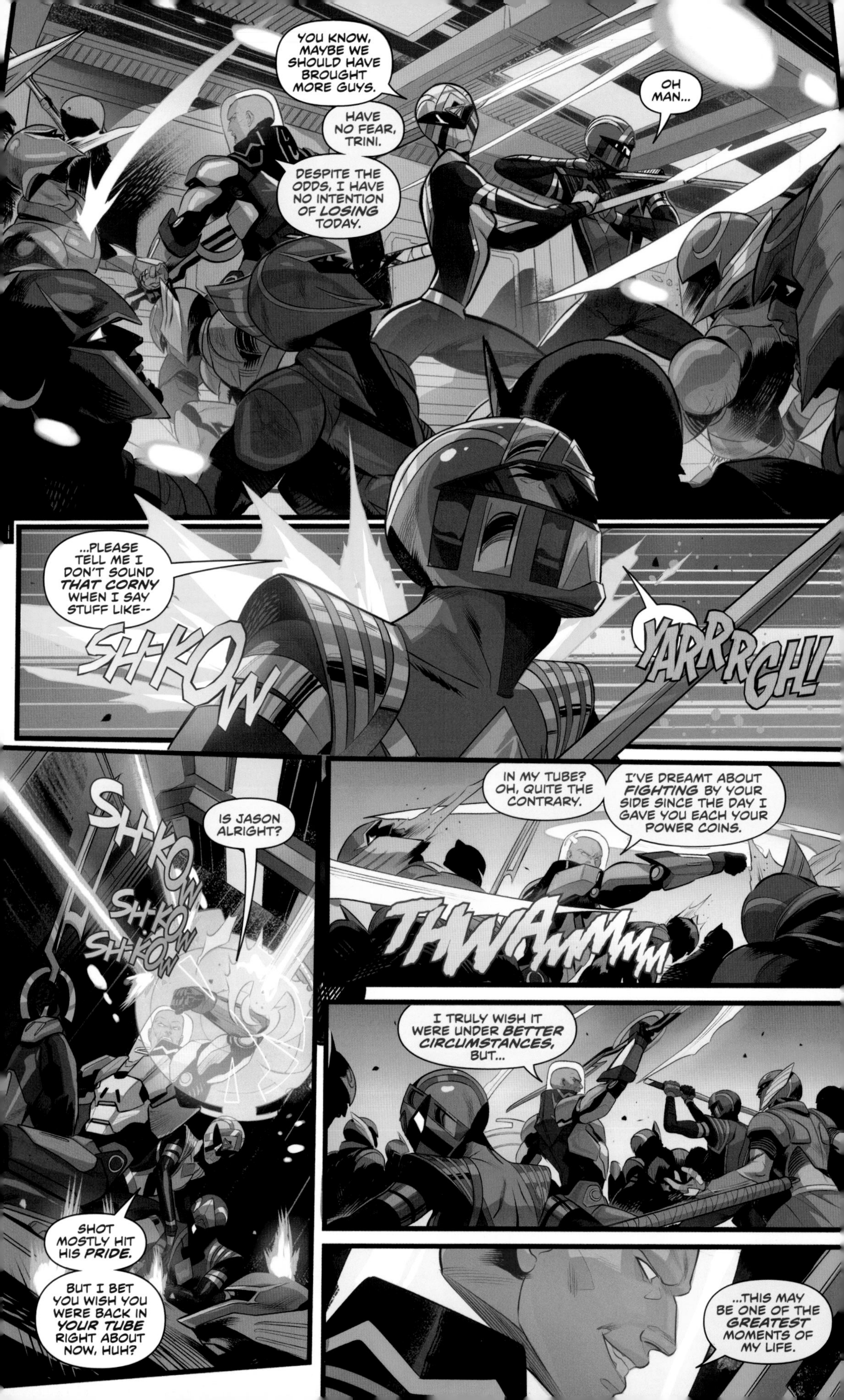
YOU KNOW, MAYBE WE SHOULD HAVE BROUGHT MORE GUYS.
OH MAN...
HAVE NO FEAR, TRINI.
DESPITE THE ODDS, I HAVE NO INTENTION OF LOSING TODAY.
...PLEASE TELL ME I DON'T SOUND THAT CORNY WHEN I SAY STUFF LIKE--
SH-KOW
YARRRGH!
SH-KOW
IS JASON ALRIGHT?
SH-KOW
SH-KOW
SHOT MOSTLY HIT HIS PRIDE.
BUT I BET YOU WISH YOU WERE BACK IN YOUR TUBE RIGHT ABOUT NOW, HUH?
IN MY TUBE? OH, QUITE THE CONTRARY.
I'VE DREAMT ABOUT FIGHTING BY YOUR SIDE SINCE THE DAY I GAVE YOU EACH YOUR POWER COINS.
THWAMMMM
I TRULY WISH IT WERE UNDER BETTER CIRCUMSTANCES, BUT...
...THIS MAY BE ONE OF THE GREATEST MOMENTS OF MY LIFE.

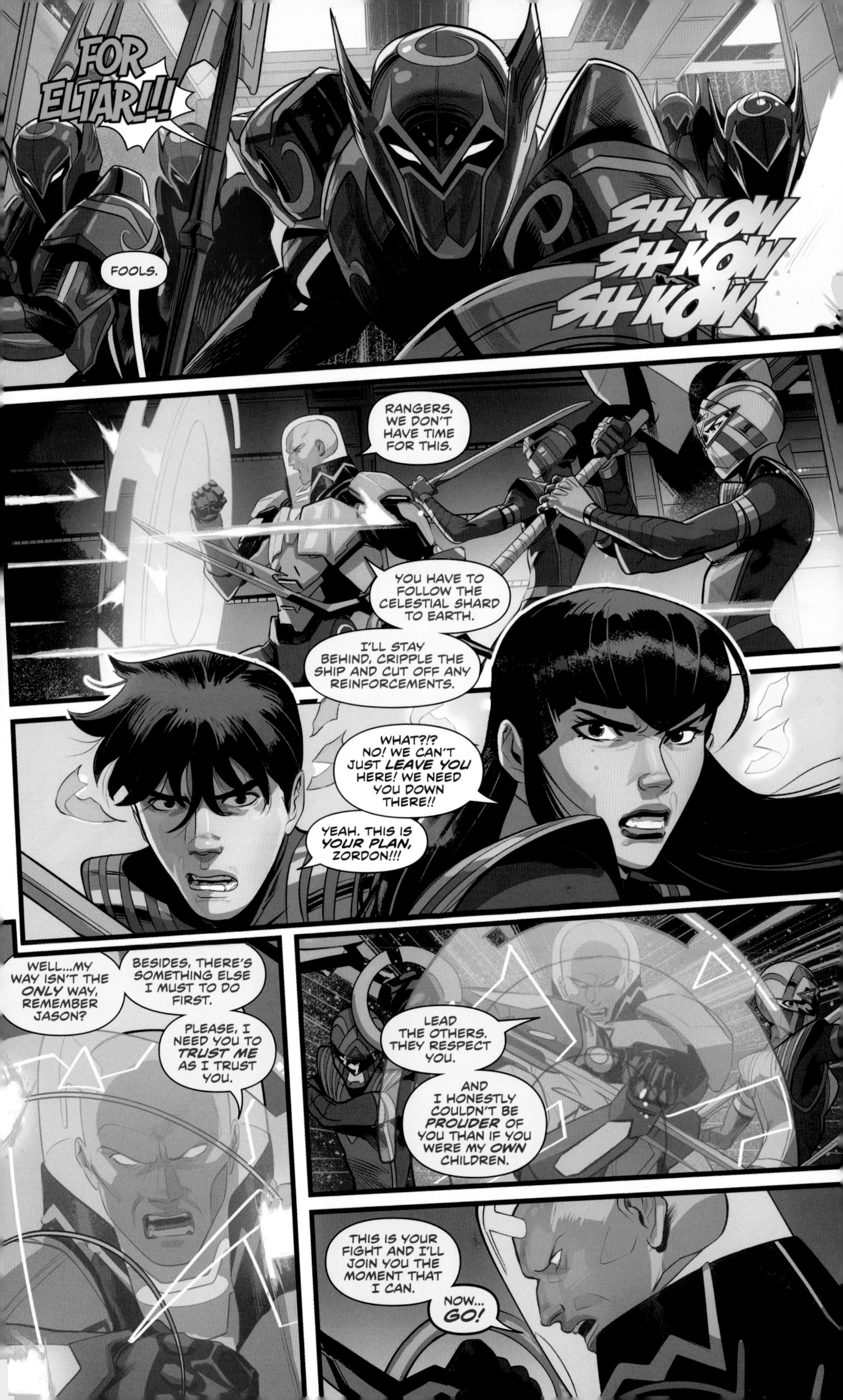
FOR ELTAR!!!
FOOLS.
SH-KOW SH-KOW SH-KOW
RANGERS, WE DON'T HAVE TIME FOR THIS.
YOU HAVE TO FOLLOW THE CELESTIAL SHARD TO EARTH.
I'LL STAY BEHIND, CRIPPLE THE SHIP AND CUT OFF ANY REINFORCEMENTS.
WHAT?!? NO! WE CAN'T JUST LEAVE YOU HERE! WE NEED YOU DOWN THERE!!
YEAH. THIS IS YOUR PLAN, ZORDON!!!
WELL...MY WAY ISN'T THE ONLY WAY, REMEMBER JASON?
BESIDES, THERE'S SOMETHING ELSE I MUST TO DO FIRST.
PLEASE, I NEED YOU TO TRUST ME AS I TRUST YOU.
LEAD THE OTHERS. THEY RESPECT YOU.
AND I HONESTLY COULDN'T BE PROUDER OF YOU THAN IF YOU WERE MY OWN CHILDREN.
THIS IS YOUR FIGHT AND I'LL JOIN YOU THE MOMENT THAT I CAN.
NOW... GO!

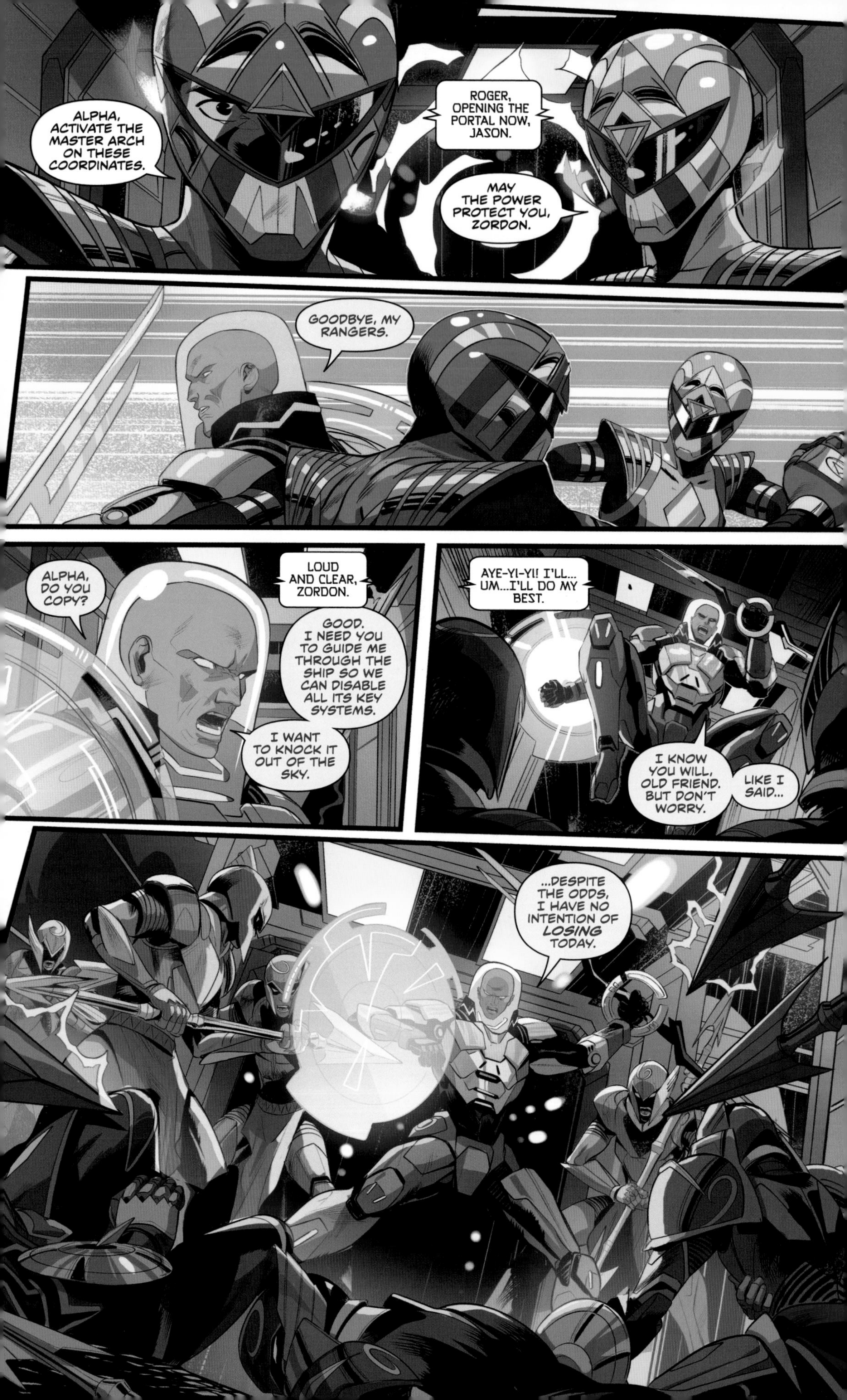
ALPHA, ACTIVATE THE MASTER ARCH ON THESE COORDINATES.
ROGER, OPENING THE PORTAL NOW, JASON.
MAY THE POWER PROTECT YOU, ZORDON.
GOODBYE, MY RANGERS.
ALPHA, DO YOU COPY?
LOUD AND CLEAR, ZORDON.
GOOD. I NEED YOU TO GUIDE ME THROUGH THE SHIP SO WE CAN DISABLE ALL ITS KEY SYSTEMS.
I WANT TO KNOCK IT OUT OF THE SKY.
AYE-YI-YI! I'LL... UM...I'LL DO MY BEST.
I KNOW YOU WILL, OLD FRIEND. BUT DON'T WORRY.
LIKE I SAID...
...DESPITE THE ODDS, I HAVE NO INTENTION OF *LOSING* TODAY.

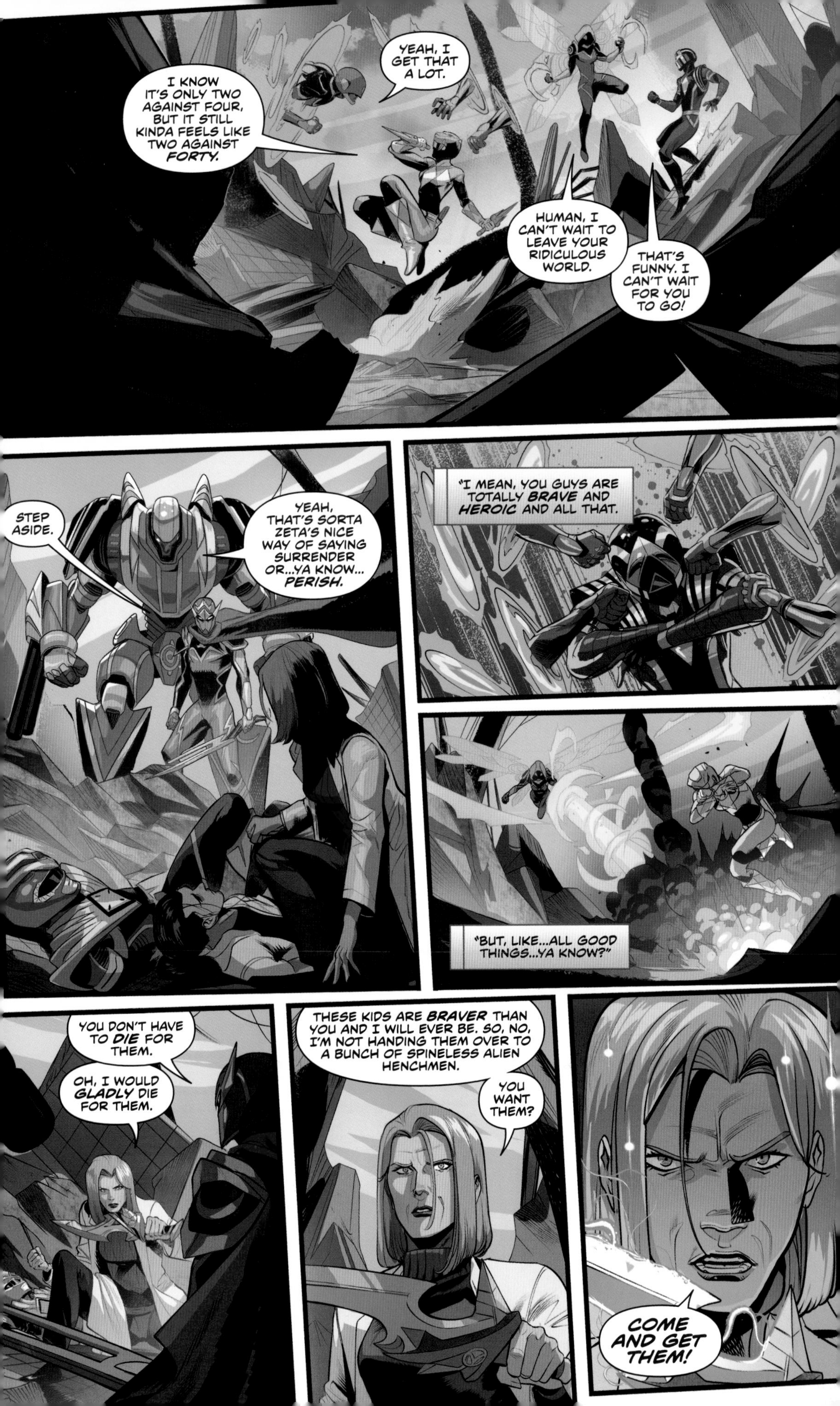
I KNOW IT'S ONLY TWO AGAINST FOUR, BUT IT STILL KINDA FEELS LIKE TWO AGAINST *FORTY.*
YEAH, I GET THAT A LOT.
HUMAN, I CAN'T WAIT TO LEAVE YOUR RIDICULOUS WORLD.
THAT'S FUNNY. I CAN'T WAIT FOR YOU TO GO!
STEP ASIDE.
YEAH, THAT'S SORTA ZETA'S NICE WAY OF SAYING SURRENDER OR...YA KNOW... *PERISH.*
"I MEAN, YOU GUYS ARE TOTALLY *BRAVE* AND *HEROIC* AND ALL THAT.
"BUT, LIKE...ALL GOOD THINGS...YA KNOW?"
YOU DON'T HAVE TO *DIE* FOR THEM.
OH, I WOULD *GLADLY* DIE FOR THEM.
THESE KIDS ARE *BRAVER* THAN YOU AND I WILL EVER BE. SO, NO, I'M NOT HANDING THEM OVER TO A BUNCH OF SPINELESS ALIEN HENCHMEN.
YOU WANT THEM?
*COME AND GET THEM!*

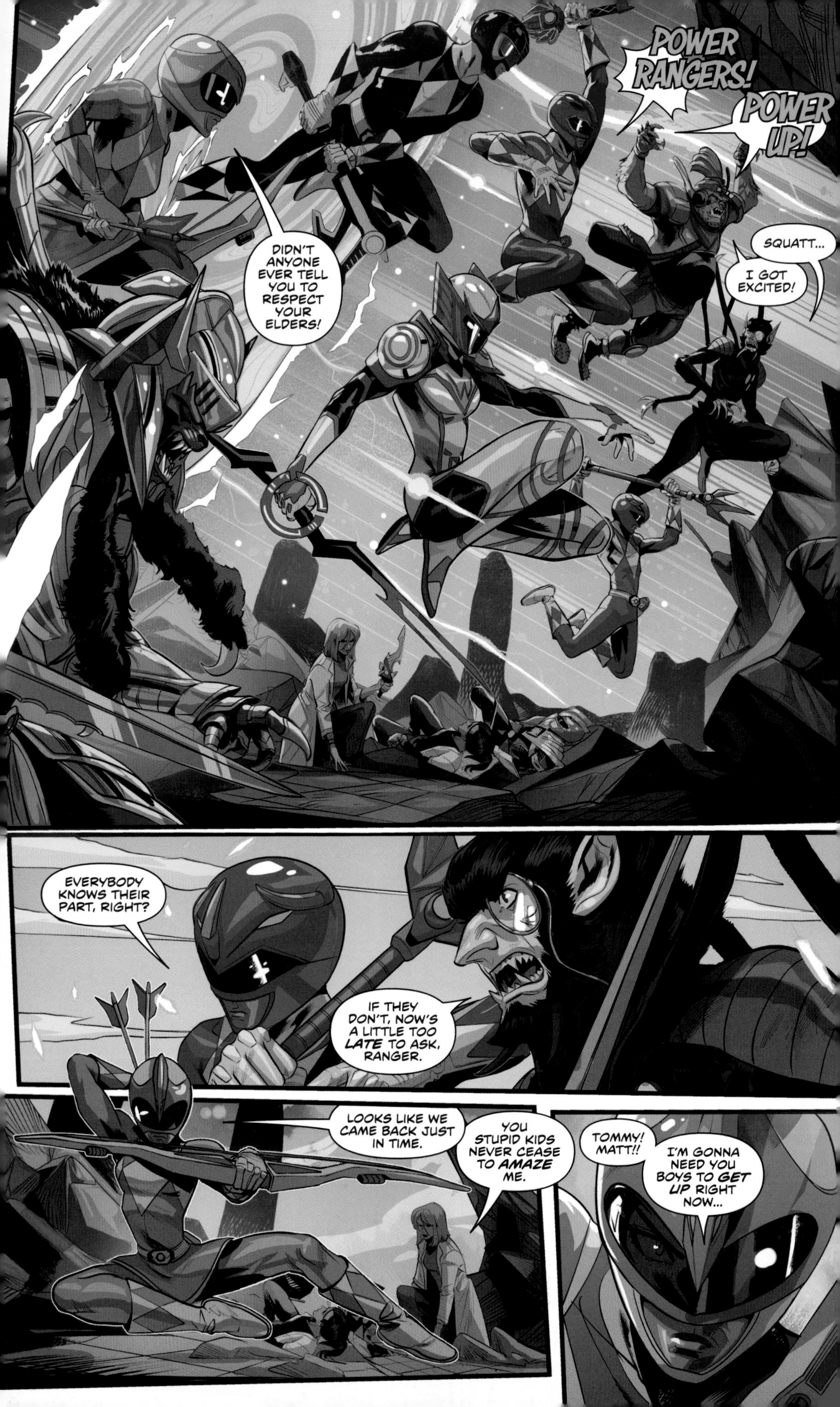
POWER RANGERS!
POWER UP!
DIDN'T ANYONE EVER TELL YOU TO RESPECT YOUR ELDERS!
SQUATT...
I GOT EXCITED!
EVERYBODY KNOWS THEIR PART, RIGHT?
IF THEY DON'T, NOW'S A LITTLE TOO *LATE* TO ASK, RANGER.
LOOKS LIKE WE CAME BACK JUST IN TIME.
YOU STUPID KIDS NEVER CEASE TO *AMAZE* ME.
TOMMY! MATT!!
I'M GONNA NEED YOU BOYS TO *GET UP* RIGHT NOW...

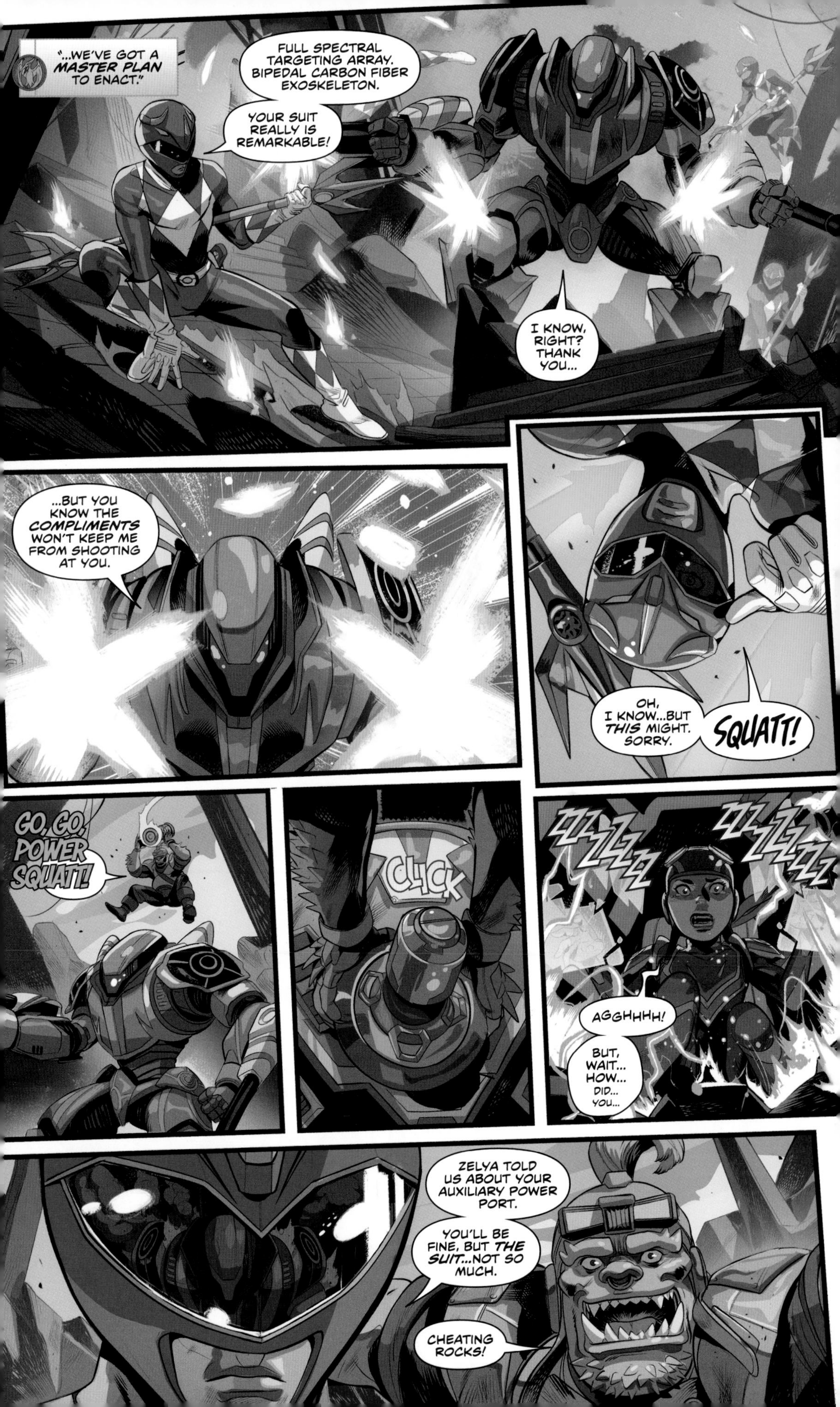
"...WE'VE GOT A MASTER PLAN TO ENACT."
FULL SPECTRAL TARGETING ARRAY. BIPEDAL CARBON FIBER EXOSKELETON.
YOUR SUIT REALLY IS REMARKABLE!
I KNOW, RIGHT? THANK YOU...
...BUT YOU KNOW THE COMPLIMENTS WON'T KEEP ME FROM SHOOTING AT YOU.
OH, I KNOW...BUT THIS MIGHT. SORRY.
SQUATT!
GO, GO, POWER SQUATT!
CLICK
AGGHHHH!
BUT, WAIT... HOW... DID... YOU...
ZELYA TOLD US ABOUT YOUR AUXILIARY POWER PORT.
YOU'LL BE FINE, BUT THE SUIT...NOT SO MUCH.
CHEATING ROCKS!

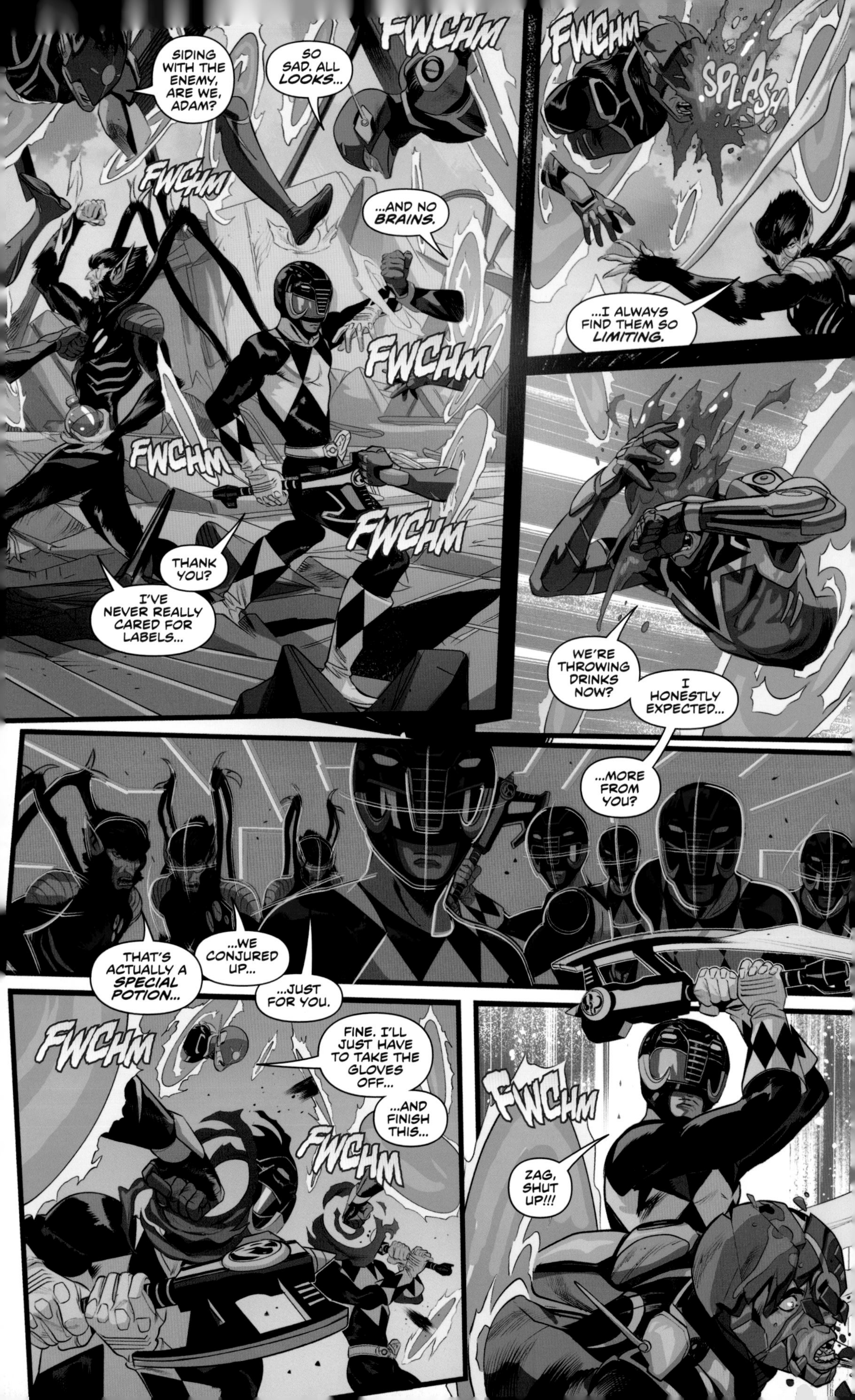
SIDING WITH THE ENEMY, ARE WE, ADAM?
SO SAD. ALL LOOKS...
FWCHM
...AND NO BRAINS.
FWCHM
FWCHM
FWCHM
FWCHM
THANK YOU?
I'VE NEVER REALLY CARED FOR LABELS...
FWCHM
SPLASH
...I ALWAYS FIND THEM SO LIMITING.
WE'RE THROWING DRINKS NOW?
I HONESTLY EXPECTED...
...MORE FROM YOU?
THAT'S ACTUALLY A SPECIAL POTION...
...WE CONJURED UP...
...JUST FOR YOU.
FWCHM
FINE. I'LL JUST HAVE TO TAKE THE GLOVES OFF...
...AND FINISH THIS...
FWCHM
FWCHM
ZAG, SHUT UP!!!

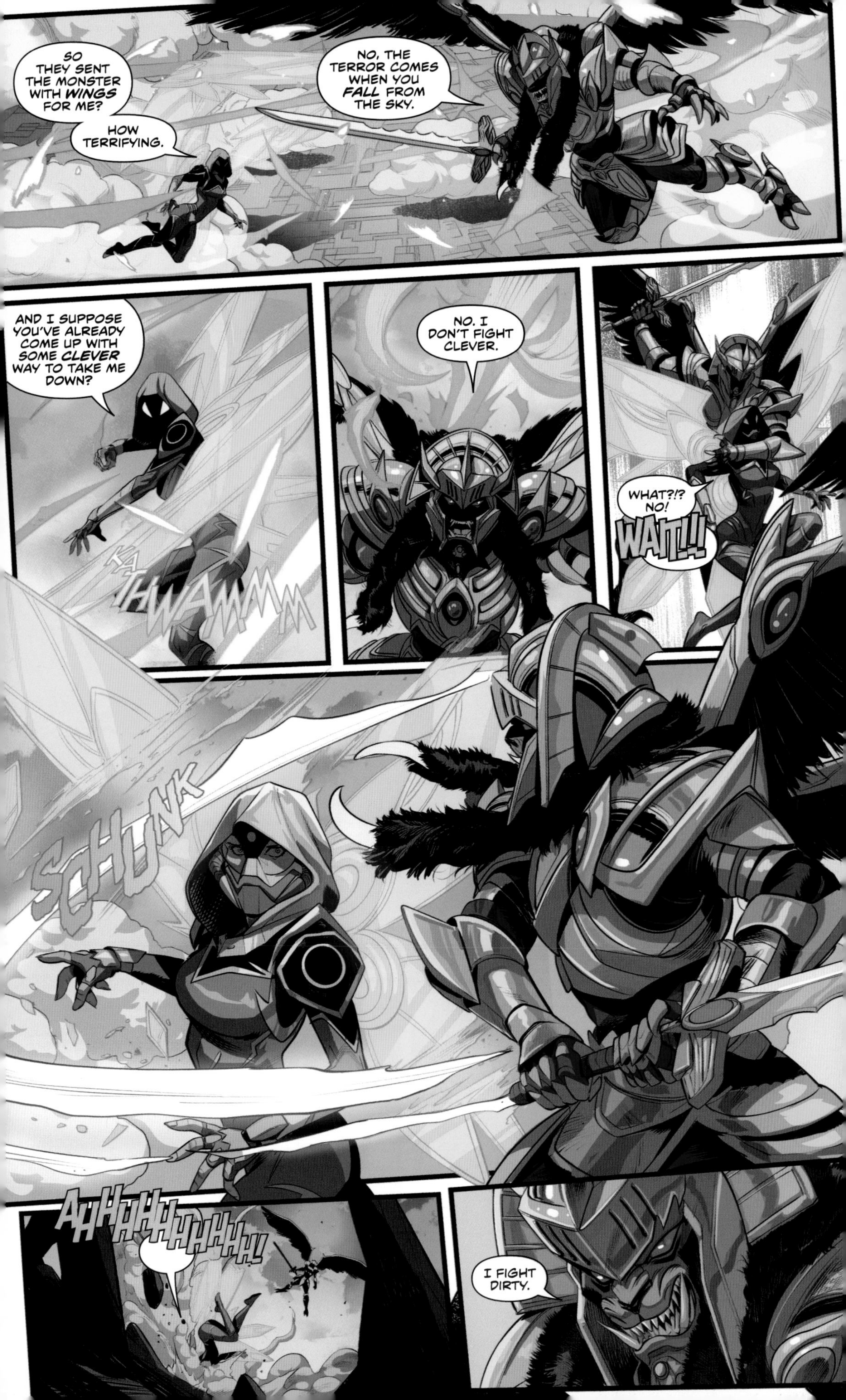
SO THEY SENT THE MONSTER WITH WINGS FOR ME?
HOW TERRIFYING.
NO, THE TERROR COMES WHEN YOU FALL FROM THE SKY.
AND I SUPPOSE YOU'VE ALREADY COME UP WITH SOME CLEVER WAY TO TAKE ME DOWN?
KATHWAMMM
NO. I DON'T FIGHT CLEVER.
WHAT?!? NO! WAIT!!!
SCHUNK
AHHHHHHHHHH!!
I FIGHT DIRTY.

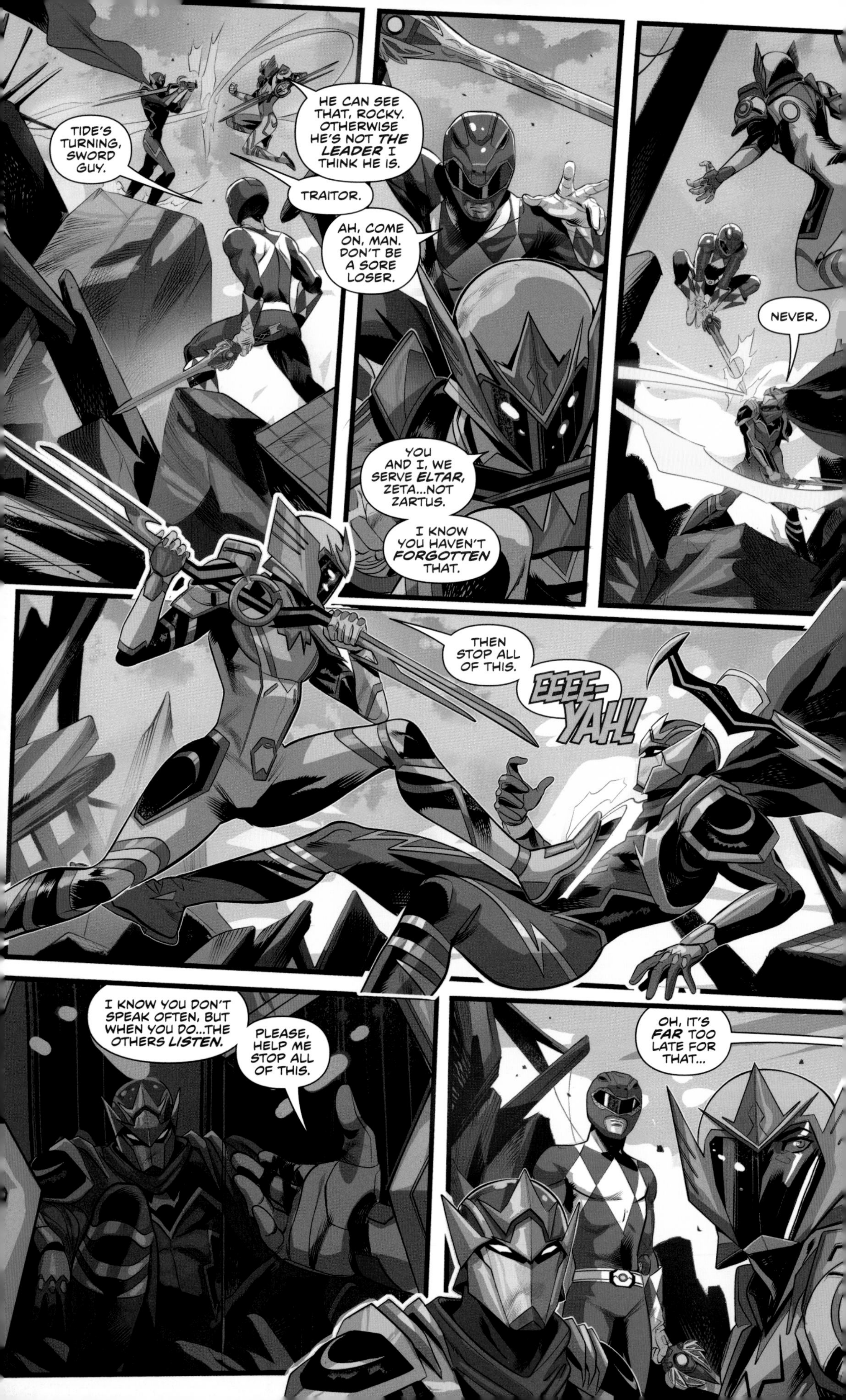
TIDE'S TURNING, SWORD GUY.
HE CAN SEE THAT, ROCKY. OTHERWISE HE'S NOT *THE LEADER* I THINK HE IS.
TRAITOR.
AH, COME ON, MAN. DON'T BE A SORE LOSER.
YOU AND I, WE SERVE *ELTAR*, ZETA...NOT ZARTUS.
I KNOW YOU HAVEN'T *FORGOTTEN* THAT.
NEVER.
THEN STOP ALL OF THIS.
EEEE-YAH!
I KNOW YOU DON'T SPEAK OFTEN, BUT WHEN YOU DO...THE OTHERS *LISTEN.*
PLEASE, HELP ME STOP ALL OF THIS.
OH, IT'S *FAR* TOO LATE FOR THAT...

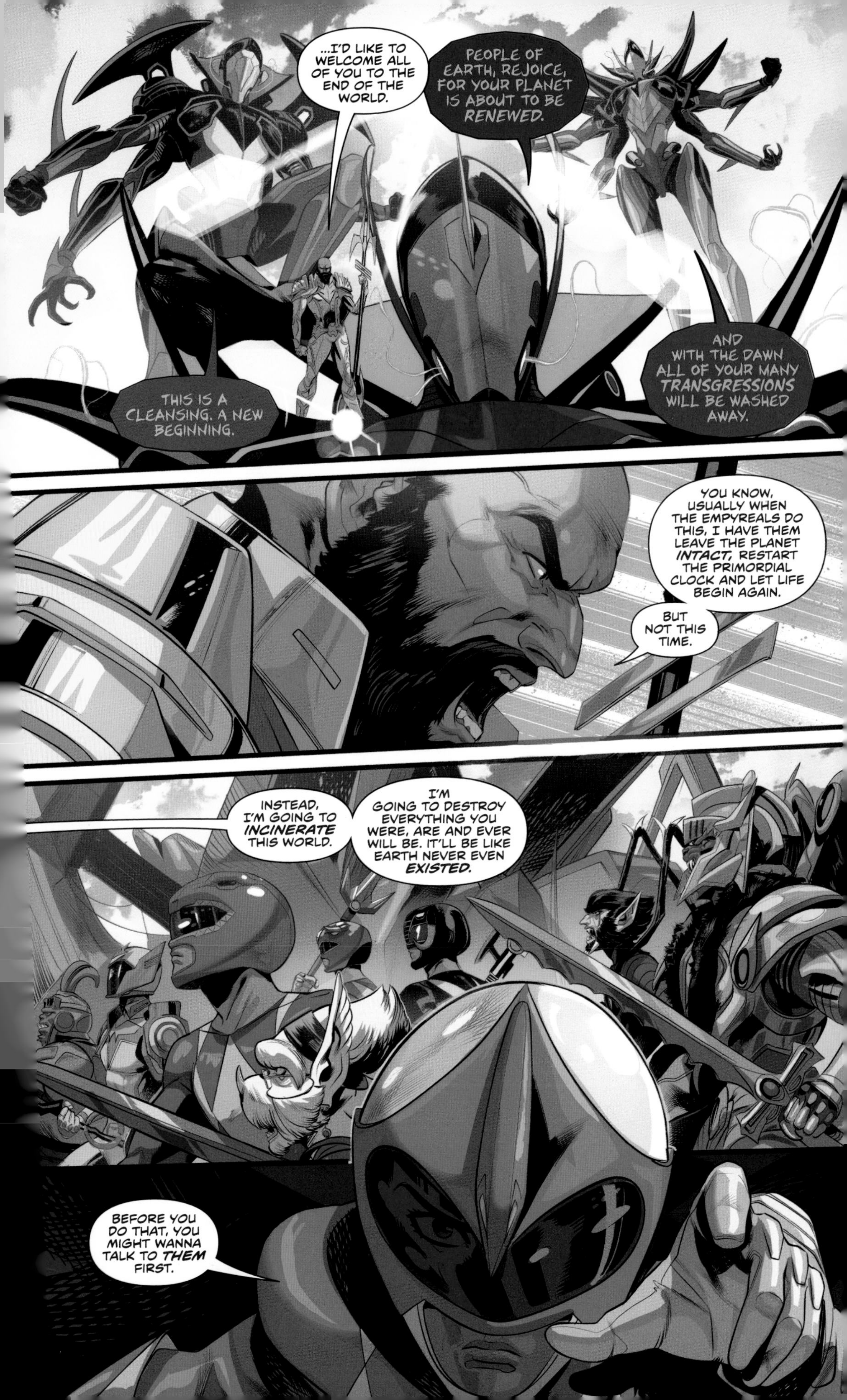
...I'D LIKE TO WELCOME ALL OF YOU TO THE END OF THE WORLD.
PEOPLE OF EARTH, REJOICE, FOR YOUR PLANET IS ABOUT TO BE RENEWED.
THIS IS A CLEANSING. A NEW BEGINNING.
AND WITH THE DAWN ALL OF YOUR MANY TRANSGRESSIONS WILL BE WASHED AWAY.
YOU KNOW, USUALLY WHEN THE EMPYREALS DO THIS, I HAVE THEM LEAVE THE PLANET INTACT, RESTART THE PRIMORDIAL CLOCK AND LET LIFE BEGIN AGAIN.
BUT NOT THIS TIME.
INSTEAD, I'M GOING TO INCINERATE THIS WORLD.
I'M GOING TO DESTROY EVERYTHING YOU WERE, ARE AND EVER WILL BE. IT'LL BE LIKE EARTH NEVER EVEN EXISTED.
BEFORE YOU DO THAT, YOU MIGHT WANNA TALK TO THEM FIRST.

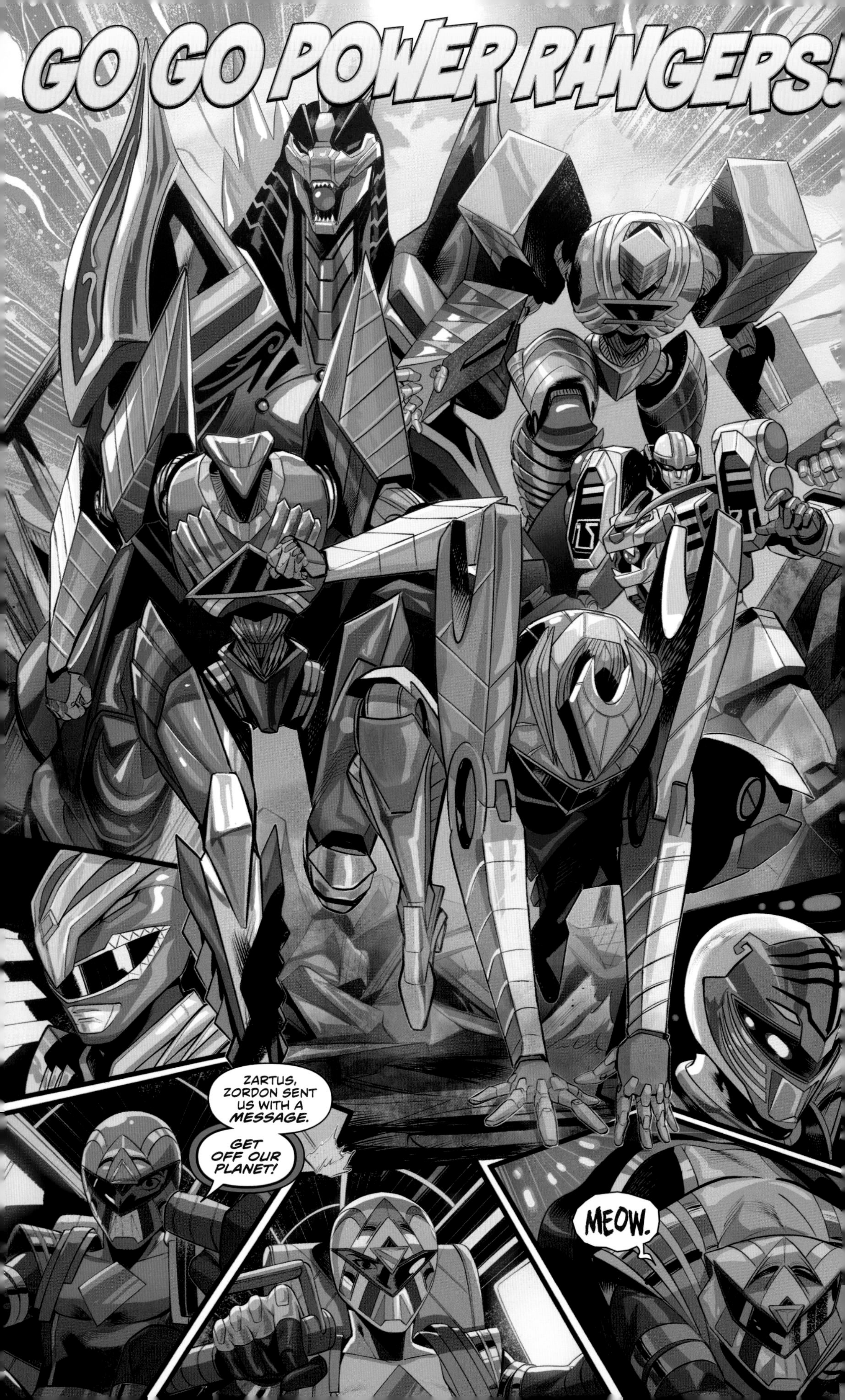
GO GO POWER RANGERS!
ZARTUS, ZORDON SENT US WITH A MESSAGE.
GET OFF OUR PLANET!
MEOW.

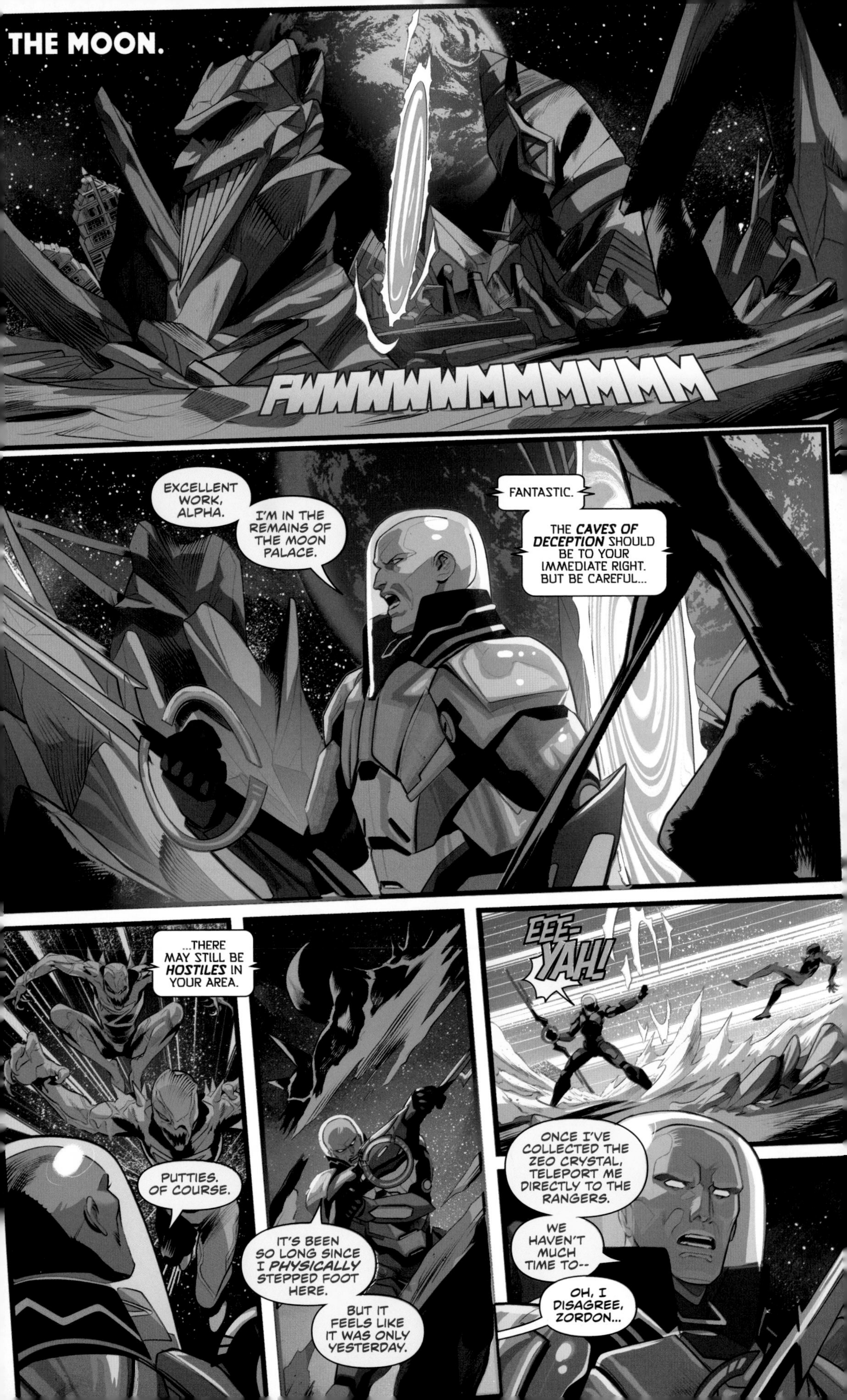
THE MOON.
FWWWWWMMMMMMM
EXCELLENT WORK, ALPHA.
I'M IN THE REMAINS OF THE MOON PALACE.
FANTASTIC.
THE CAVES OF DECEPTION SHOULD BE TO YOUR IMMEDIATE RIGHT. BUT BE CAREFUL...
...THERE MAY STILL BE HOSTILES IN YOUR AREA.
PUTTIES. OF COURSE.
IT'S BEEN SO LONG SINCE I PHYSICALLY STEPPED FOOT HERE.
BUT IT FEELS LIKE IT WAS ONLY YESTERDAY.
EEE-YAH!
ONCE I'VE COLLECTED THE ZEO CRYSTAL, TELEPORT ME DIRECTLY TO THE RANGERS.
WE HAVEN'T MUCH TIME TO--
OH, I DISAGREE, ZORDON...

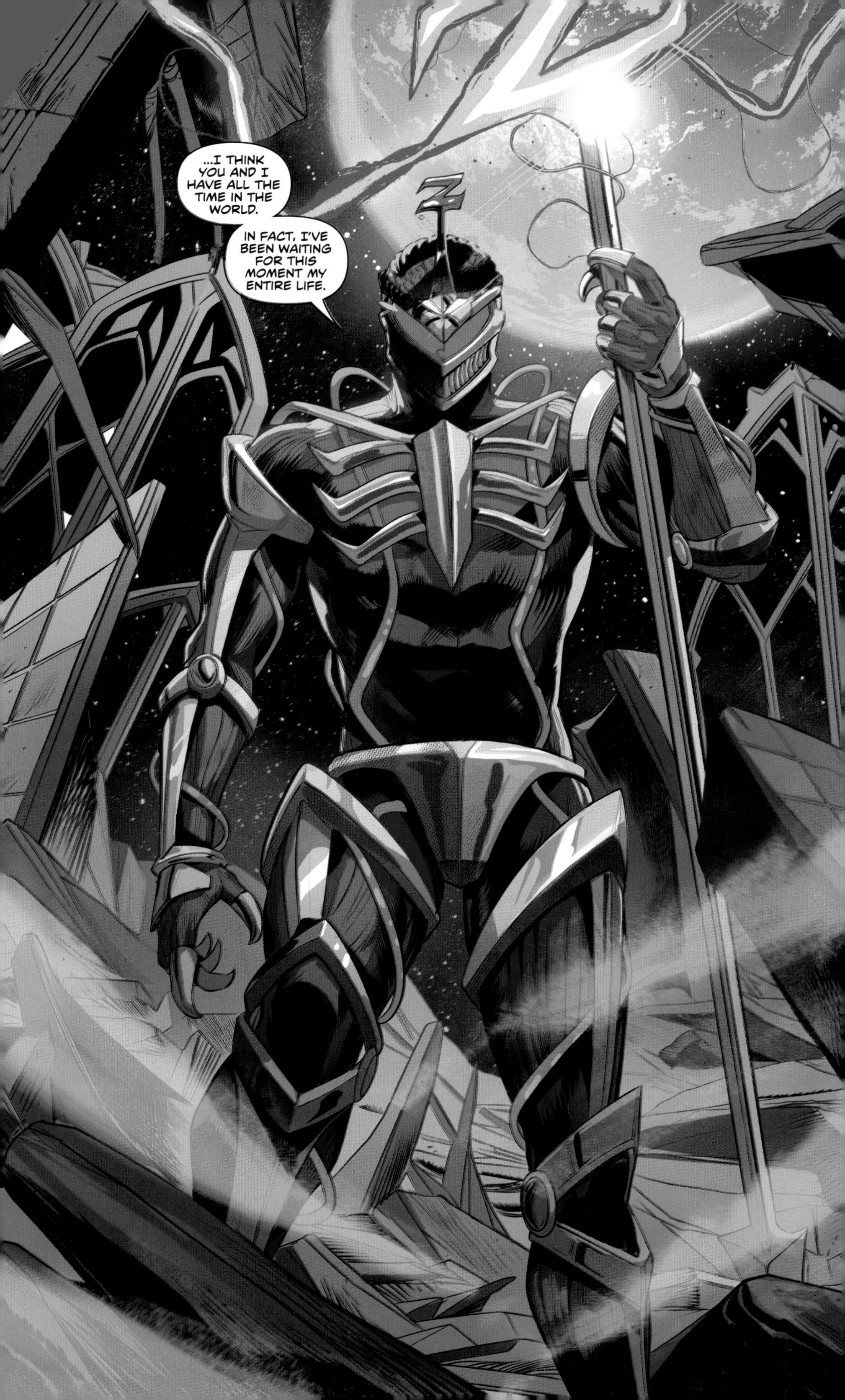
...I THINK YOU AND I HAVE ALL THE TIME IN THE WORLD.
IN FACT, I'VE BEEN WAITING FOR THIS MOMENT MY ENTIRE LIFE.

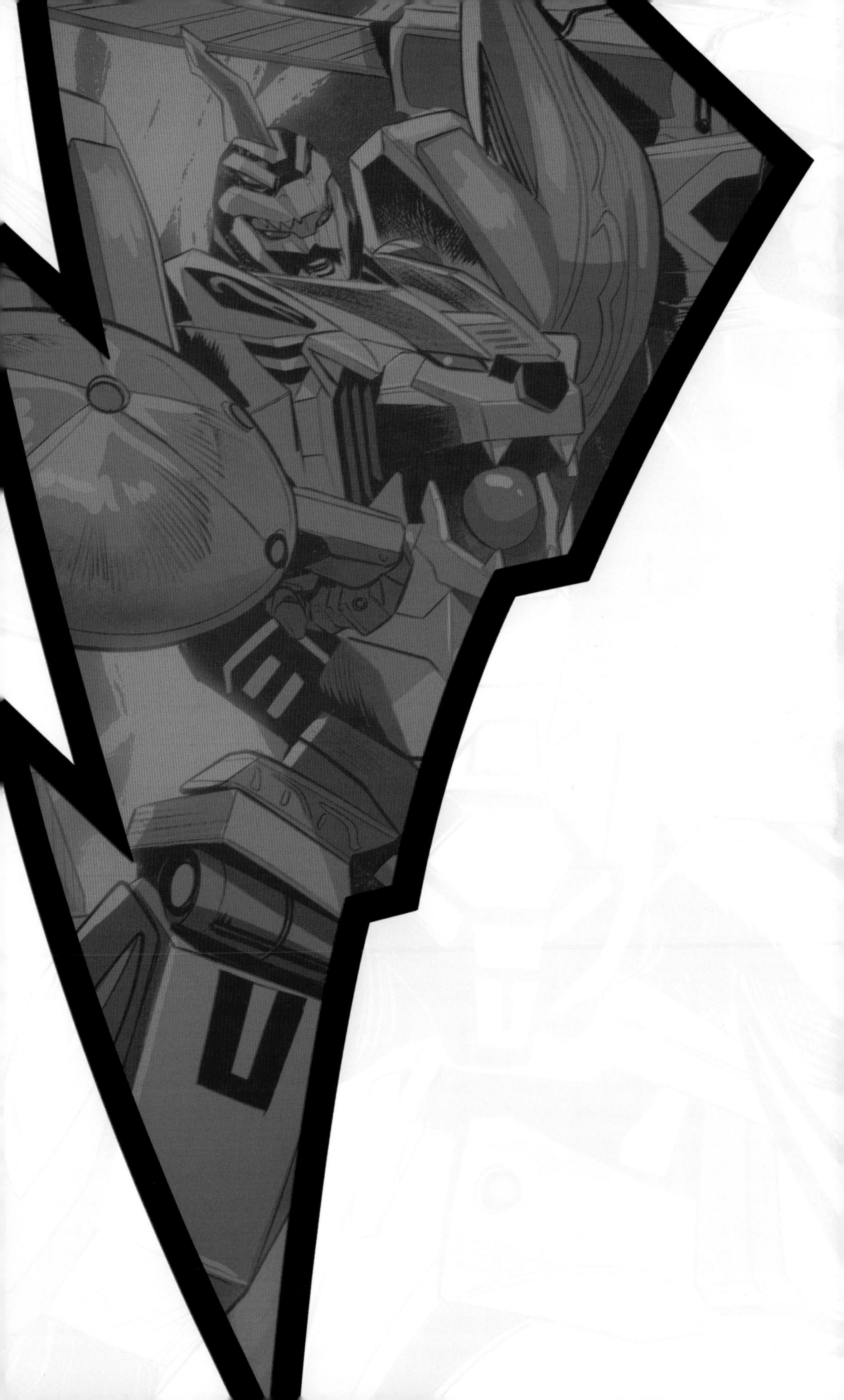

CHAPTER
# FIFTEEN

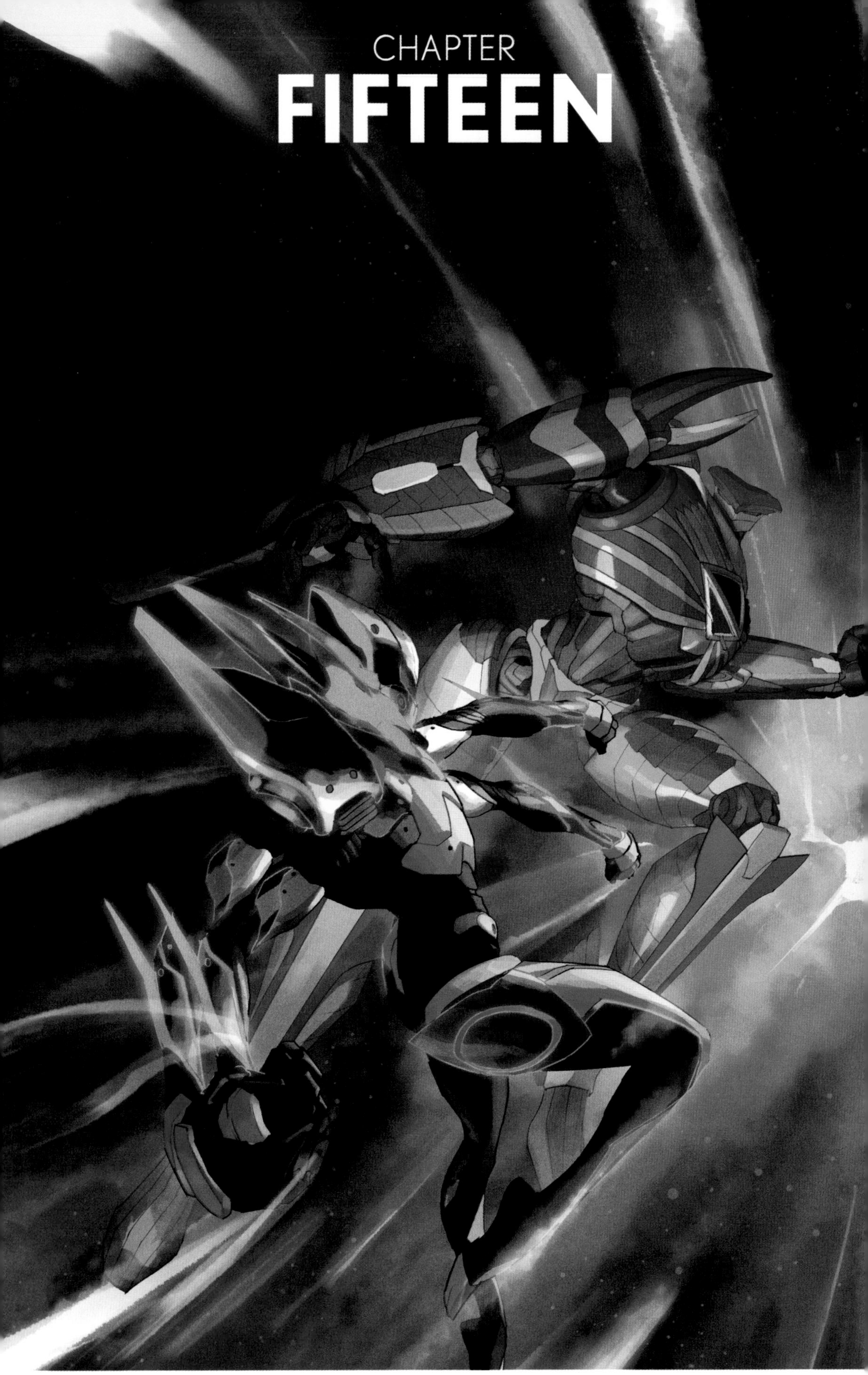

GERALD PAREL | ISSUE FIFTEEN COVER

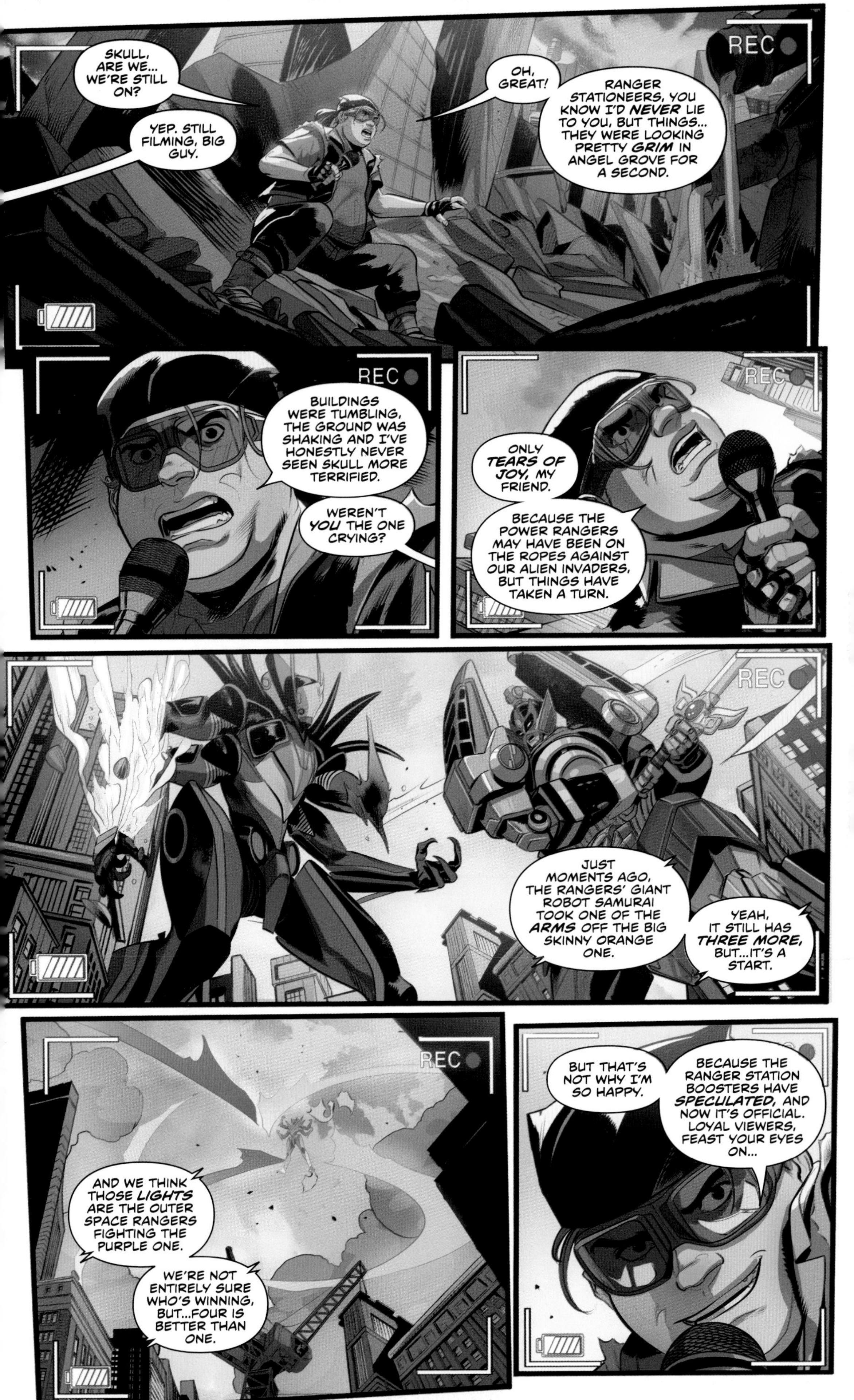
REC
SKULL, ARE WE... WE'RE STILL ON?
YEP. STILL FILMING, BIG GUY.
OH, GREAT!
RANGER STATIONEERS, YOU KNOW I'D NEVER LIE TO YOU, BUT THINGS... THEY WERE LOOKING PRETTY GRIM IN ANGEL GROVE FOR A SECOND.
REC
BUILDINGS WERE TUMBLING, THE GROUND WAS SHAKING AND I'VE HONESTLY NEVER SEEN SKULL MORE TERRIFIED.
WEREN'T YOU THE ONE CRYING?
REC
ONLY TEARS OF JOY, MY FRIEND.
BECAUSE THE POWER RANGERS MAY HAVE BEEN ON THE ROPES AGAINST OUR ALIEN INVADERS, BUT THINGS HAVE TAKEN A TURN.
REC
JUST MOMENTS AGO, THE RANGERS' GIANT ROBOT SAMURAI TOOK ONE OF THE ARMS OFF THE BIG SKINNY ORANGE ONE.
YEAH, IT STILL HAS THREE MORE, BUT...IT'S A START.
REC
AND WE THINK THOSE LIGHTS ARE THE OUTER SPACE RANGERS FIGHTING THE PURPLE ONE.
WE'RE NOT ENTIRELY SURE WHO'S WINNING, BUT...FOUR IS BETTER THAN ONE.
BUT THAT'S NOT WHY I'M SO HAPPY.
BECAUSE THE RANGER STATION BOOSTERS HAVE SPECULATED, AND NOW IT'S OFFICIAL. LOYAL VIEWERS, FEAST YOUR EYES ON...

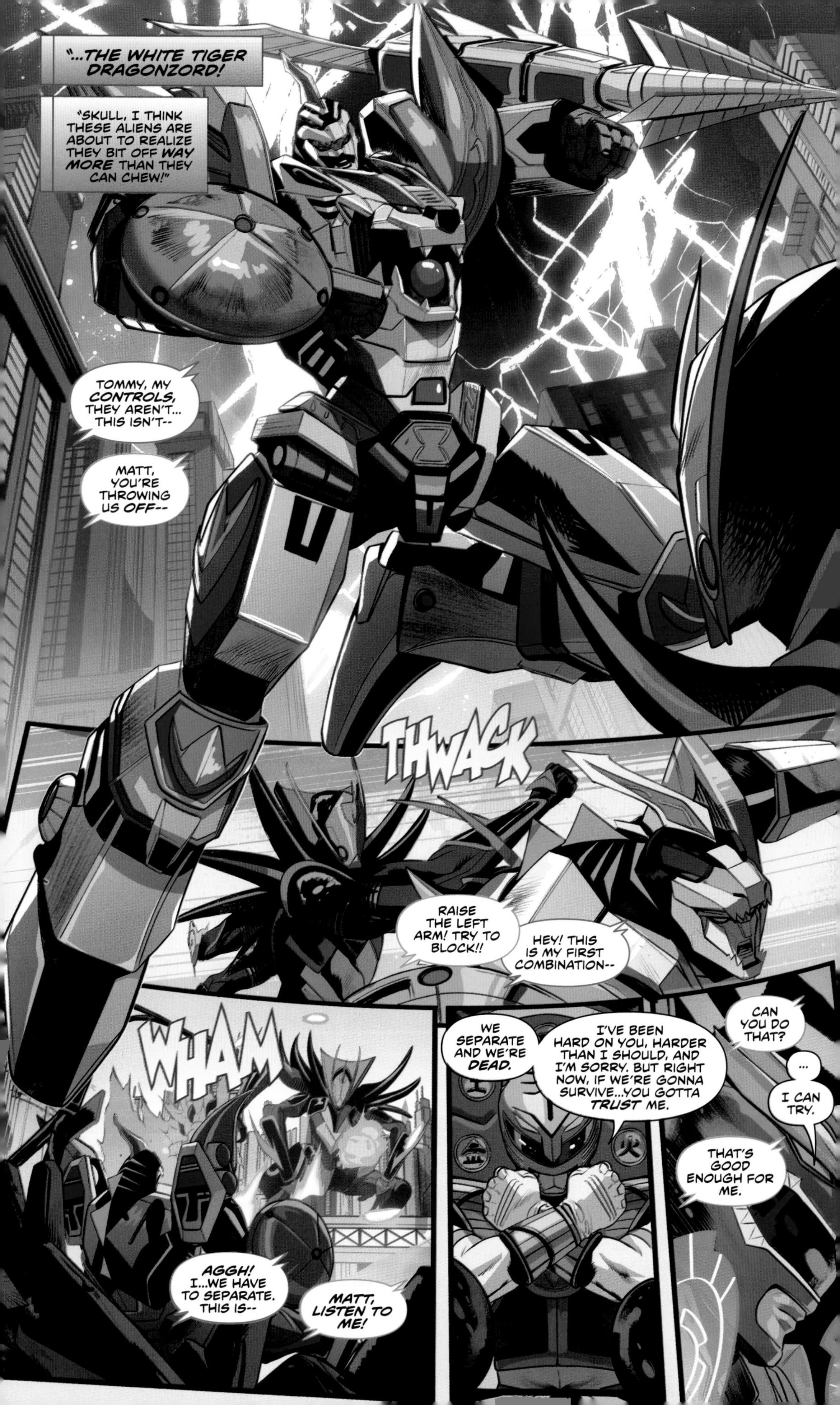

"...THE WHITE TIGER DRAGONZORD!
"SKULL, I THINK THESE ALIENS ARE ABOUT TO REALIZE THEY BIT OFF WAY MORE THAN THEY CAN CHEW!"
TOMMY, MY CONTROLS, THEY AREN'T... THIS ISN'T--
MATT, YOU'RE THROWING US OFF--
THWACK
RAISE THE LEFT ARM! TRY TO BLOCK!!
HEY! THIS IS MY FIRST COMBINATION--
WHAM
AGGH! I...WE HAVE TO SEPARATE. THIS IS--
MATT, LISTEN TO ME!
WE SEPARATE AND WE'RE DEAD.
I'VE BEEN HARD ON YOU, HARDER THAN I SHOULD, AND I'M SORRY. BUT RIGHT NOW, IF WE'RE GONNA SURVIVE...YOU GOTTA TRUST ME.
CAN YOU DO THAT?
...
I CAN TRY.
THAT'S GOOD ENOUGH FOR ME.

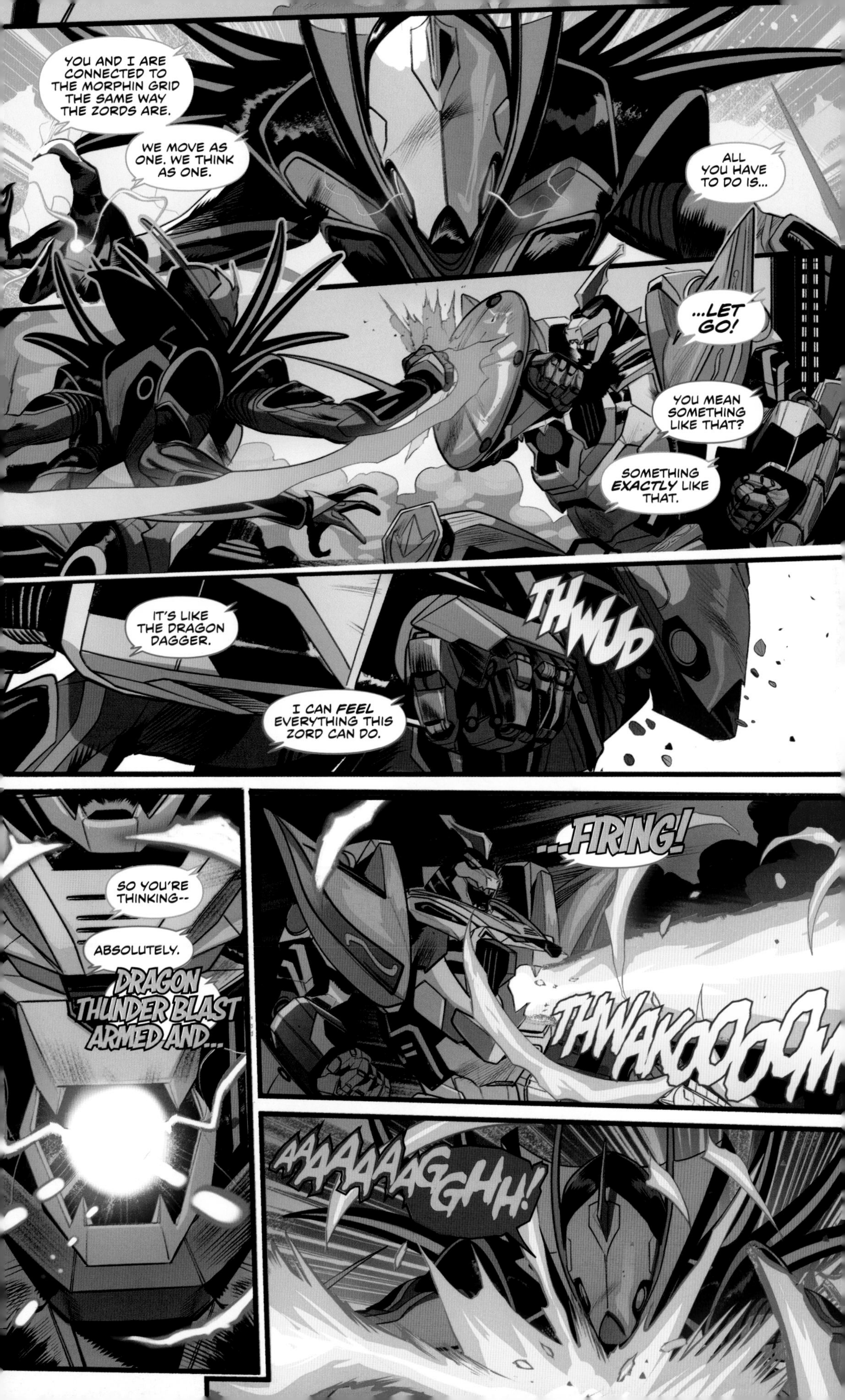
YOU AND I ARE CONNECTED TO THE MORPHIN GRID THE SAME WAY THE ZORDS ARE.
WE MOVE AS ONE. WE THINK AS ONE.
ALL YOU HAVE TO DO IS...
...LET GO!
YOU MEAN SOMETHING LIKE THAT?
SOMETHING EXACTLY LIKE THAT.
THWUD
IT'S LIKE THE DRAGON DAGGER.
I CAN FEEL EVERYTHING THIS ZORD CAN DO.
SO YOU'RE THINKING--
ABSOLUTELY.
DRAGON THUNDER BLAST ARMED AND...
...FIRING!
THWAKOOOOM
AAAAAAAGGHH!

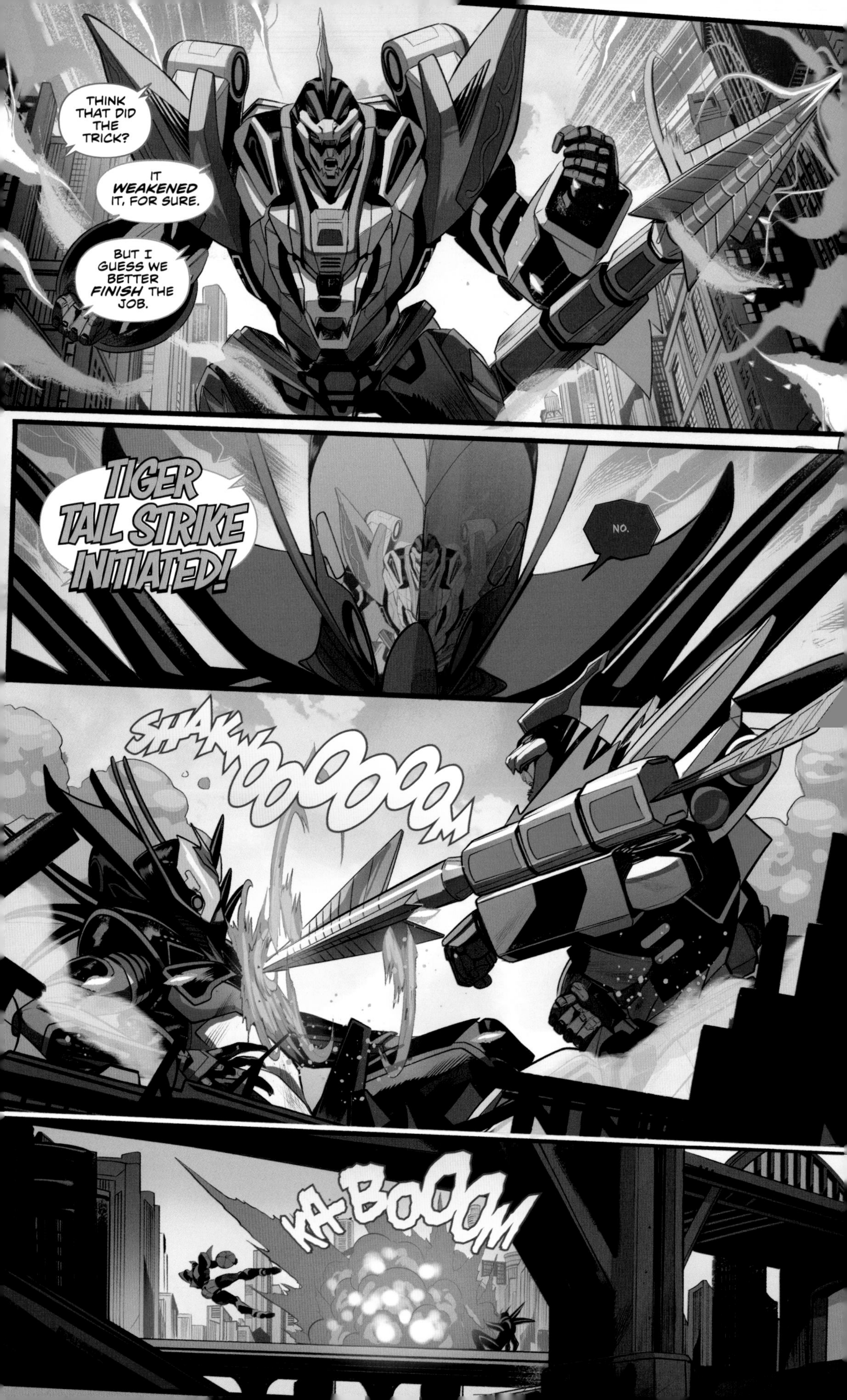
THINK THAT DID THE TRICK?
IT WEAKENED IT, FOR SURE.
BUT I GUESS WE BETTER FINISH THE JOB.
TIGER TAIL STRIKE INITIATED!
NO.
SHAKOOOOOOM
KA BOOOM

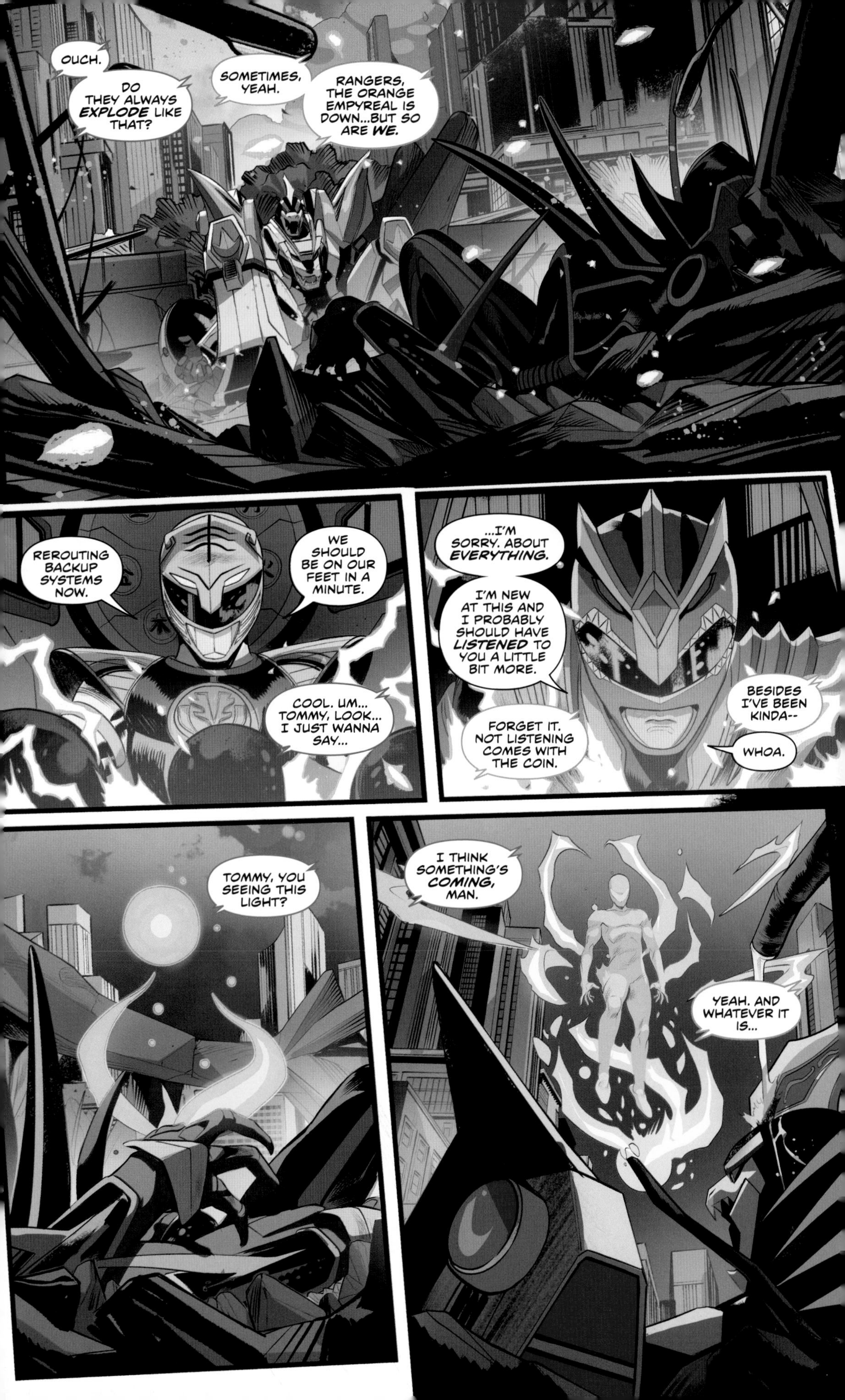
OUCH.
DO THEY ALWAYS EXPLODE LIKE THAT?
SOMETIMES, YEAH.
RANGERS, THE ORANGE EMPYREAL IS DOWN...BUT SO ARE WE.
REROUTING BACKUP SYSTEMS NOW.
WE SHOULD BE ON OUR FEET IN A MINUTE.
COOL. UM... TOMMY, LOOK... I JUST WANNA SAY...
...I'M SORRY. ABOUT EVERYTHING.
I'M NEW AT THIS AND I PROBABLY SHOULD HAVE LISTENED TO YOU A LITTLE BIT MORE.
FORGET IT. NOT LISTENING COMES WITH THE COIN.
BESIDES I'VE BEEN KINDA--
WHOA.
TOMMY, YOU SEEING THIS LIGHT?
I THINK SOMETHING'S COMING, MAN.
YEAH. AND WHATEVER IT IS...

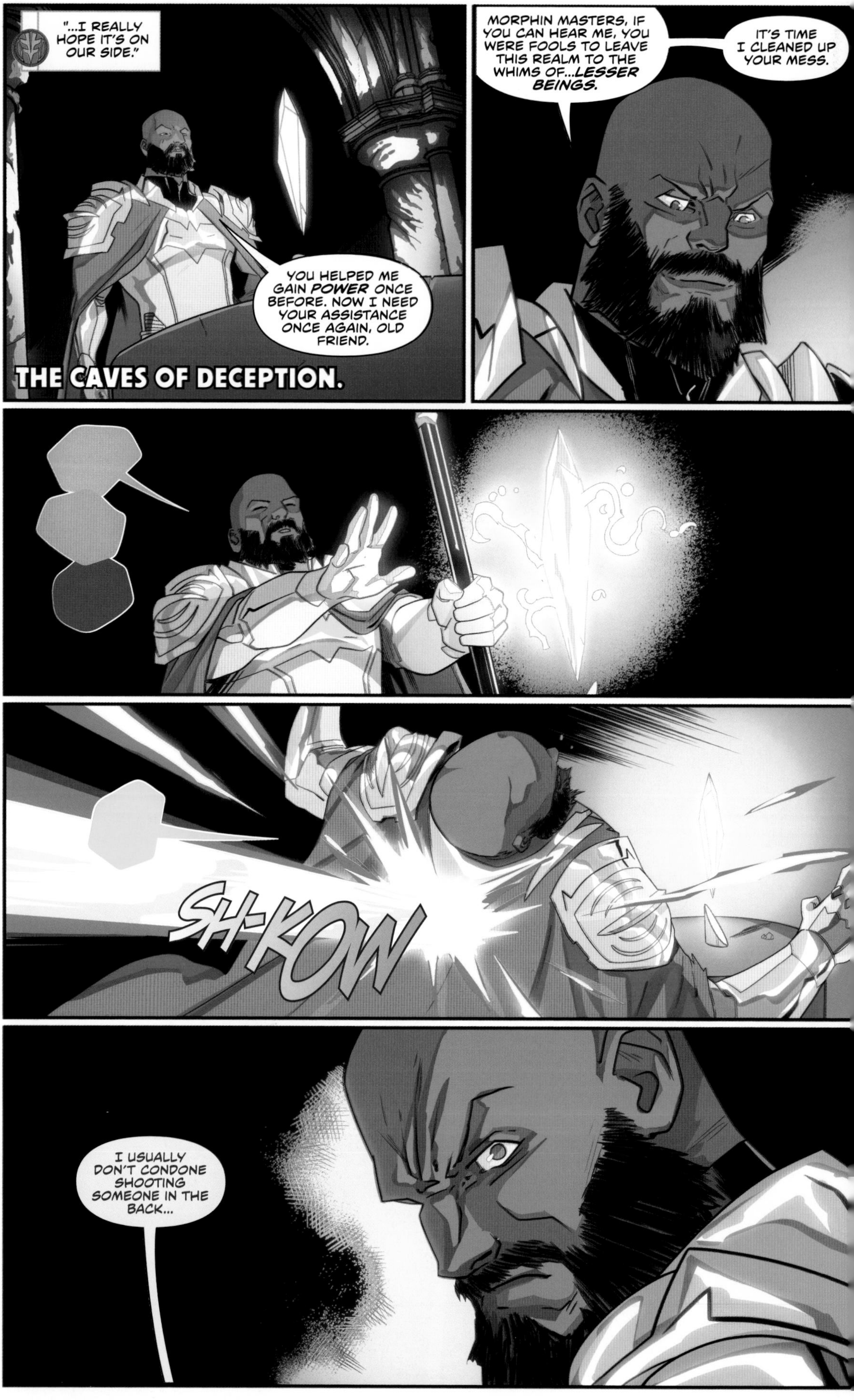
"...I REALLY HOPE IT'S ON OUR SIDE."
YOU HELPED ME GAIN POWER ONCE BEFORE. NOW I NEED YOUR ASSISTANCE ONCE AGAIN, OLD FRIEND.
THE CAVES OF DECEPTION.
MORPHIN MASTERS, IF YOU CAN HEAR ME, YOU WERE FOOLS TO LEAVE THIS REALM TO THE WHIMS OF...LESSER BEINGS.
IT'S TIME I CLEANED UP YOUR MESS.
SH-KOW
I USUALLY DON'T CONDONE SHOOTING SOMEONE IN THE BACK...

...BUT FOR YOU, I FIGURED I'D MAKE *AN EXCEPTION.*

WHAT'S THE MATTER, ZARTUS? DID *SOMEBODY* BREAK YOUR LITTLE *CRYS--*

WHO SAID I WAS *DONE* WITH YOU, SAGE?

THERE'S NO PLACE ON THIS MOON YOU CAN RUN FROM--

*KTHWAM*

AH, I SEE. YOU *WEREN'T* RUNNING, WERE YOU?

WELL, LOOK AT THIS. ZORDON, ZARTUS AND ZEDD.

BACK WHERE IT ALL STARTED.

FORGIVE ME FOR NOT INTERRUPTING YOUR *SPARRING SESSION* UPSTAIRS.

BUT IT SEEMED LIKE YOU TWO WERE WORKING OUT SOME... ISSUES.

ZARTUS, TAKE ANOTHER STEP TOWARD THE ZEO CRYSTAL AND--

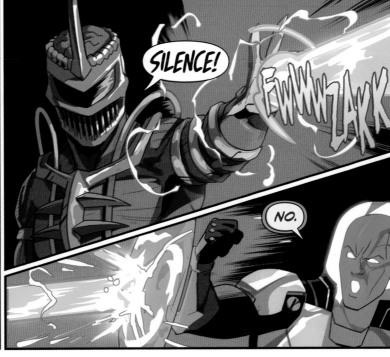

SILENCE!

*FWWWZAKK*

NO.

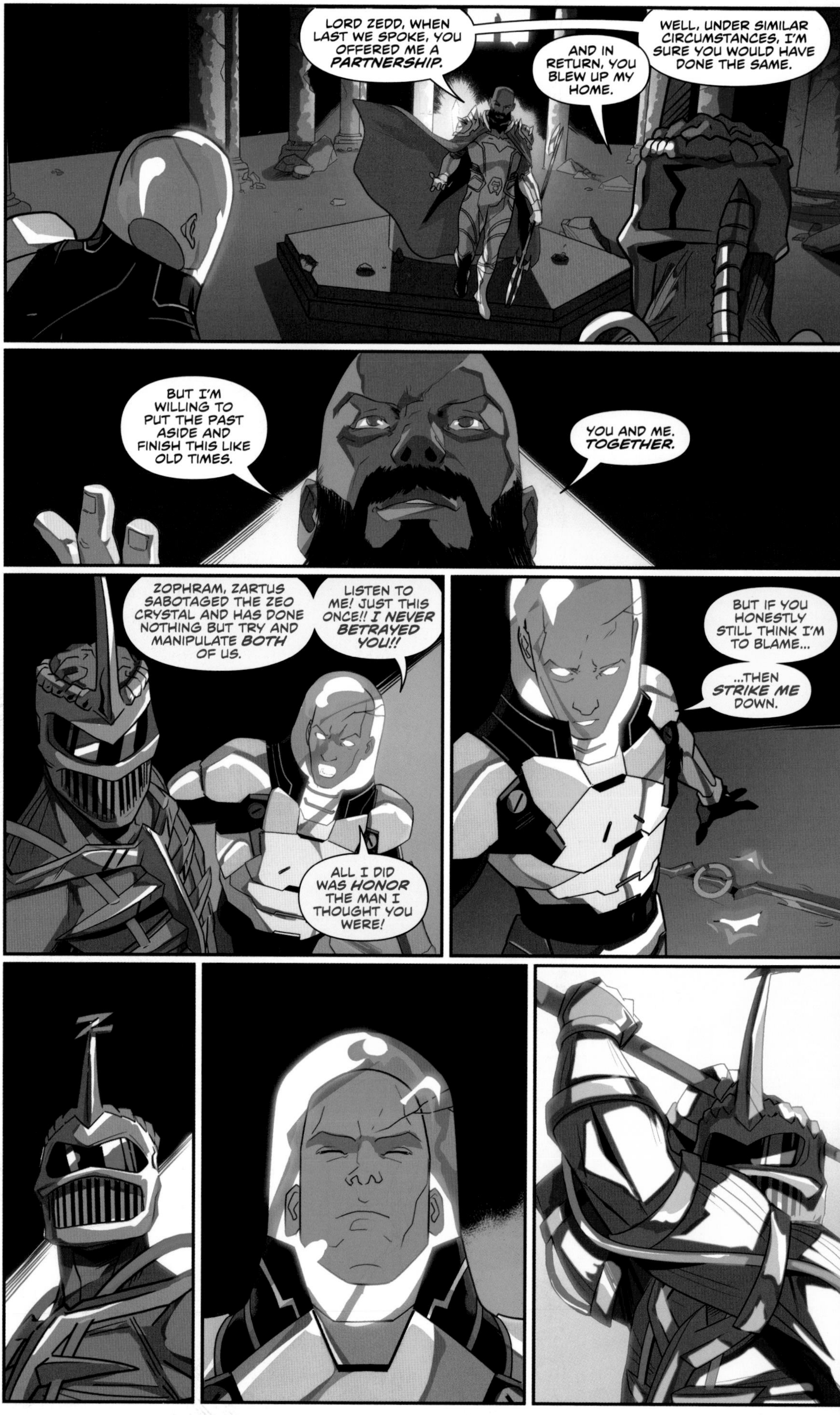
LORD ZEDD, WHEN LAST WE SPOKE, YOU OFFERED ME A PARTNERSHIP.
AND IN RETURN, YOU BLEW UP MY HOME.
WELL, UNDER SIMILAR CIRCUMSTANCES, I'M SURE YOU WOULD HAVE DONE THE SAME.
BUT I'M WILLING TO PUT THE PAST ASIDE AND FINISH THIS LIKE OLD TIMES.
YOU AND ME. TOGETHER.
ZOPHRAM, ZARTUS SABOTAGED THE ZEO CRYSTAL AND HAS DONE NOTHING BUT TRY AND MANIPULATE BOTH OF US.
LISTEN TO ME! JUST THIS ONCE!! I NEVER BETRAYED YOU!!
ALL I DID WAS HONOR THE MAN I THOUGHT YOU WERE!
BUT IF YOU HONESTLY STILL THINK I'M TO BLAME...
...THEN STRIKE ME DOWN.

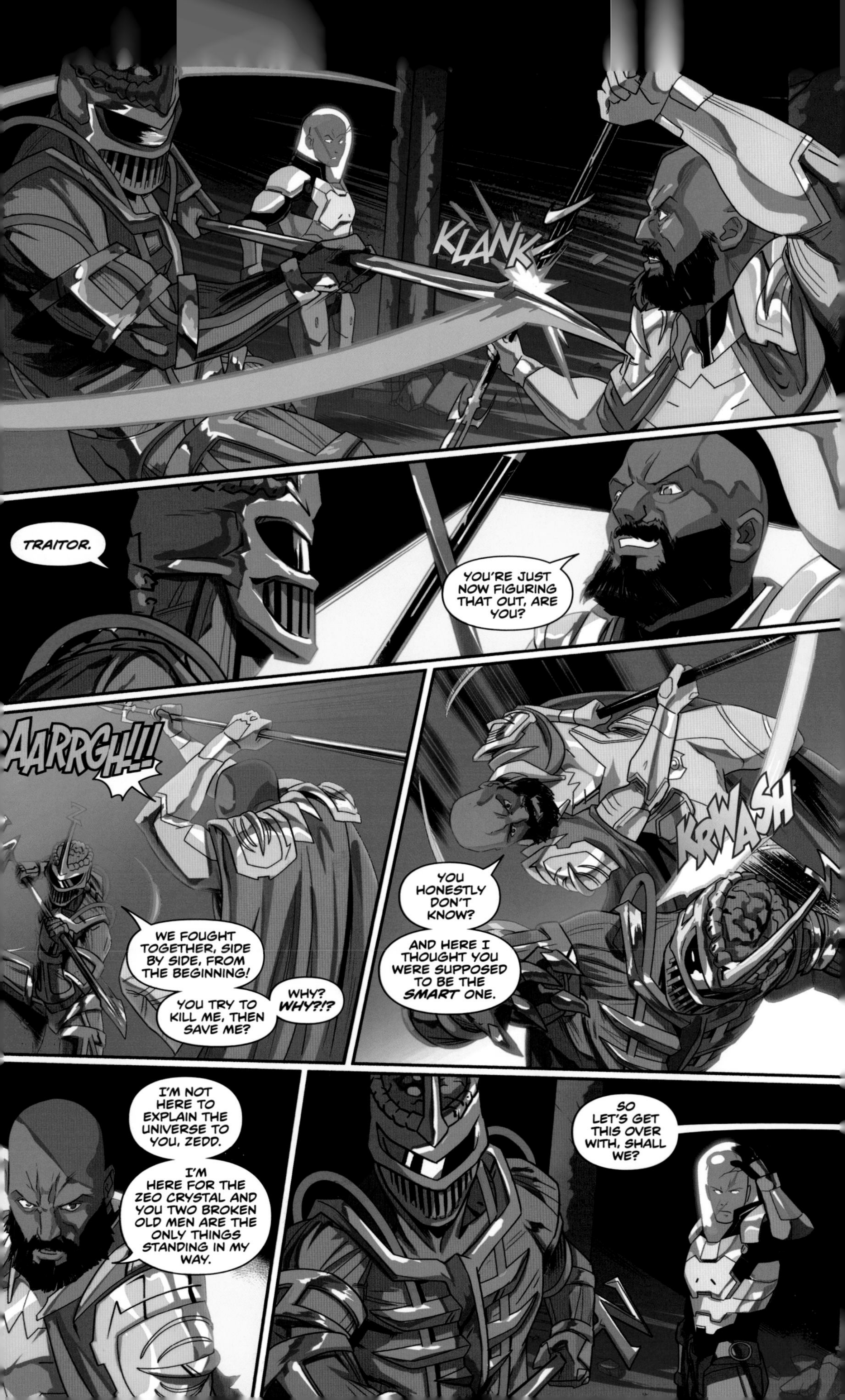
KLANK
TRAITOR.
YOU'RE JUST NOW FIGURING THAT OUT, ARE YOU?
AARRGH!!!
WE FOUGHT TOGETHER, SIDE BY SIDE, FROM THE BEGINNING!
YOU TRY TO KILL ME, THEN SAVE ME?
WHY? *WHY?!?*
KRASH
YOU HONESTLY DON'T KNOW?
AND HERE I THOUGHT YOU WERE SUPPOSED TO BE THE *SMART* ONE.
I'M NOT HERE TO EXPLAIN THE UNIVERSE TO YOU, ZEDD.
I'M HERE FOR THE ZEO CRYSTAL AND YOU TWO BROKEN OLD MEN ARE THE ONLY THINGS STANDING IN MY WAY.
SO LET'S GET THIS OVER WITH, SHALL WE?

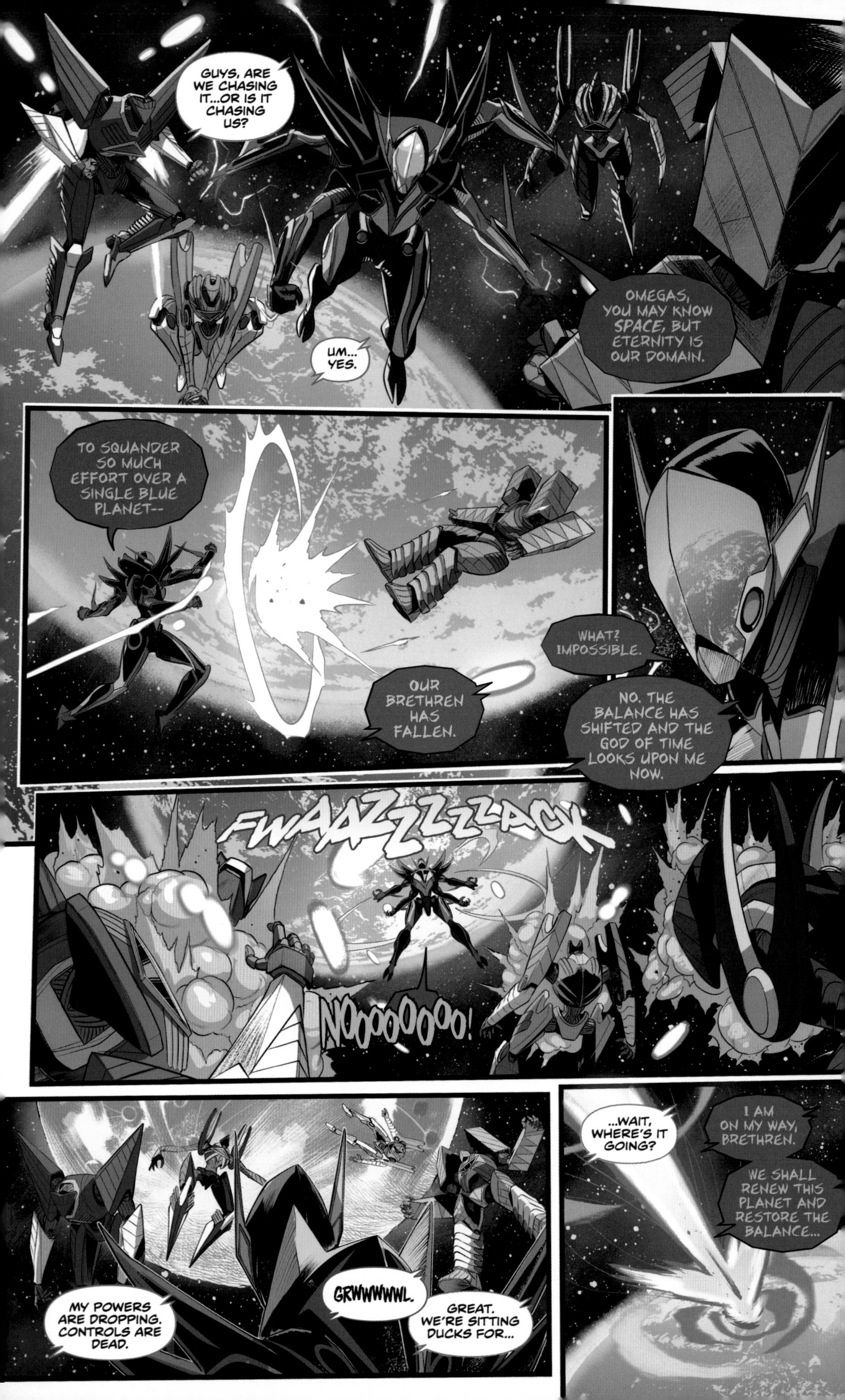
GUYS, ARE WE CHASING IT...OR IS IT CHASING US?
UM... YES.
OMEGAS, YOU MAY KNOW SPACE, BUT ETERNITY IS OUR DOMAIN.
TO SQUANDER SO MUCH EFFORT OVER A SINGLE BLUE PLANET--
OUR BRETHREN HAS FALLEN.
WHAT? IMPOSSIBLE.
NO. THE BALANCE HAS SHIFTED AND THE GOD OF TIME LOOKS UPON ME NOW.
FWAAZZZZZACK
NOOOOOOOO!
MY POWERS ARE DROPPING. CONTROLS ARE DEAD.
GRWWWWWL.
GREAT. WE'RE SITTING DUCKS FOR...
...WAIT, WHERE'S IT GOING?
I AM ON MY WAY, BRETHREN.
WE SHALL RENEW THIS PLANET AND RESTORE THE BALANCE...

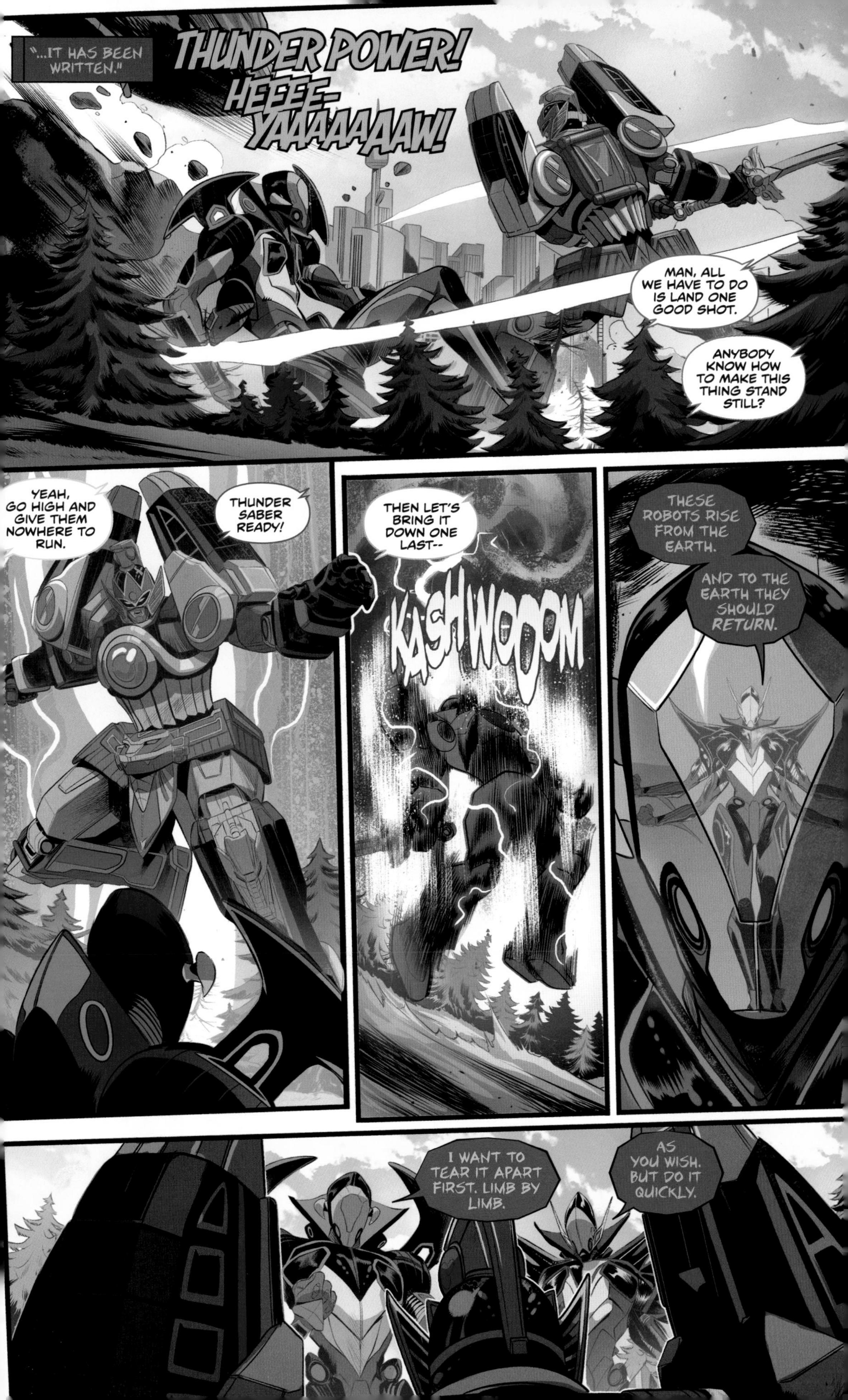
"...IT HAS BEEN WRITTEN."
THUNDER POWER! HEEEE-YAAAAAAAW!
MAN, ALL WE HAVE TO DO IS LAND ONE GOOD SHOT.
ANYBODY KNOW HOW TO MAKE THIS THING STAND STILL?
YEAH, GO HIGH AND GIVE THEM NOWHERE TO RUN.
THUNDER SABER READY!
THEN LET'S BRING IT DOWN ONE LAST--
KASHWOOOM
THESE ROBOTS RISE FROM THE EARTH.
AND TO THE EARTH THEY SHOULD RETURN.
I WANT TO TEAR IT APART FIRST. LIMB BY LIMB.
AS YOU WISH. BUT DO IT QUICKLY.

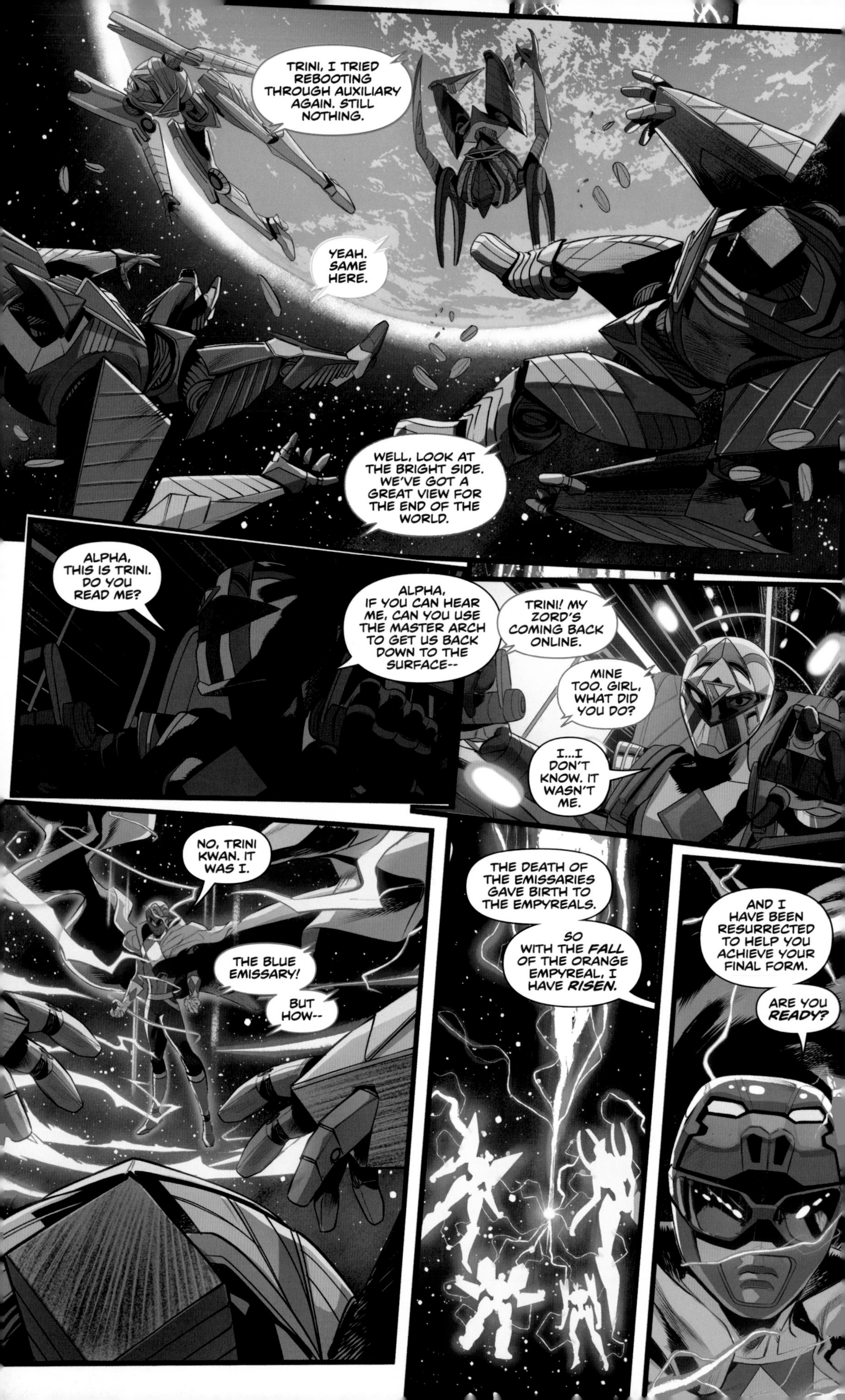
TRINI, I TRIED REBOOTING THROUGH AUXILIARY AGAIN. STILL NOTHING.
YEAH. SAME HERE.
WELL, LOOK AT THE BRIGHT SIDE. WE'VE GOT A GREAT VIEW FOR THE END OF THE WORLD.
ALPHA, THIS IS TRINI. DO YOU READ ME?
ALPHA, IF YOU CAN HEAR ME, CAN YOU USE THE MASTER ARCH TO GET US BACK DOWN TO THE SURFACE--
TRINI! MY ZORD'S COMING BACK ONLINE.
MINE TOO. GIRL, WHAT DID YOU DO?
I...I DON'T KNOW. IT WASN'T ME.
NO, TRINI KWAN. IT WAS I.
THE BLUE EMISSARY!
BUT HOW--
THE DEATH OF THE EMISSARIES GAVE BIRTH TO THE EMPYREALS.
SO WITH THE *FALL* OF THE ORANGE EMPYREAL, I HAVE *RISEN.*
AND I HAVE BEEN RESURRECTED TO HELP YOU ACHIEVE YOUR FINAL FORM.
ARE YOU *READY?*

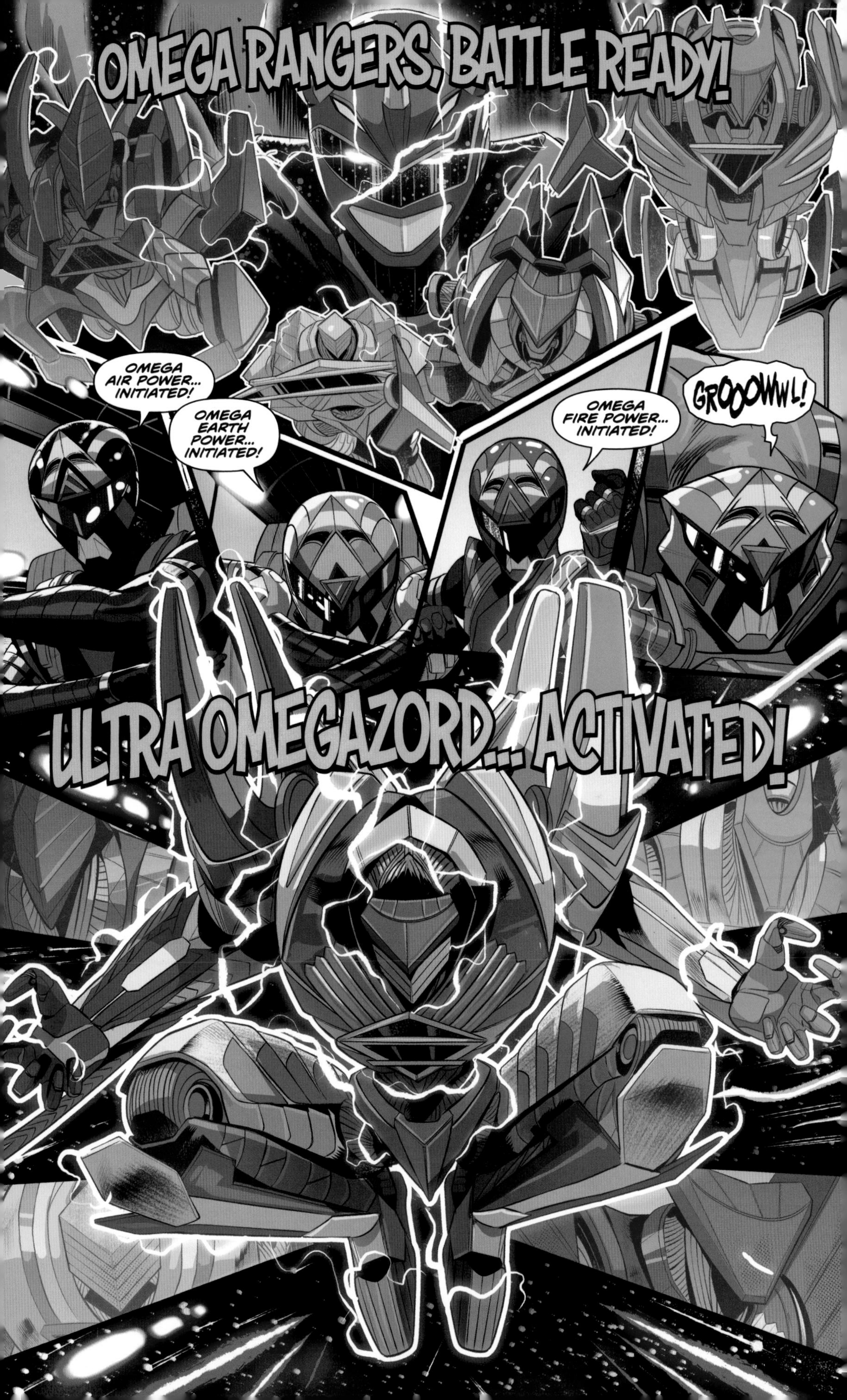
OMEGA RANGERS, BATTLE READY!
OMEGA AIR POWER... INITIATED!
OMEGA EARTH POWER... INITIATED!
OMEGA FIRE POWER... INITIATED!
GROOOWWL!
ULTRA OMEGAZORD... ACTIVATED!

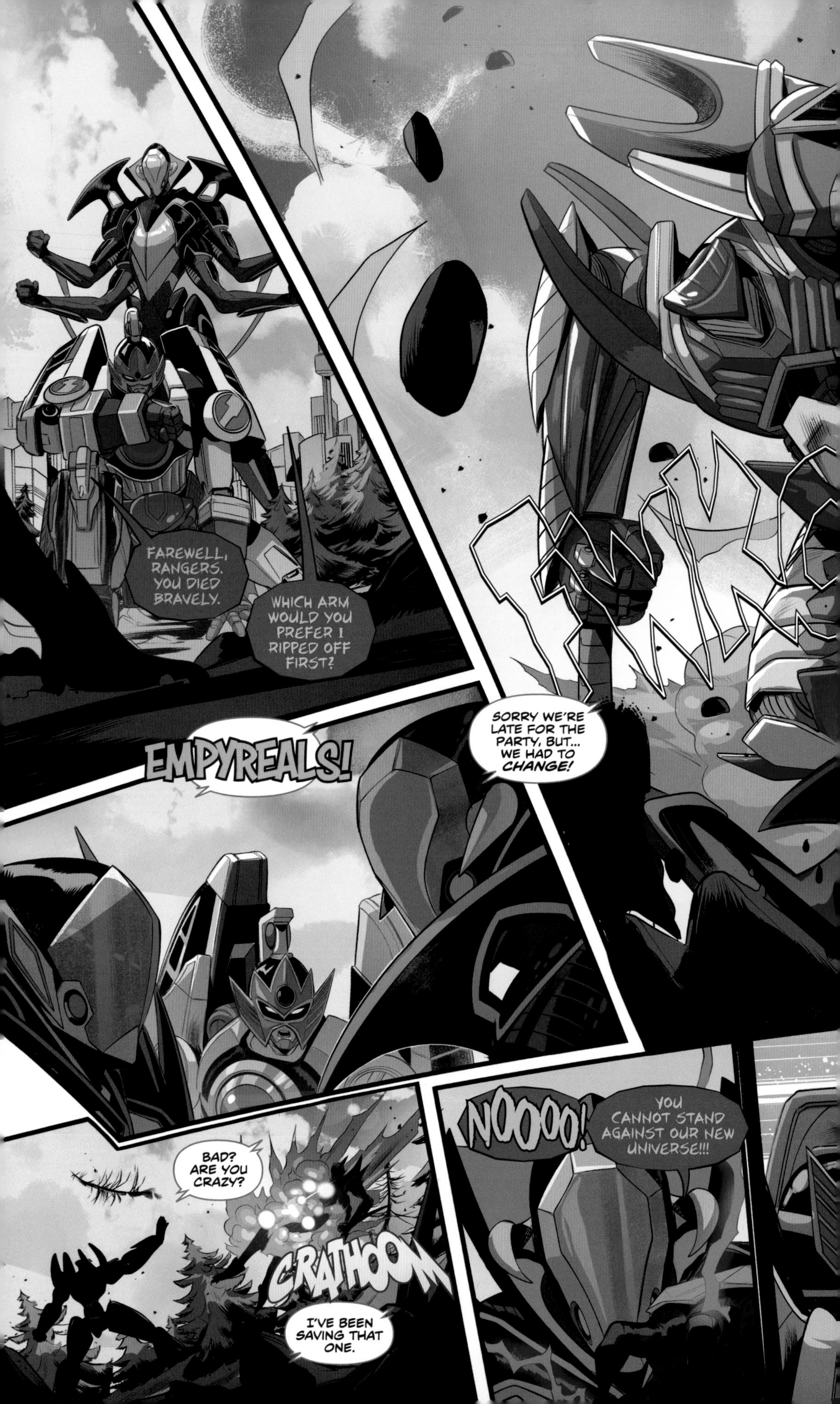
FAREWELL, RANGERS. YOU DIED BRAVELY.
WHICH ARM WOULD YOU PREFER I RIPPED OFF FIRST?
SORRY WE'RE LATE FOR THE PARTY, BUT... WE HAD TO CHANGE!
EMPYREALS!
BAD? ARE YOU CRAZY?
CRATHOOM
I'VE BEEN SAVING THAT ONE.
NOOOO!
YOU CANNOT STAND AGAINST OUR NEW UNIVERSE!!!

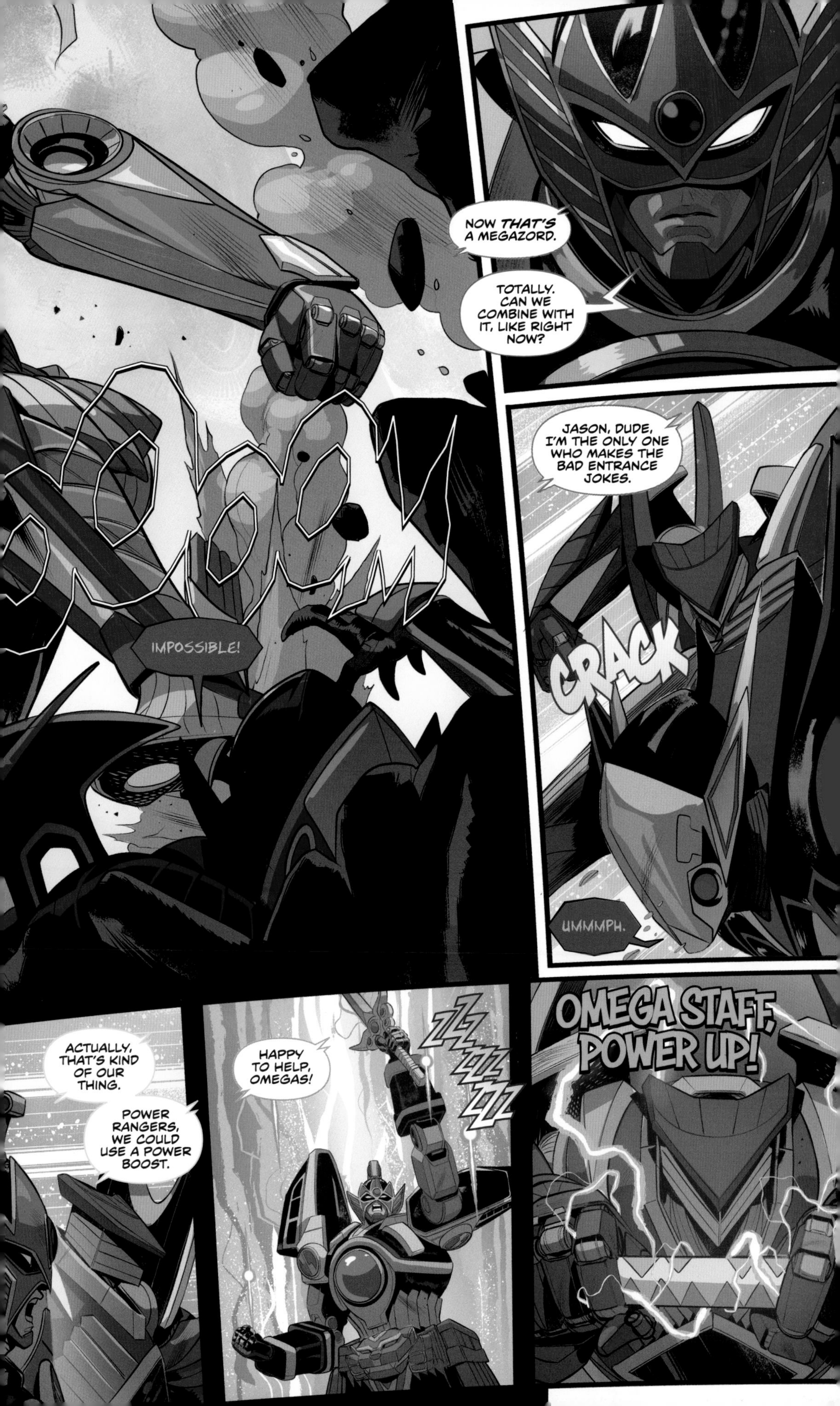
NOW THAT'S A MEGAZORD.
TOTALLY. CAN WE COMBINE WITH IT, LIKE RIGHT NOW?
BOOOOOOM
IMPOSSIBLE!
JASON, DUDE, I'M THE ONLY ONE WHO MAKES THE BAD ENTRANCE JOKES.
CRACK
UMMMPH.
ACTUALLY, THAT'S KIND OF OUR THING.
POWER RANGERS, WE COULD USE A POWER BOOST.
HAPPY TO HELP, OMEGAS!
ZZZZZZZ
OMEGA STAFF, POWER UP!

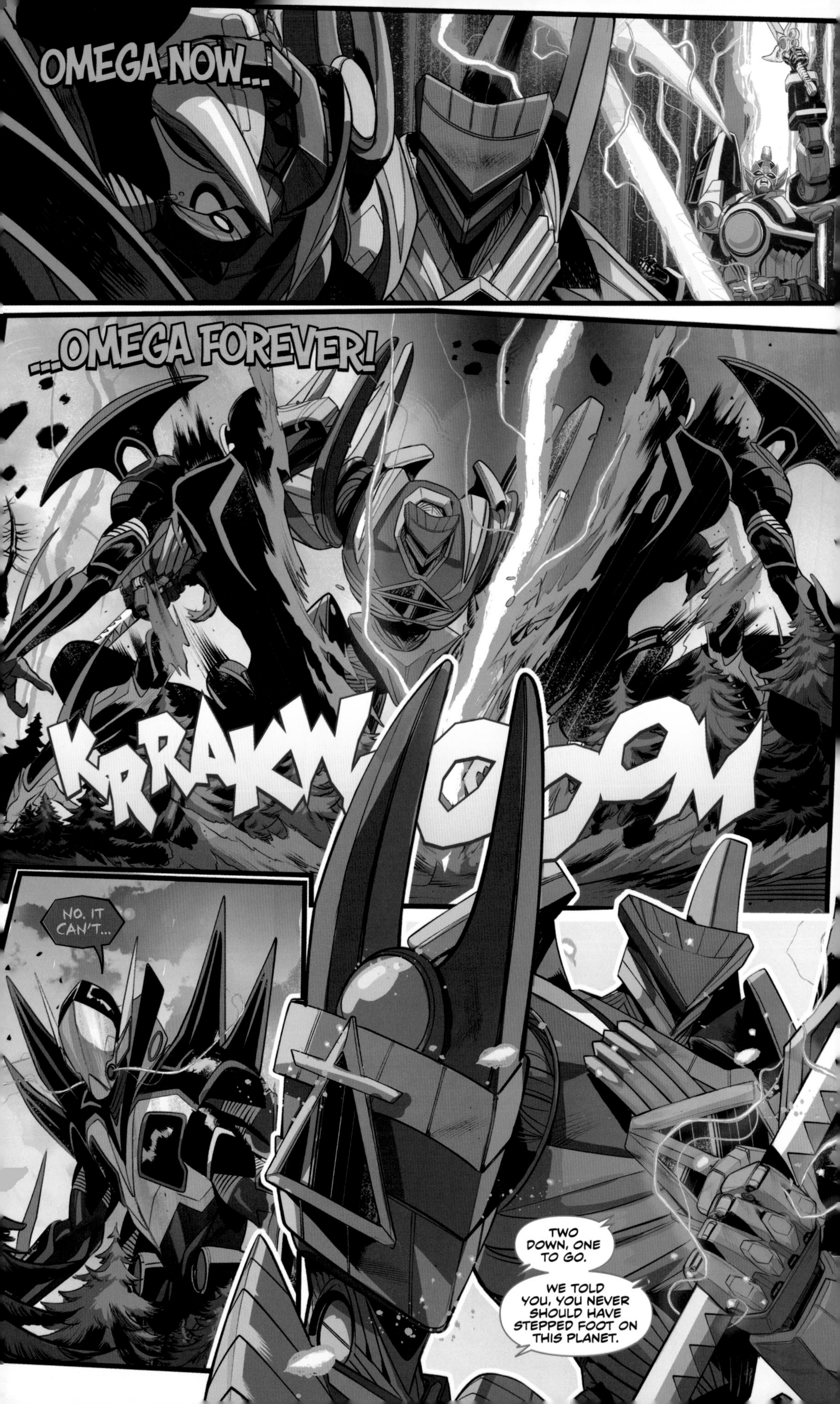
OMEGA NOW...
...OMEGA FOREVER!
KRRAKWOOOM
NO. IT CAN'T...
TWO DOWN, ONE TO GO.
WE TOLD YOU, YOU NEVER SHOULD HAVE STEPPED FOOT ON THIS PLANET.

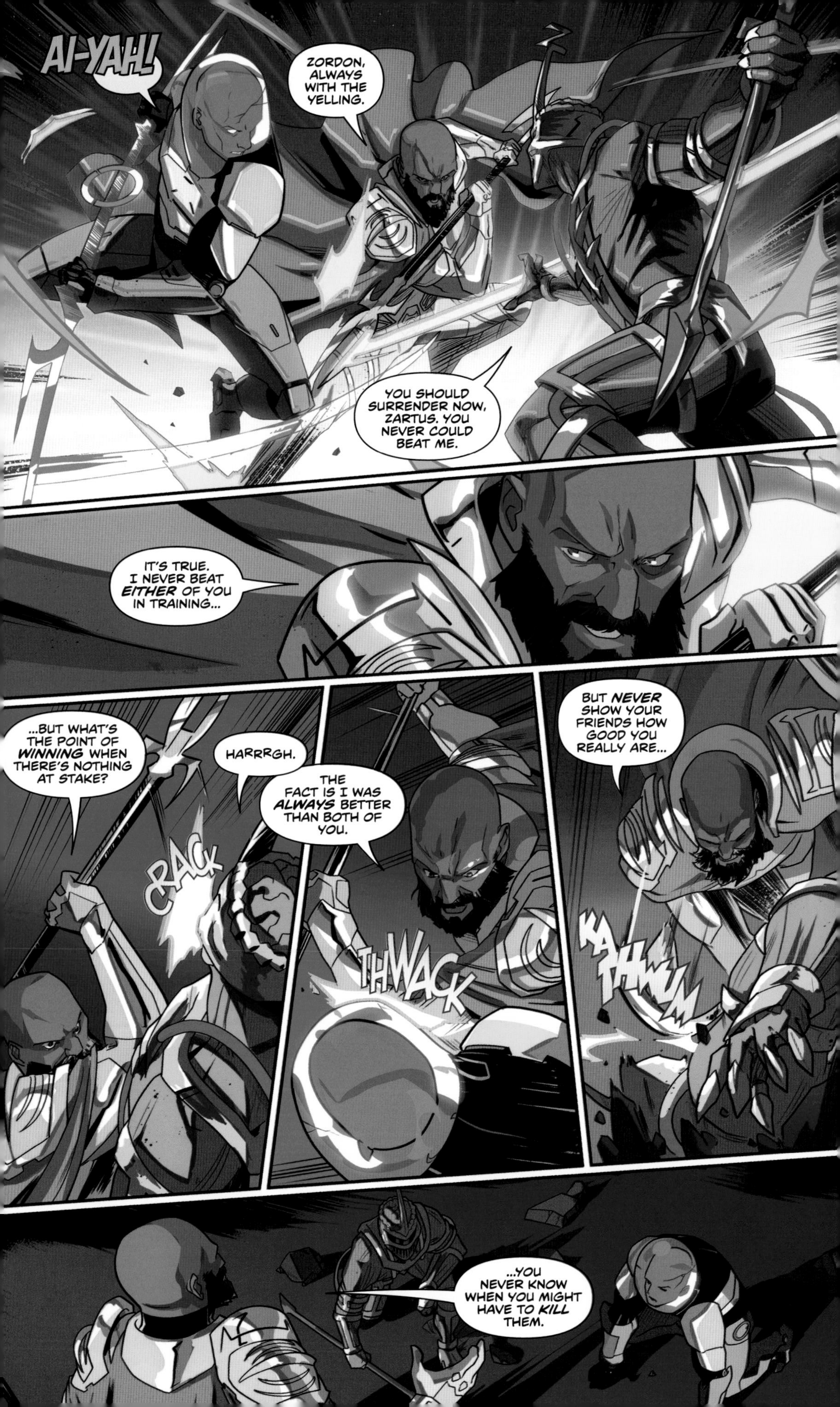
AI-YAH!
ZORDON, ALWAYS WITH THE YELLING.
YOU SHOULD SURRENDER NOW, ZARTUS. YOU NEVER COULD BEAT ME.
IT'S TRUE. I NEVER BEAT *EITHER* OF YOU IN TRAINING...
...BUT WHAT'S THE POINT OF *WINNING* WHEN THERE'S NOTHING AT STAKE?
HARRRGH.
CRACK
THE FACT IS I WAS *ALWAYS* BETTER THAN BOTH OF YOU.
THWACK
BUT *NEVER* SHOW YOUR FRIENDS HOW GOOD YOU REALLY ARE...
KATHUM
...YOU NEVER KNOW WHEN YOU MIGHT HAVE TO *KILL* THEM.

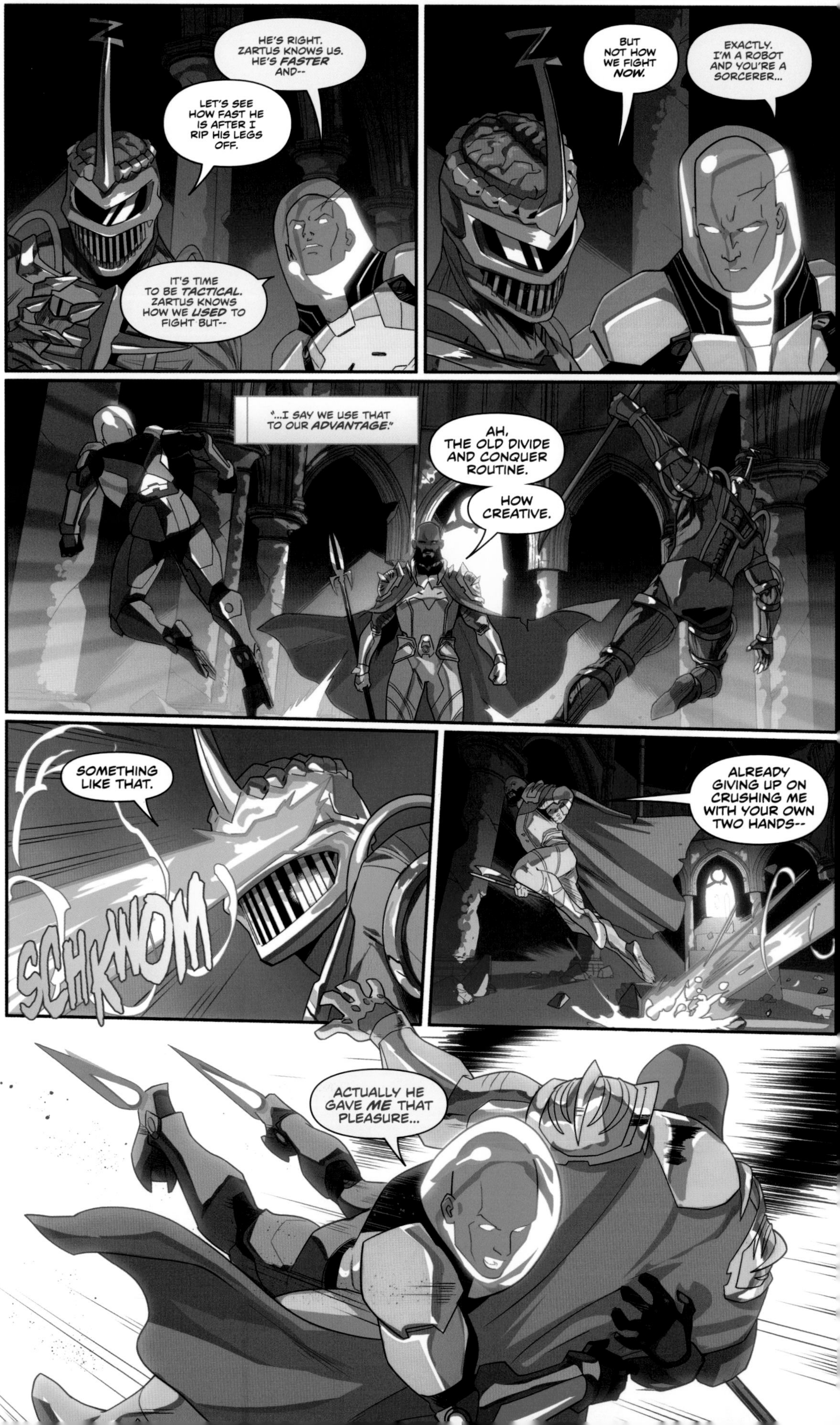
HE'S RIGHT. ZARTUS KNOWS US. HE'S FASTER AND--
LET'S SEE HOW FAST HE IS AFTER I RIP HIS LEGS OFF.
IT'S TIME TO BE TACTICAL. ZARTUS KNOWS HOW WE USED TO FIGHT BUT--
BUT NOT HOW WE FIGHT NOW.
EXACTLY. I'M A ROBOT AND YOU'RE A SORCERER...
"...I SAY WE USE THAT TO OUR ADVANTAGE."
AH, THE OLD DIVIDE AND CONQUER ROUTINE.
HOW CREATIVE.
SOMETHING LIKE THAT.
SCHKWOM
ALREADY GIVING UP ON CRUSHING ME WITH YOUR OWN TWO HANDS--
ACTUALLY HE GAVE ME THAT PLEASURE...

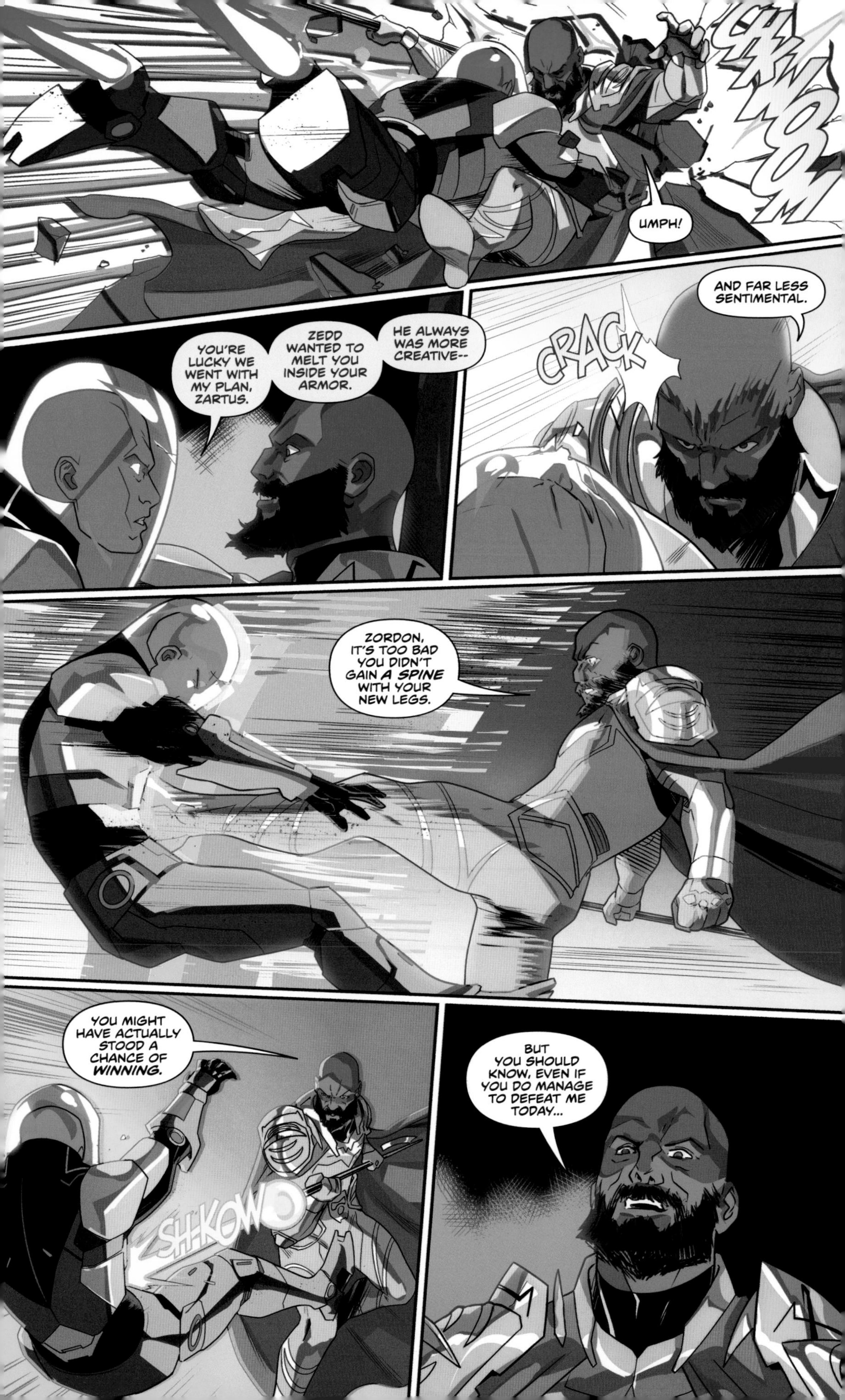
KRAKOOM
UMPH!
YOU'RE LUCKY WE WENT WITH MY PLAN, ZARTUS.
ZEDD WANTED TO MELT YOU INSIDE YOUR ARMOR.
HE ALWAYS WAS MORE CREATIVE--
CRACK
AND FAR LESS SENTIMENTAL.
ZORDON, IT'S TOO BAD YOU DIDN'T GAIN *A SPINE* WITH YOUR NEW LEGS.
YOU MIGHT HAVE ACTUALLY STOOD A CHANCE OF *WINNING*.
SH-KOW
BUT YOU SHOULD KNOW, EVEN IF YOU DO MANAGE TO DEFEAT ME TODAY...

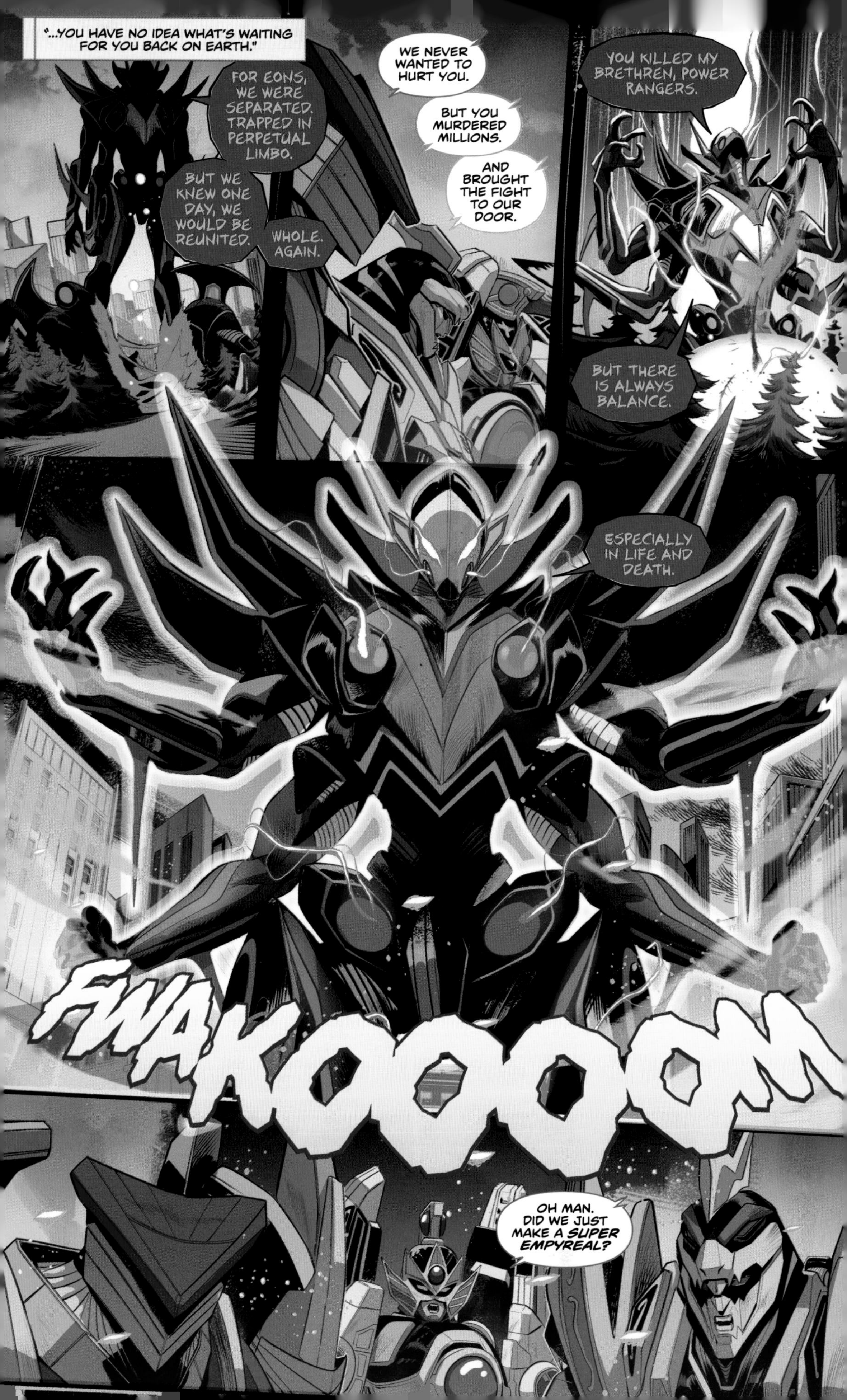
"...YOU HAVE NO IDEA WHAT'S WAITING FOR YOU BACK ON EARTH."
FOR EONS, WE WERE SEPARATED. TRAPPED IN PERPETUAL LIMBO.
BUT WE KNEW ONE DAY, WE WOULD BE REUNITED.
WHOLE. AGAIN.
WE NEVER WANTED TO HURT YOU.
BUT YOU MURDERED MILLIONS.
AND BROUGHT THE FIGHT TO OUR DOOR.
YOU KILLED MY BRETHREN, POWER RANGERS.
BUT THERE IS ALWAYS BALANCE.
ESPECIALLY IN LIFE AND DEATH.
FWAKOOOOM
OH MAN. DID WE JUST MAKE A *SUPER EMPYREAL?*

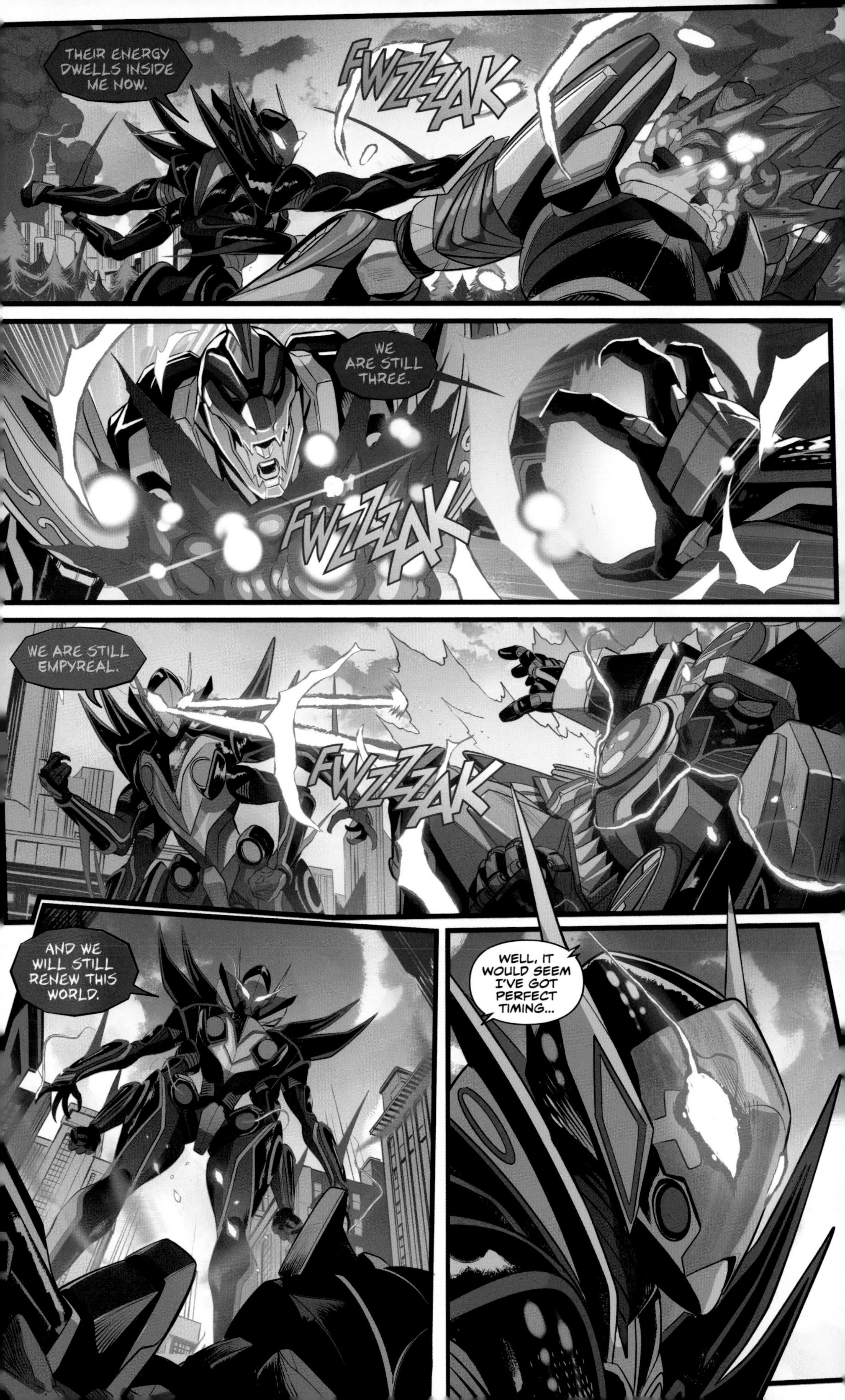
THEIR ENERGY DWELLS INSIDE ME NOW.
FWZZZAK
WE ARE STILL THREE.
FWZZZAK
WE ARE STILL EMPYREAL.
FWZZZAK
AND WE WILL STILL RENEW THIS WORLD.
WELL, IT WOULD SEEM I'VE GOT PERFECT TIMING...

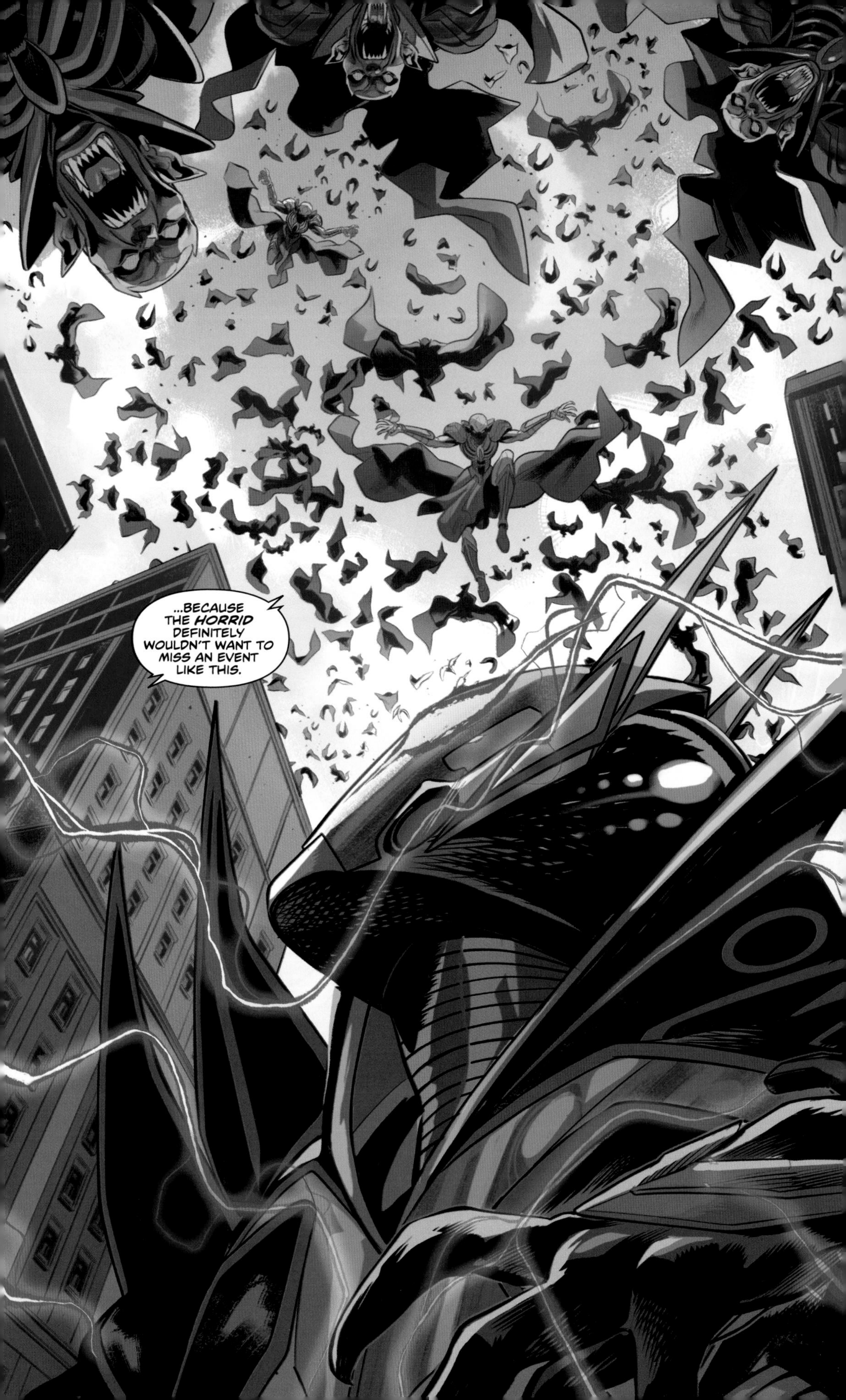
...BECAUSE THE HORRID DEFINITELY WOULDN'T WANT TO MISS AN EVENT LIKE THIS.

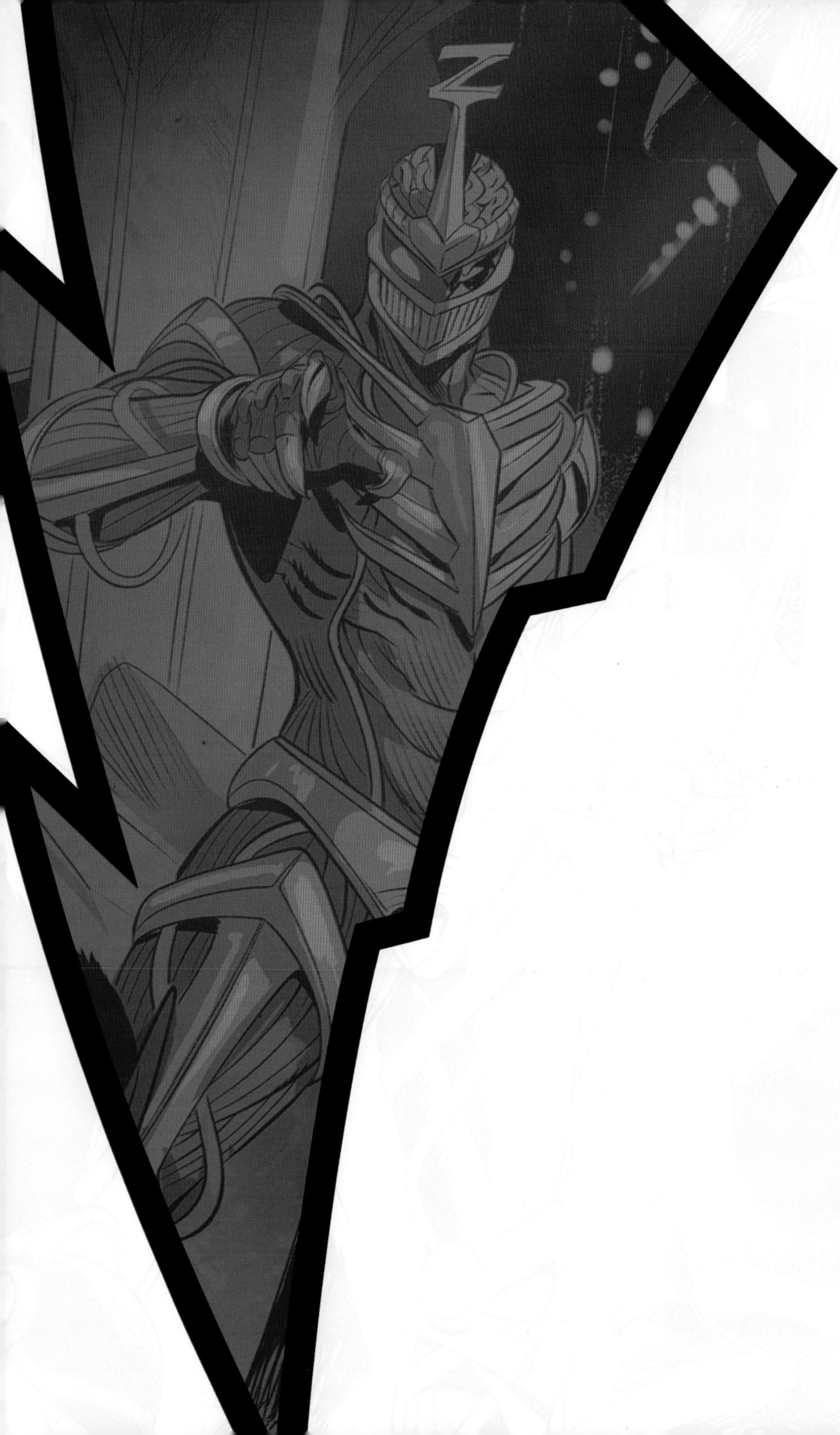

# CHAPTER
# SIXTEEN

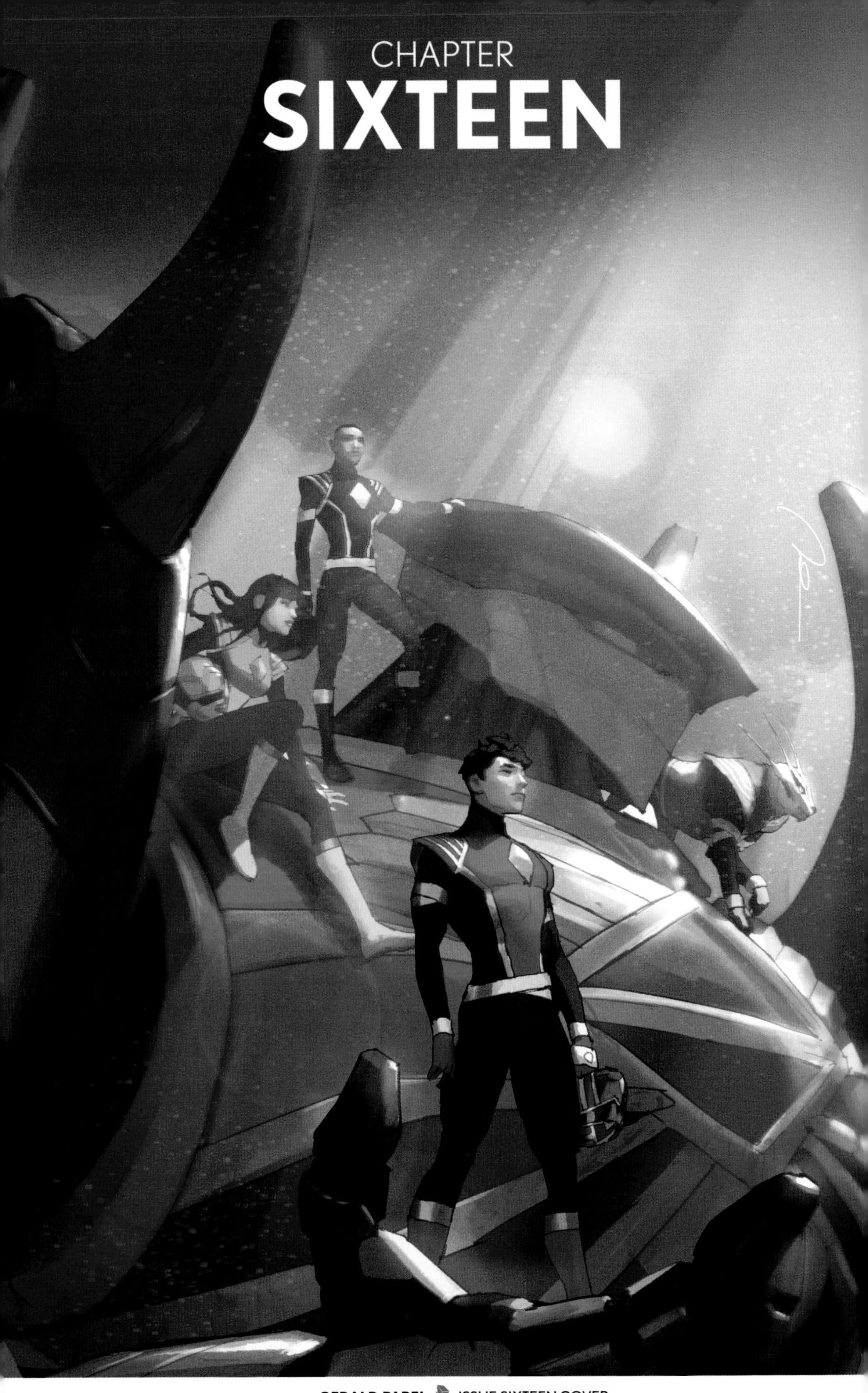

**GERALD PAREL** ISSUE SIXTEEN COVER

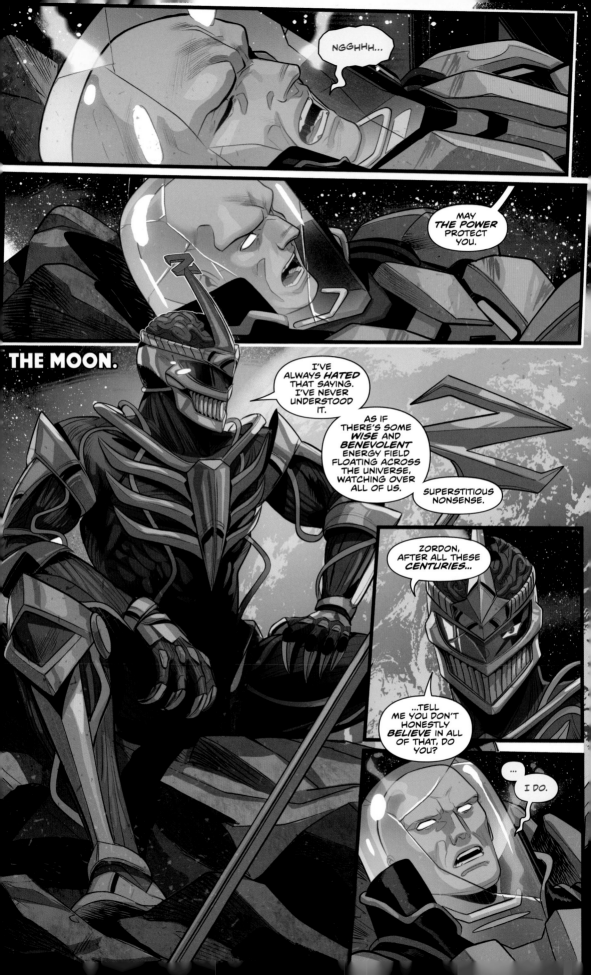

NGGHHH...

MAY **THE POWER** PROTECT YOU.

**THE MOON.**

I'VE ALWAYS **HATED** THAT SAYING. I'VE NEVER UNDERSTOOD IT.

AS IF THERE'S SOME **WISE** AND **BENEVOLENT** ENERGY FIELD FLOATING ACROSS THE UNIVERSE, WATCHING OVER ALL OF US.

SUPERSTITIOUS NONSENSE.

ZORDON, AFTER ALL THESE **CENTURIES**...

...TELL ME YOU DON'T HONESTLY **BELIEVE** IN ALL OF THAT, DO YOU?

...

I DO.

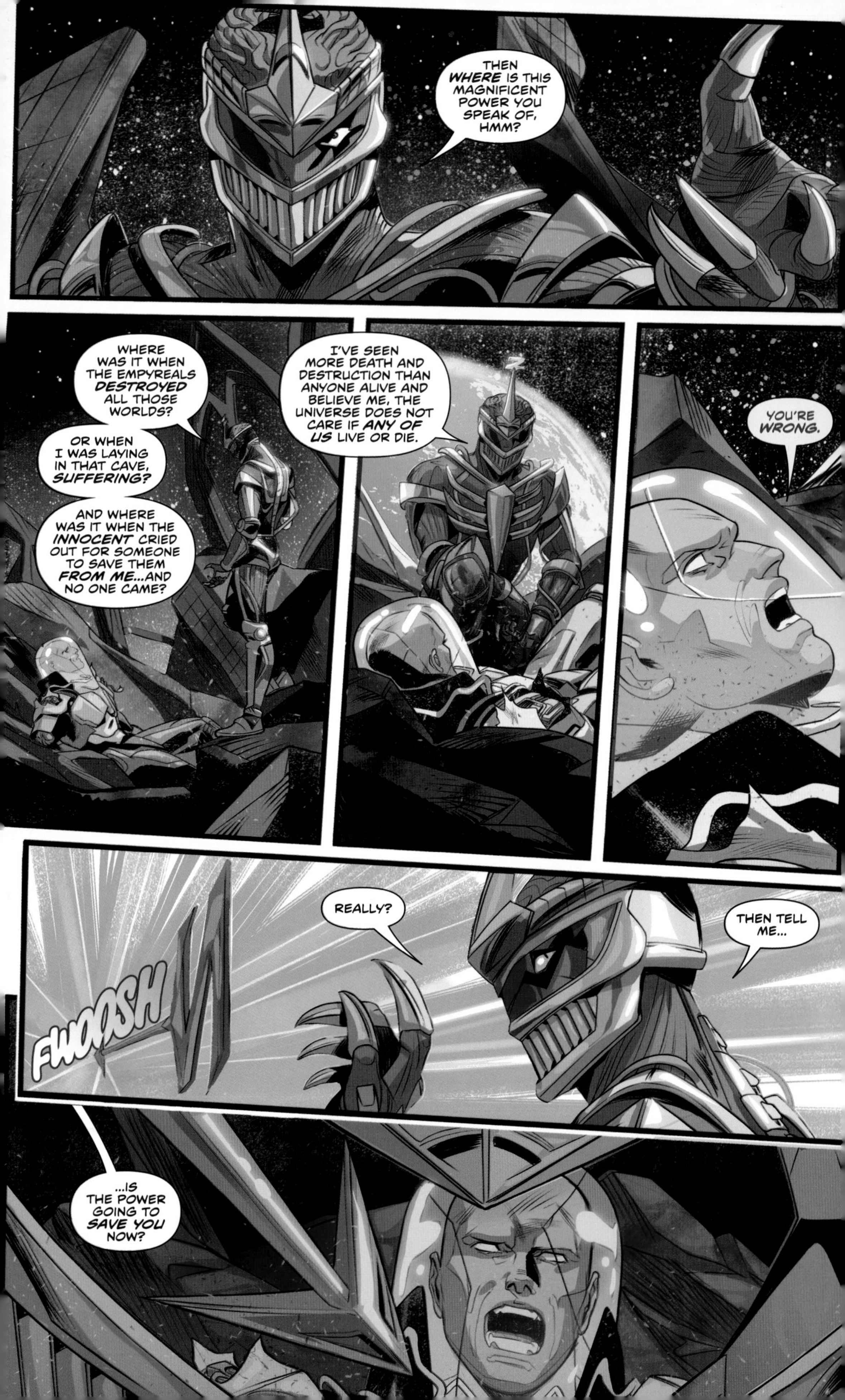
THEN WHERE IS THIS MAGNIFICENT POWER YOU SPEAK OF, HMM?
WHERE WAS IT WHEN THE EMPYREALS DESTROYED ALL THOSE WORLDS?
OR WHEN I WAS LAYING IN THAT CAVE, SUFFERING?
AND WHERE WAS IT WHEN THE INNOCENT CRIED OUT FOR SOMEONE TO SAVE THEM FROM ME...AND NO ONE CAME?
I'VE SEEN MORE DEATH AND DESTRUCTION THAN ANYONE ALIVE AND BELIEVE ME, THE UNIVERSE DOES NOT CARE IF ANY OF US LIVE OR DIE.
YOU'RE WRONG.
FWOOSH
REALLY?
THEN TELL ME...
...IS THE POWER GOING TO SAVE YOU NOW?

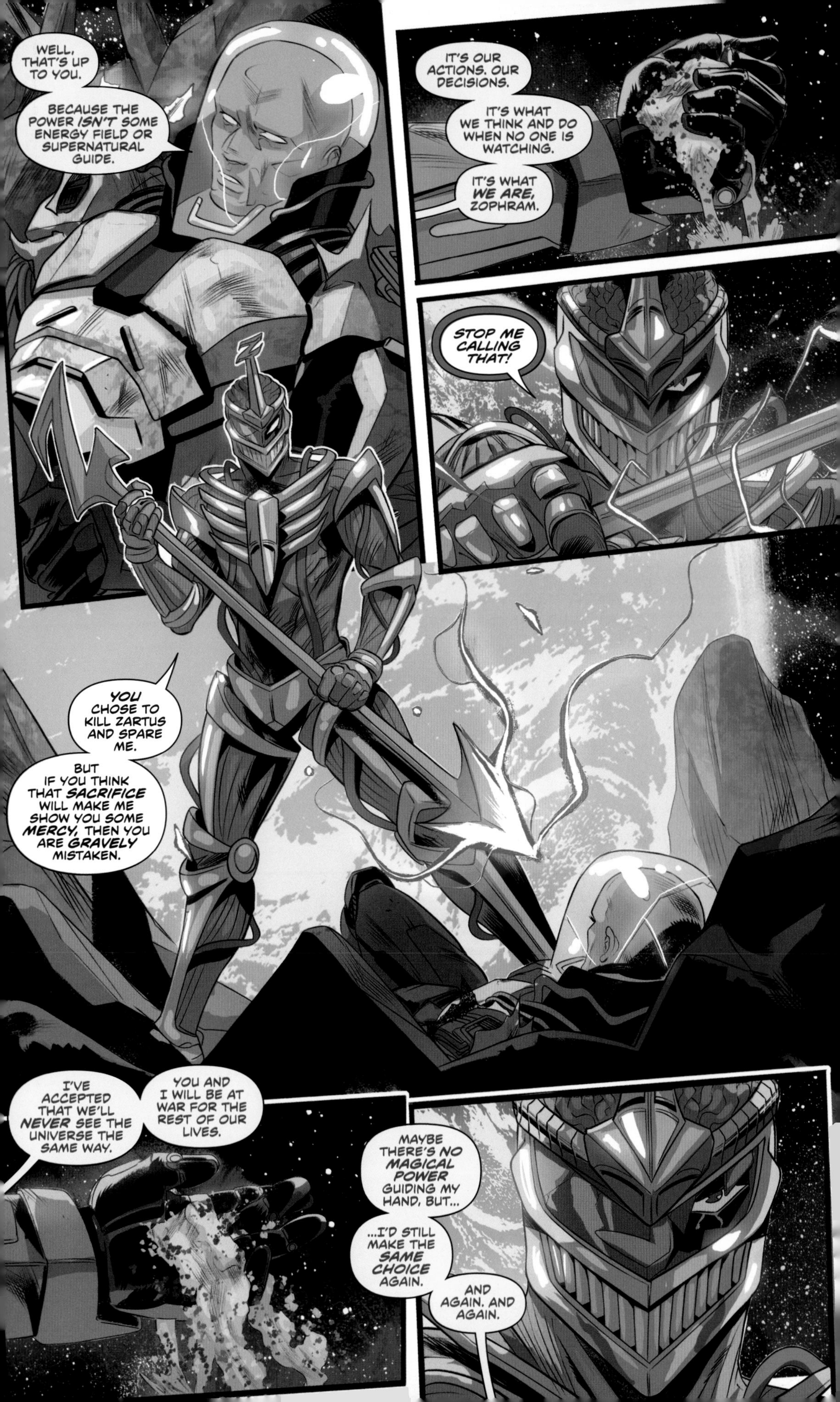
WELL, THAT'S UP TO YOU.
BECAUSE THE POWER ISN'T SOME ENERGY FIELD OR SUPERNATURAL GUIDE.
IT'S OUR ACTIONS. OUR DECISIONS.
IT'S WHAT WE THINK AND DO WHEN NO ONE IS WATCHING.
IT'S WHAT WE ARE, ZOPHRAM.
STOP ME CALLING THAT!
YOU CHOSE TO KILL ZARTUS AND SPARE ME.
BUT IF YOU THINK THAT SACRIFICE WILL MAKE ME SHOW YOU SOME MERCY, THEN YOU ARE GRAVELY MISTAKEN.
I'VE ACCEPTED THAT WE'LL NEVER SEE THE UNIVERSE THE SAME WAY.
YOU AND I WILL BE AT WAR FOR THE REST OF OUR LIVES.
MAYBE THERE'S NO MAGICAL POWER GUIDING MY HAND, BUT...
...I'D STILL MAKE THE SAME CHOICE AGAIN.
AND AGAIN. AND AGAIN.

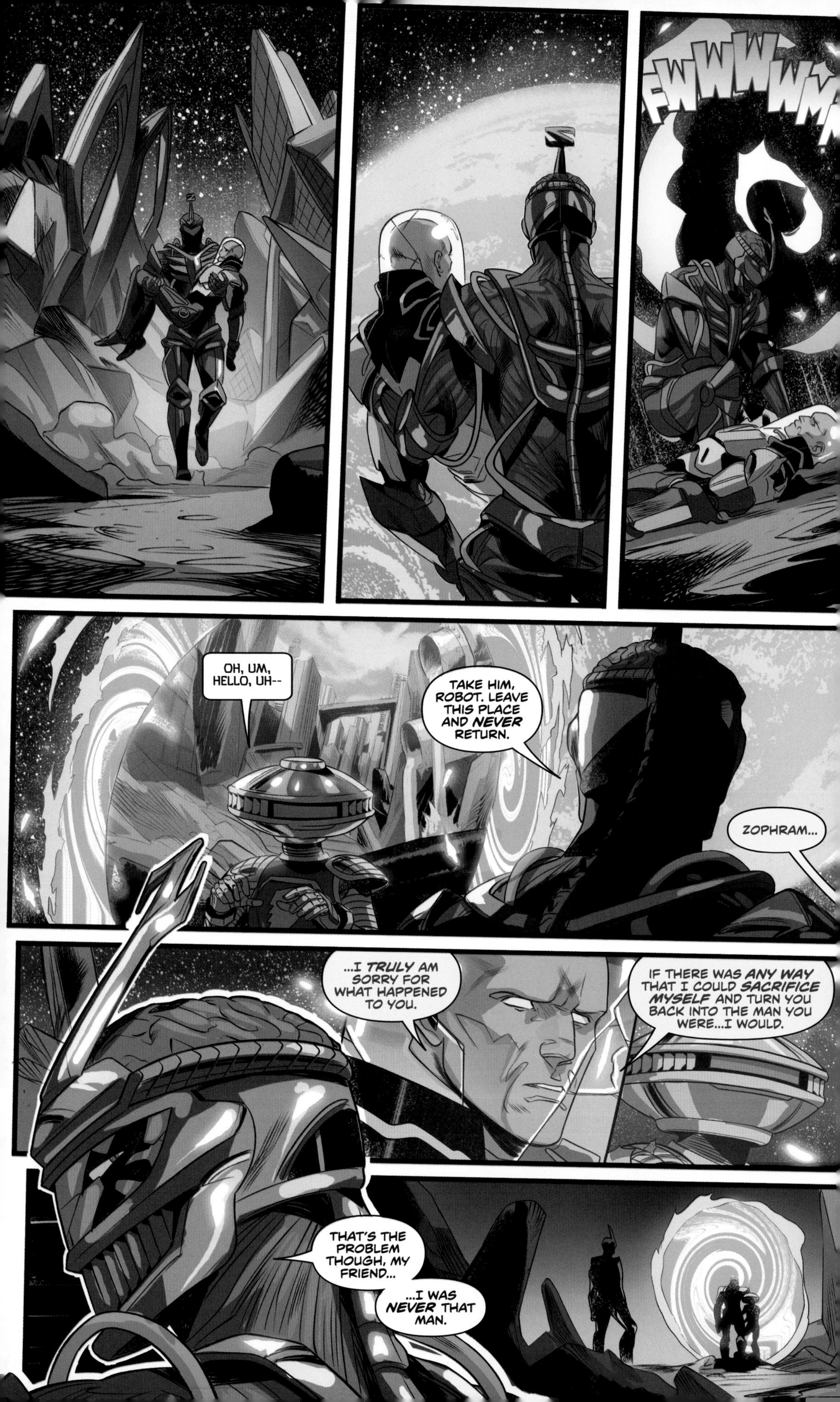
FWWWWM
OH, UM, HELLO, UH--
TAKE HIM, ROBOT. LEAVE THIS PLACE AND *NEVER* RETURN.
ZOPHRAM...
...I *TRULY* AM SORRY FOR WHAT HAPPENED TO YOU.
IF THERE WAS *ANY WAY* THAT I COULD *SACRIFICE MYSELF* AND TURN YOU BACK INTO THE MAN YOU WERE...I WOULD.
THAT'S THE PROBLEM THOUGH, MY FRIEND...
...I WAS *NEVER* THAT MAN.

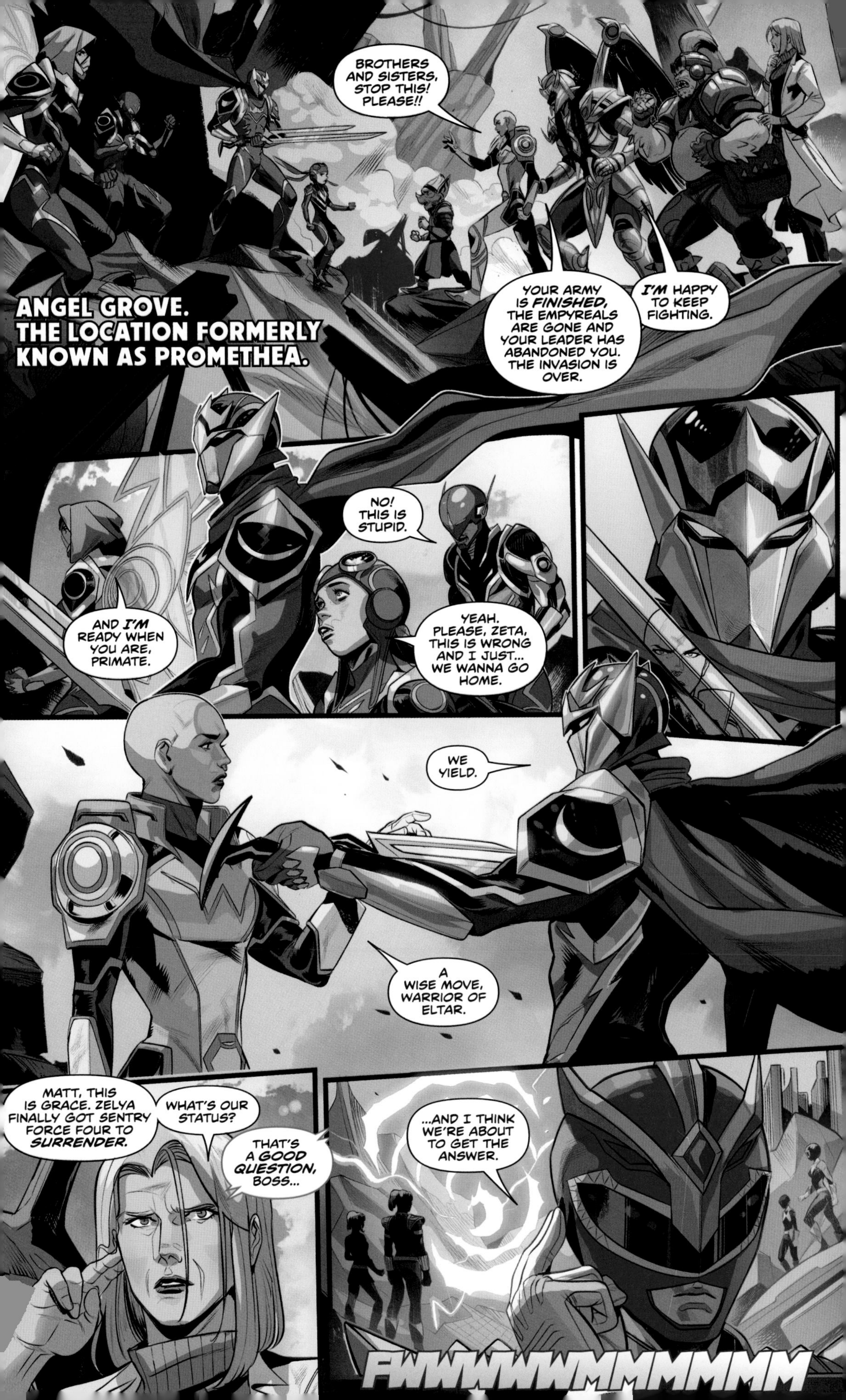
BROTHERS AND SISTERS, STOP THIS! PLEASE!!
ANGEL GROVE. THE LOCATION FORMERLY KNOWN AS PROMETHEA.
YOUR ARMY IS FINISHED, THE EMPYREALS ARE GONE AND YOUR LEADER HAS ABANDONED YOU. THE INVASION IS OVER.
I'M HAPPY TO KEEP FIGHTING.
NO! THIS IS STUPID.
AND I'M READY WHEN YOU ARE, PRIMATE.
YEAH. PLEASE, ZETA, THIS IS WRONG AND I JUST... WE WANNA GO HOME.
WE YIELD.
A WISE MOVE, WARRIOR OF ELTAR.
MATT, THIS IS GRACE. ZELYA FINALLY GOT SENTRY FORCE FOUR TO SURRENDER.
WHAT'S OUR STATUS?
THAT'S A GOOD QUESTION, BOSS...
...AND I THINK WE'RE ABOUT TO GET THE ANSWER.
FWWWWWMMMMMM

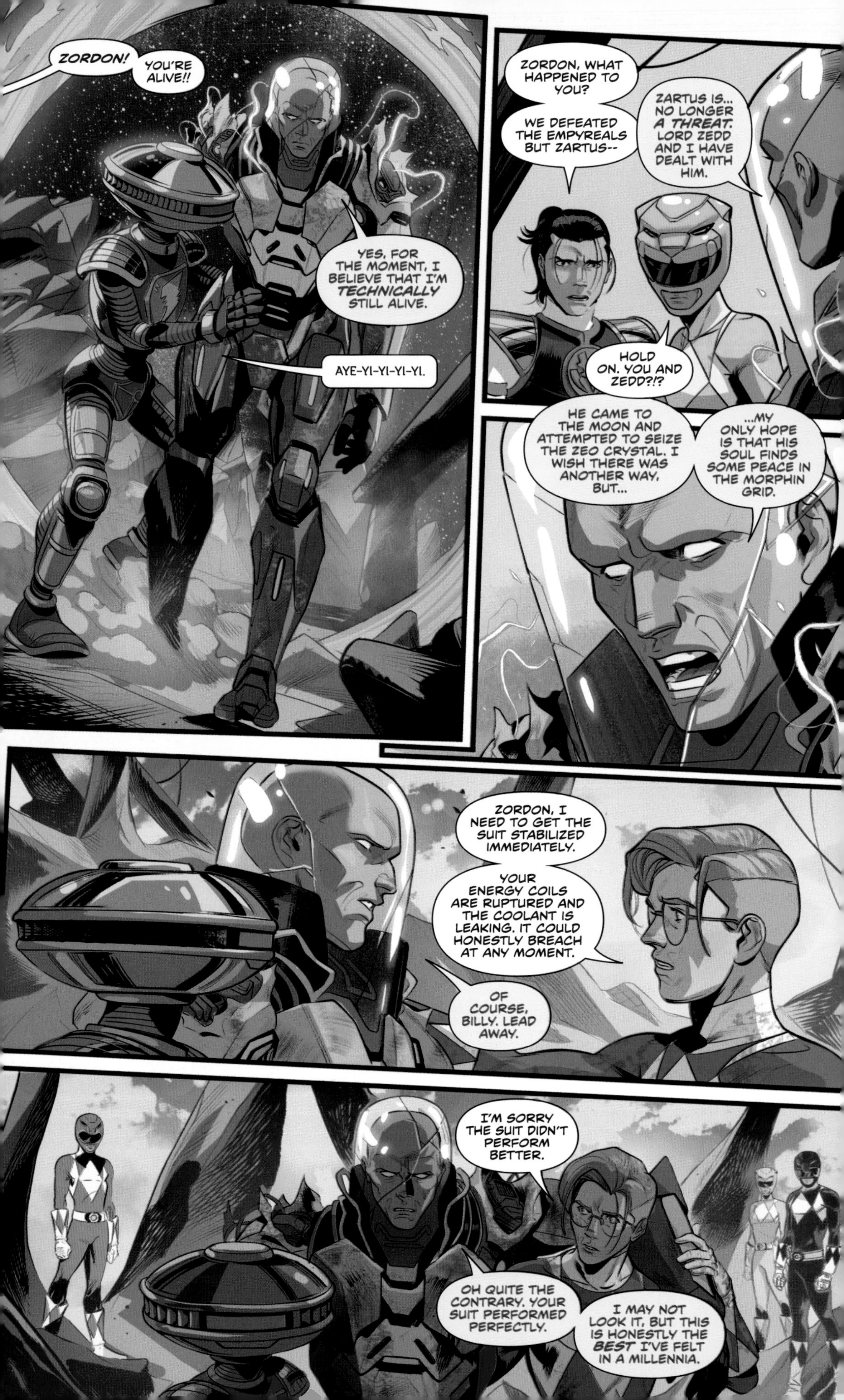
ZORDON!
YOU'RE ALIVE!!
YES, FOR THE MOMENT. I BELIEVE THAT I'M TECHNICALLY STILL ALIVE.
AYE-YI-YI-YI-YI.
ZORDON, WHAT HAPPENED TO YOU?
WE DEFEATED THE EMPYREALS BUT ZARTUS--
ZARTUS IS... NO LONGER A THREAT. LORD ZEDD AND I HAVE DEALT WITH HIM.
HOLD ON. YOU AND ZEDD?!?
HE CAME TO THE MOON AND ATTEMPTED TO SEIZE THE ZEO CRYSTAL. I WISH THERE WAS ANOTHER WAY, BUT...
...MY ONLY HOPE IS THAT HIS SOUL FINDS SOME PEACE IN THE MORPHIN GRID.
ZORDON, I NEED TO GET THE SUIT STABILIZED IMMEDIATELY.
YOUR ENERGY COILS ARE RUPTURED AND THE COOLANT IS LEAKING. IT COULD HONESTLY BREACH AT ANY MOMENT.
OF COURSE, BILLY. LEAD AWAY.
I'M SORRY THE SUIT DIDN'T PERFORM BETTER.
OH QUITE THE CONTRARY. YOUR SUIT PERFORMED PERFECTLY.
I MAY NOT LOOK IT, BUT THIS IS HONESTLY THE BEST I'VE FELT IN A MILLENNIA.

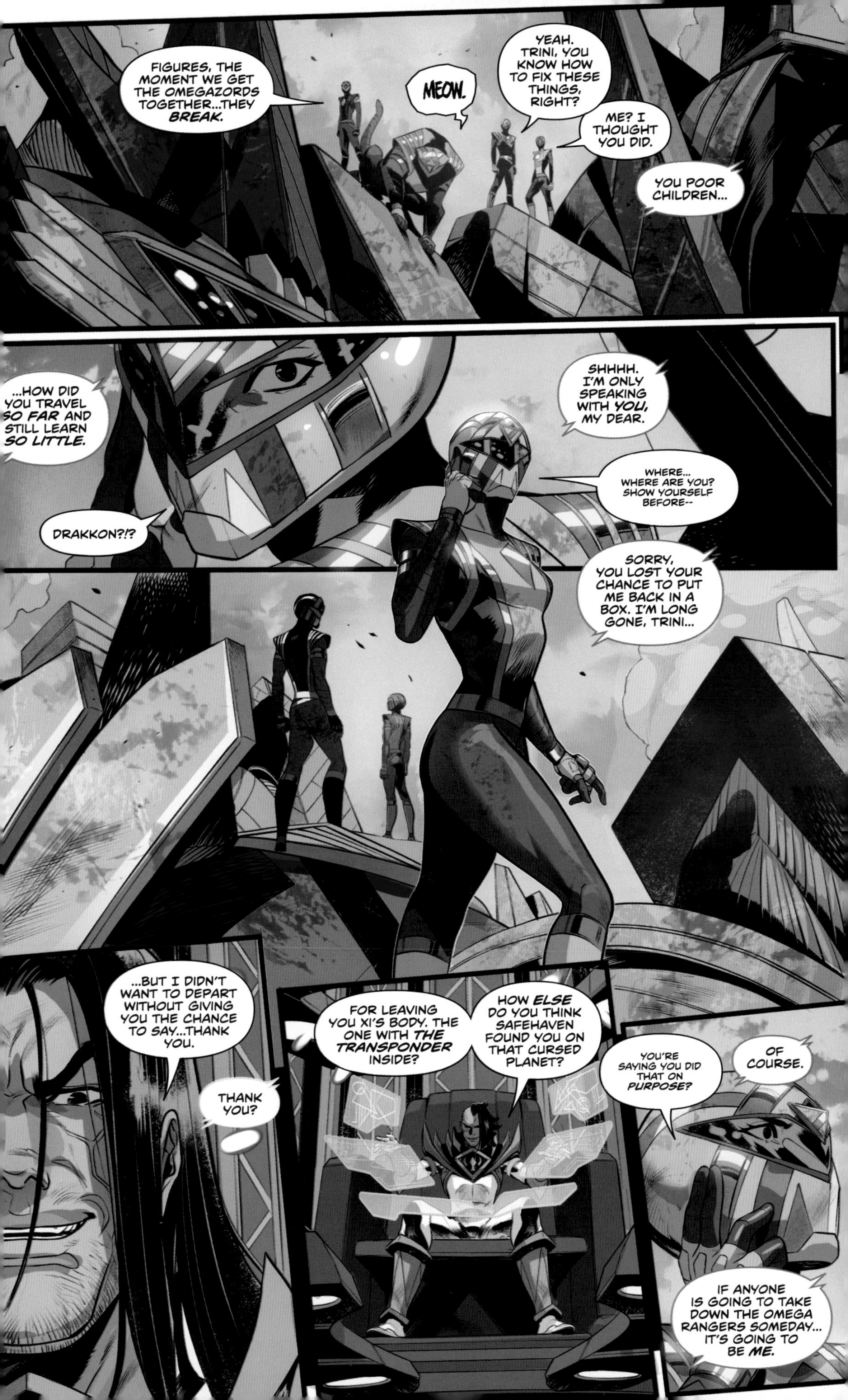
FIGURES, THE MOMENT WE GET THE OMEGAZORDS TOGETHER...THEY BREAK.
MEOW.
YEAH. TRINI, YOU KNOW HOW TO FIX THESE THINGS, RIGHT?
ME? I THOUGHT YOU DID.
YOU POOR CHILDREN...
...HOW DID YOU TRAVEL SO FAR AND STILL LEARN SO LITTLE.
DRAKKON?!?
SHHHH. I'M ONLY SPEAKING WITH YOU, MY DEAR.
WHERE... WHERE ARE YOU? SHOW YOURSELF BEFORE--
SORRY, YOU LOST YOUR CHANCE TO PUT ME BACK IN A BOX. I'M LONG GONE, TRINI...
...BUT I DIDN'T WANT TO DEPART WITHOUT GIVING YOU THE CHANCE TO SAY...THANK YOU.
THANK YOU?
FOR LEAVING YOU XI'S BODY. THE ONE WITH THE TRANSPONDER INSIDE?
HOW ELSE DO YOU THINK SAFEHAVEN FOUND YOU ON THAT CURSED PLANET?
YOU'RE SAYING YOU DID THAT ON PURPOSE?
OF COURSE.
IF ANYONE IS GOING TO TAKE DOWN THE OMEGA RANGERS SOMEDAY... IT'S GOING TO BE ME.

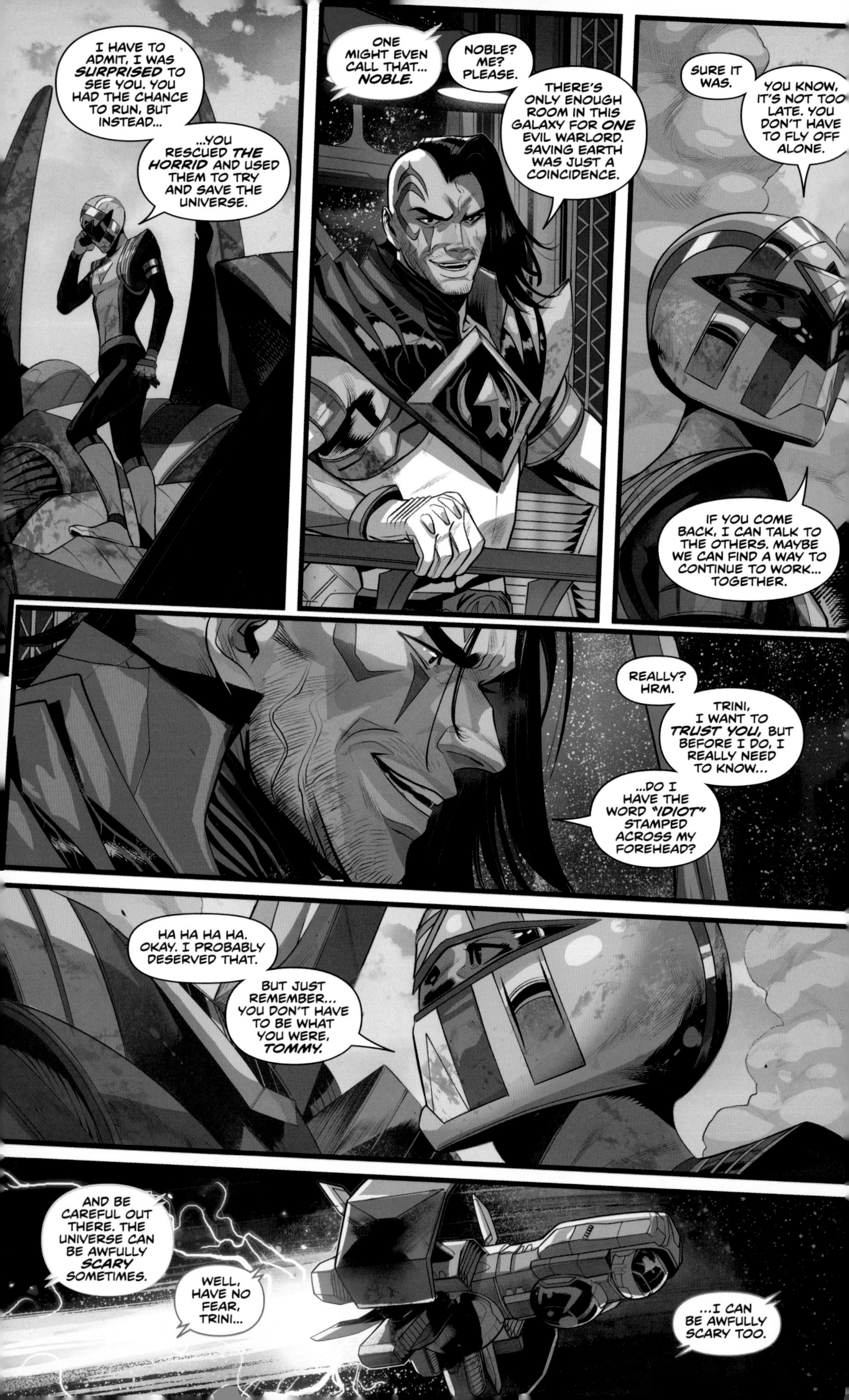
I HAVE TO ADMIT, I WAS SURPRISED TO SEE YOU. YOU HAD THE CHANCE TO RUN, BUT INSTEAD...
...YOU RESCUED THE HORRID AND USED THEM TO TRY AND SAVE THE UNIVERSE.
ONE MIGHT EVEN CALL THAT... NOBLE.
NOBLE? ME? PLEASE.
THERE'S ONLY ENOUGH ROOM IN THIS GALAXY FOR ONE EVIL WARLORD. SAVING EARTH WAS JUST A COINCIDENCE.
SURE IT WAS.
YOU KNOW, IT'S NOT TOO LATE. YOU DON'T HAVE TO FLY OFF ALONE.
IF YOU COME BACK, I CAN TALK TO THE OTHERS. MAYBE WE CAN FIND A WAY TO CONTINUE TO WORK... TOGETHER.
REALLY? HRM.
TRINI, I WANT TO TRUST YOU, BUT BEFORE I DO, I REALLY NEED TO KNOW...
...DO I HAVE THE WORD "IDIOT" STAMPED ACROSS MY FOREHEAD?
HA HA HA HA. OKAY. I PROBABLY DESERVED THAT.
BUT JUST REMEMBER... YOU DON'T HAVE TO BE WHAT YOU WERE, TOMMY.
AND BE CAREFUL OUT THERE. THE UNIVERSE CAN BE AWFULLY SCARY SOMETIMES.
WELL, HAVE NO FEAR, TRINI...
...I CAN BE AWFULLY SCARY TOO.

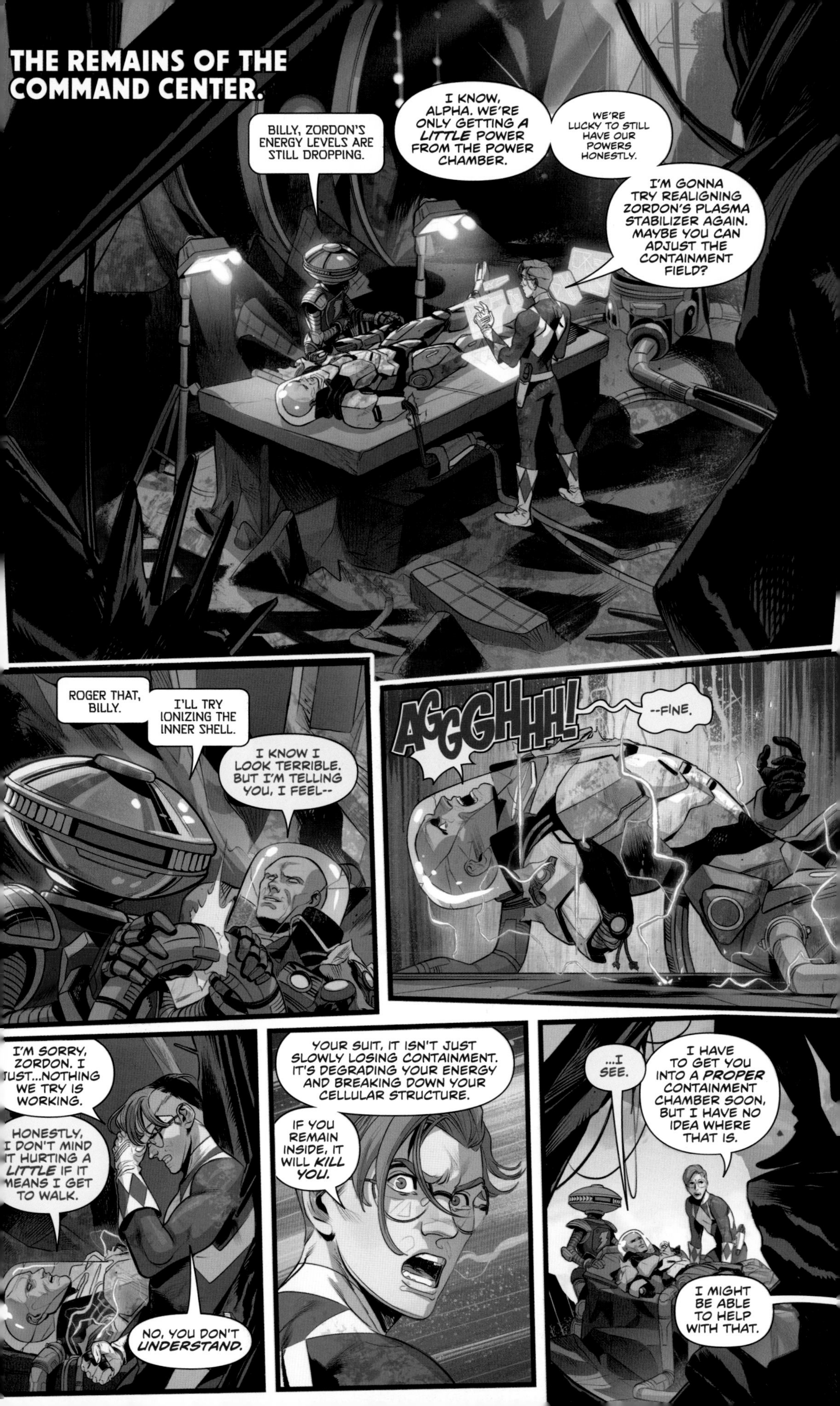
THE REMAINS OF THE COMMAND CENTER.
BILLY, ZORDON'S ENERGY LEVELS ARE STILL DROPPING.
I KNOW, ALPHA. WE'RE ONLY GETTING A *LITTLE* POWER FROM THE POWER CHAMBER.
WE'RE LUCKY TO STILL HAVE OUR POWERS HONESTLY.
I'M GONNA TRY REALIGNING ZORDON'S PLASMA STABILIZER AGAIN. MAYBE YOU CAN ADJUST THE CONTAINMENT FIELD?
ROGER THAT, BILLY.
I'LL TRY IONIZING THE INNER SHELL.
I KNOW I LOOK TERRIBLE. BUT I'M TELLING YOU, I FEEL--
AGGGHHH!
--FINE.
I'M SORRY, ZORDON. I JUST...NOTHING WE TRY IS WORKING.
HONESTLY, I DON'T MIND IT HURTING A *LITTLE* IF IT MEANS I GET TO WALK.
NO, YOU DON'T *UNDERSTAND.*
YOUR SUIT, IT ISN'T JUST SLOWLY LOSING CONTAINMENT. IT'S DEGRADING YOUR ENERGY AND BREAKING DOWN YOUR CELLULAR STRUCTURE.
IF YOU REMAIN INSIDE, IT WILL *KILL YOU.*
...I SEE.
I HAVE TO GET YOU INTO A *PROPER* CONTAINMENT CHAMBER SOON, BUT I HAVE NO IDEA WHERE THAT IS.
I MIGHT BE ABLE TO HELP WITH THAT.

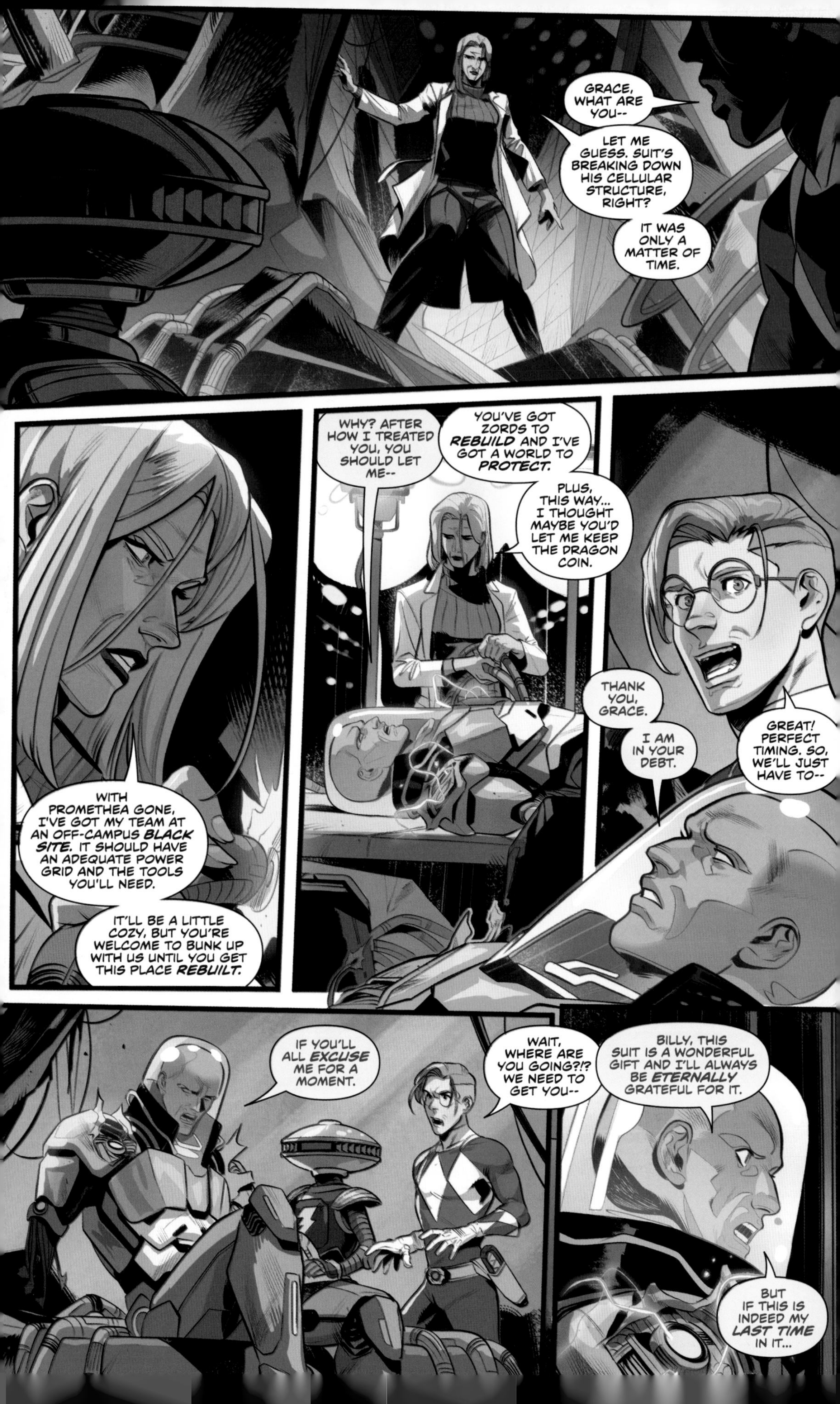
GRACE, WHAT ARE YOU--
LET ME GUESS. SUIT'S BREAKING DOWN HIS CELLULAR STRUCTURE, RIGHT?
IT WAS ONLY A MATTER OF TIME.
WITH PROMETHEA GONE, I'VE GOT MY TEAM AT AN OFF-CAMPUS BLACK SITE. IT SHOULD HAVE AN ADEQUATE POWER GRID AND THE TOOLS YOU'LL NEED.
IT'LL BE A LITTLE COZY, BUT YOU'RE WELCOME TO BUNK UP WITH US UNTIL YOU GET THIS PLACE REBUILT.
WHY? AFTER HOW I TREATED YOU, YOU SHOULD LET ME--
YOU'VE GOT ZORDS TO REBUILD AND I'VE GOT A WORLD TO PROTECT.
PLUS, THIS WAY... I THOUGHT MAYBE YOU'D LET ME KEEP THE DRAGON COIN.
THANK YOU, GRACE.
I AM IN YOUR DEBT.
GREAT! PERFECT TIMING. SO, WE'LL JUST HAVE TO--
IF YOU'LL ALL EXCUSE ME FOR A MOMENT.
WAIT, WHERE ARE YOU GOING?!? WE NEED TO GET YOU--
BILLY, THIS SUIT IS A WONDERFUL GIFT AND I'LL ALWAYS BE ETERNALLY GRATEFUL FOR IT.
BUT IF THIS IS INDEED MY LAST TIME IN IT...

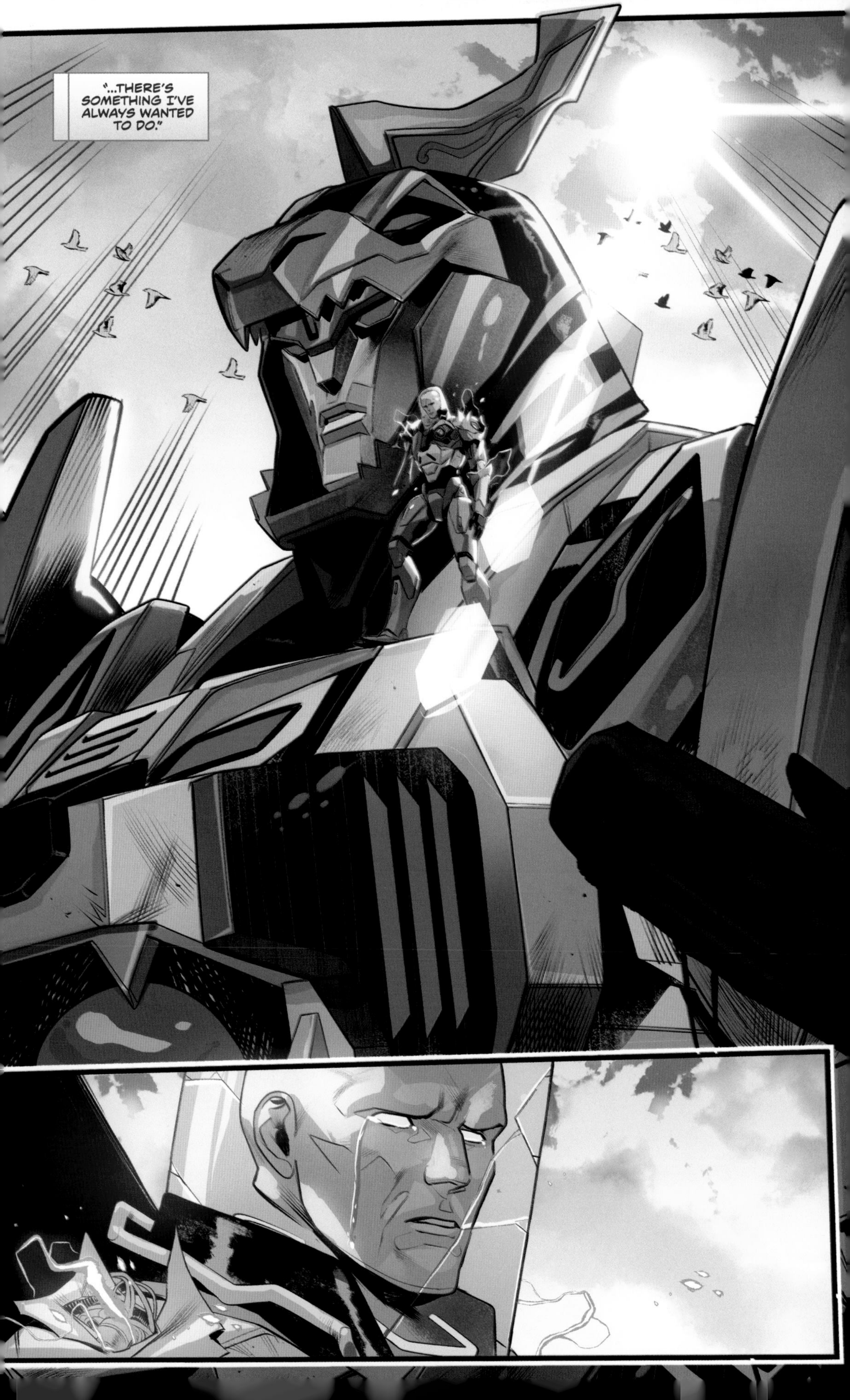
"...THERE'S SOMETHING I'VE ALWAYS WANTED TO DO."

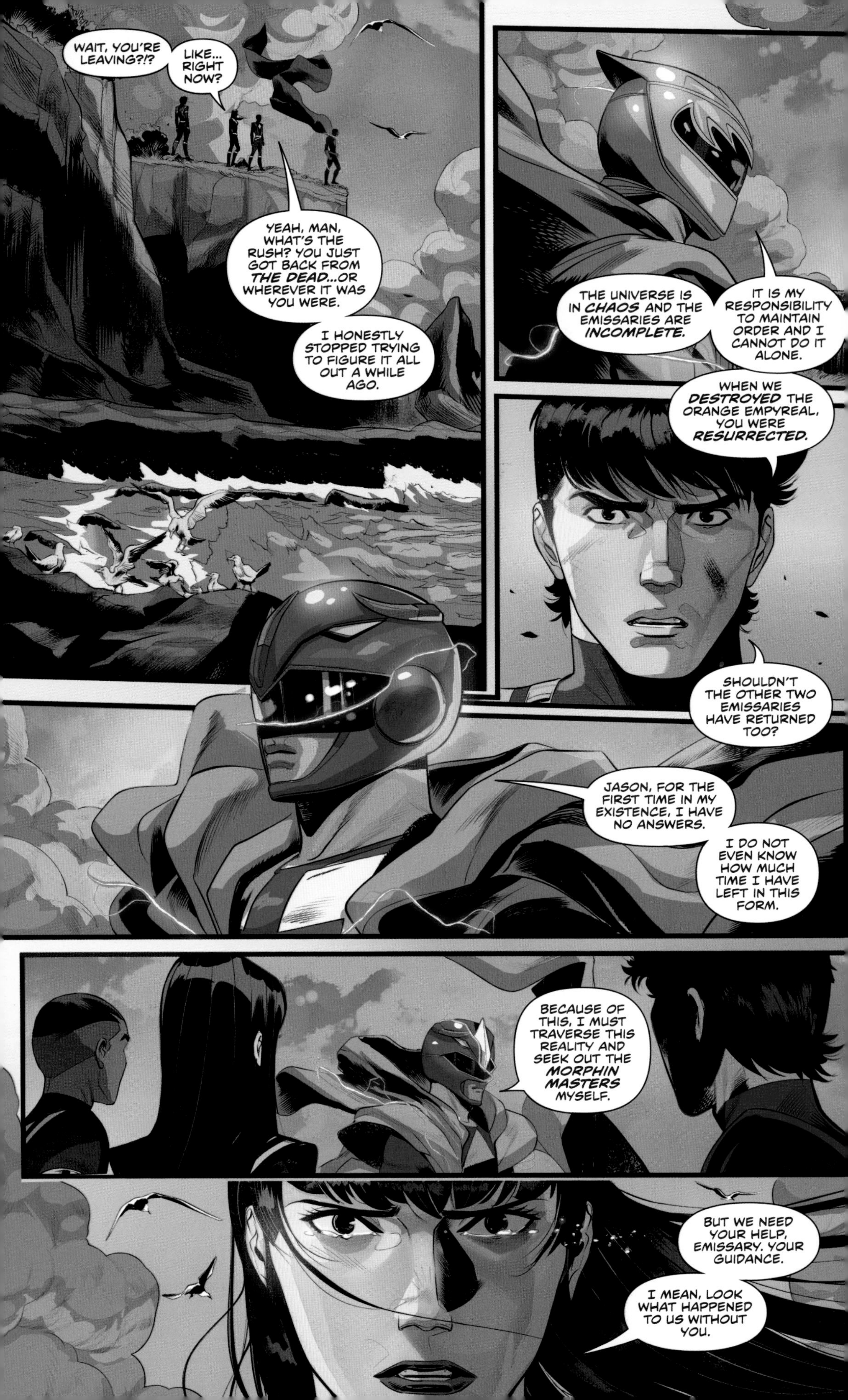
WAIT, YOU'RE LEAVING?!?
LIKE... RIGHT NOW?
YEAH, MAN, WHAT'S THE RUSH? YOU JUST GOT BACK FROM THE DEAD...OR WHEREVER IT WAS YOU WERE.
I HONESTLY STOPPED TRYING TO FIGURE IT ALL OUT A WHILE AGO.
THE UNIVERSE IS IN CHAOS AND THE EMISSARIES ARE INCOMPLETE.
IT IS MY RESPONSIBILITY TO MAINTAIN ORDER AND I CANNOT DO IT ALONE.
WHEN WE DESTROYED THE ORANGE EMPYREAL, YOU WERE RESURRECTED.
SHOULDN'T THE OTHER TWO EMISSARIES HAVE RETURNED TOO?
JASON, FOR THE FIRST TIME IN MY EXISTENCE, I HAVE NO ANSWERS.
I DO NOT EVEN KNOW HOW MUCH TIME I HAVE LEFT IN THIS FORM.
BECAUSE OF THIS, I MUST TRAVERSE THIS REALITY AND SEEK OUT THE MORPHIN MASTERS MYSELF.
BUT WE NEED YOUR HELP, EMISSARY. YOUR GUIDANCE.
I MEAN, LOOK WHAT HAPPENED TO US WITHOUT YOU.

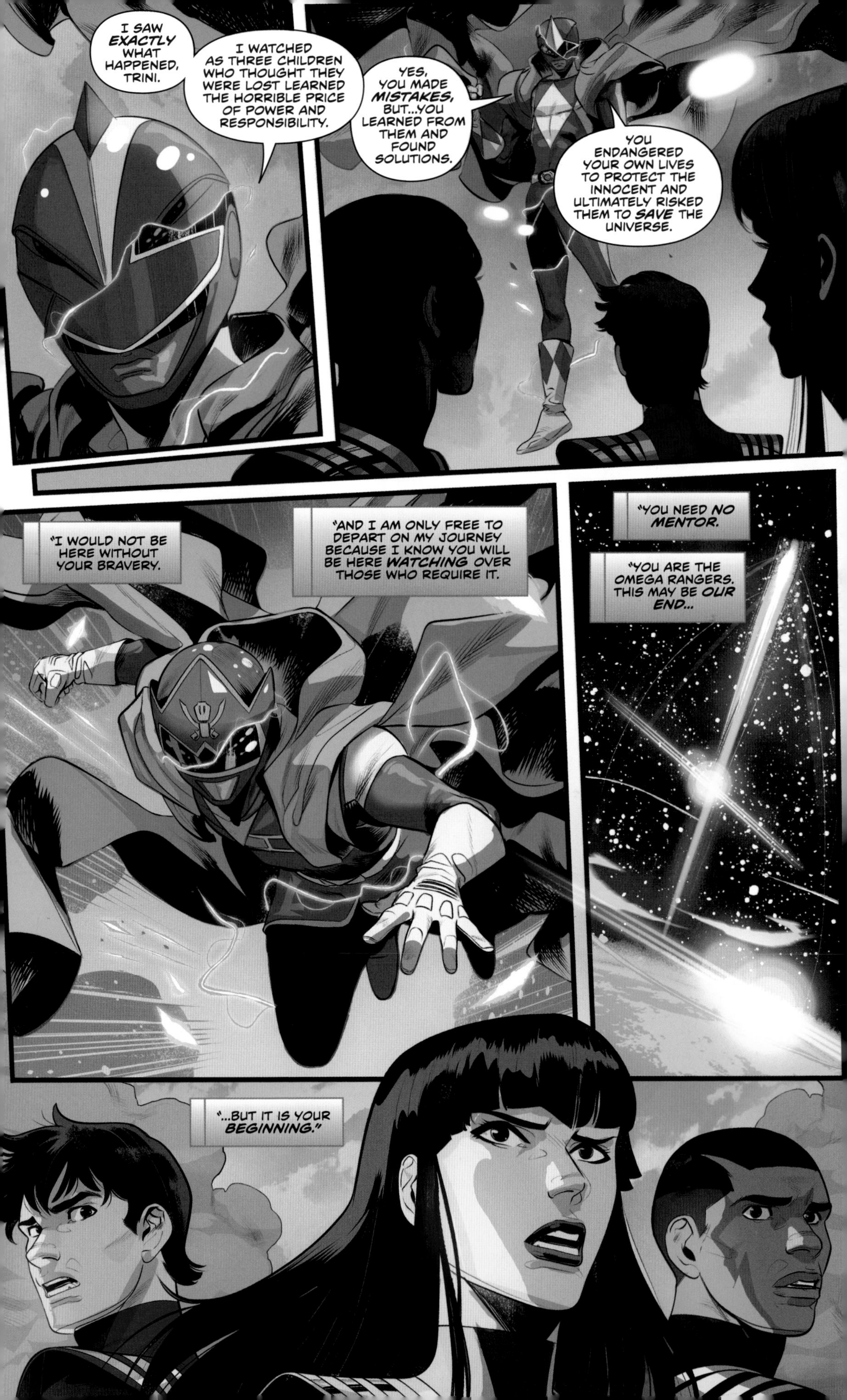
I SAW EXACTLY WHAT HAPPENED, TRINI.
I WATCHED AS THREE CHILDREN WHO THOUGHT THEY WERE LOST LEARNED THE HORRIBLE PRICE OF POWER AND RESPONSIBILITY.
YES, YOU MADE MISTAKES, BUT...YOU LEARNED FROM THEM AND FOUND SOLUTIONS.
YOU ENDANGERED YOUR OWN LIVES TO PROTECT THE INNOCENT AND ULTIMATELY RISKED THEM TO SAVE THE UNIVERSE.
"I WOULD NOT BE HERE WITHOUT YOUR BRAVERY.
"AND I AM ONLY FREE TO DEPART ON MY JOURNEY BECAUSE I KNOW YOU WILL BE HERE WATCHING OVER THOSE WHO REQUIRE IT.
"YOU NEED NO MENTOR.
"YOU ARE THE OMEGA RANGERS. THIS MAY BE OUR END...
"...BUT IT IS YOUR BEGINNING."

ALRIGHT, HERE WE GO.

ACTIVATING TRANSFER PROTOCOL.

LEVELS ARE PEAKING, ALPHA.

COMPENSATING.

AAAAHHH!

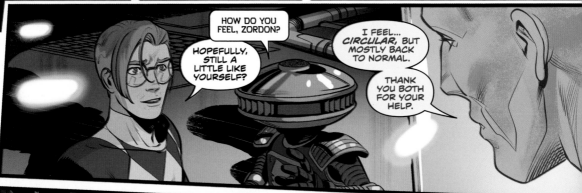

HOW DO YOU FEEL, ZORDON?

HOPEFULLY, STILL A LITTLE LIKE YOURSELF?

I FEEL... CIRCULAR, BUT MOSTLY BACK TO NORMAL.

THANK YOU BOTH FOR YOUR HELP.

SO... THIS IS HOME.

AYE-YI-YI.

IT WAS EITHER THIS OR THE JUICE BAR.

ZORDON, I KNOW YOU JUST GOT SQUEEZED INTO A TUBE, BUT IF YOU'RE UP FOR IT...

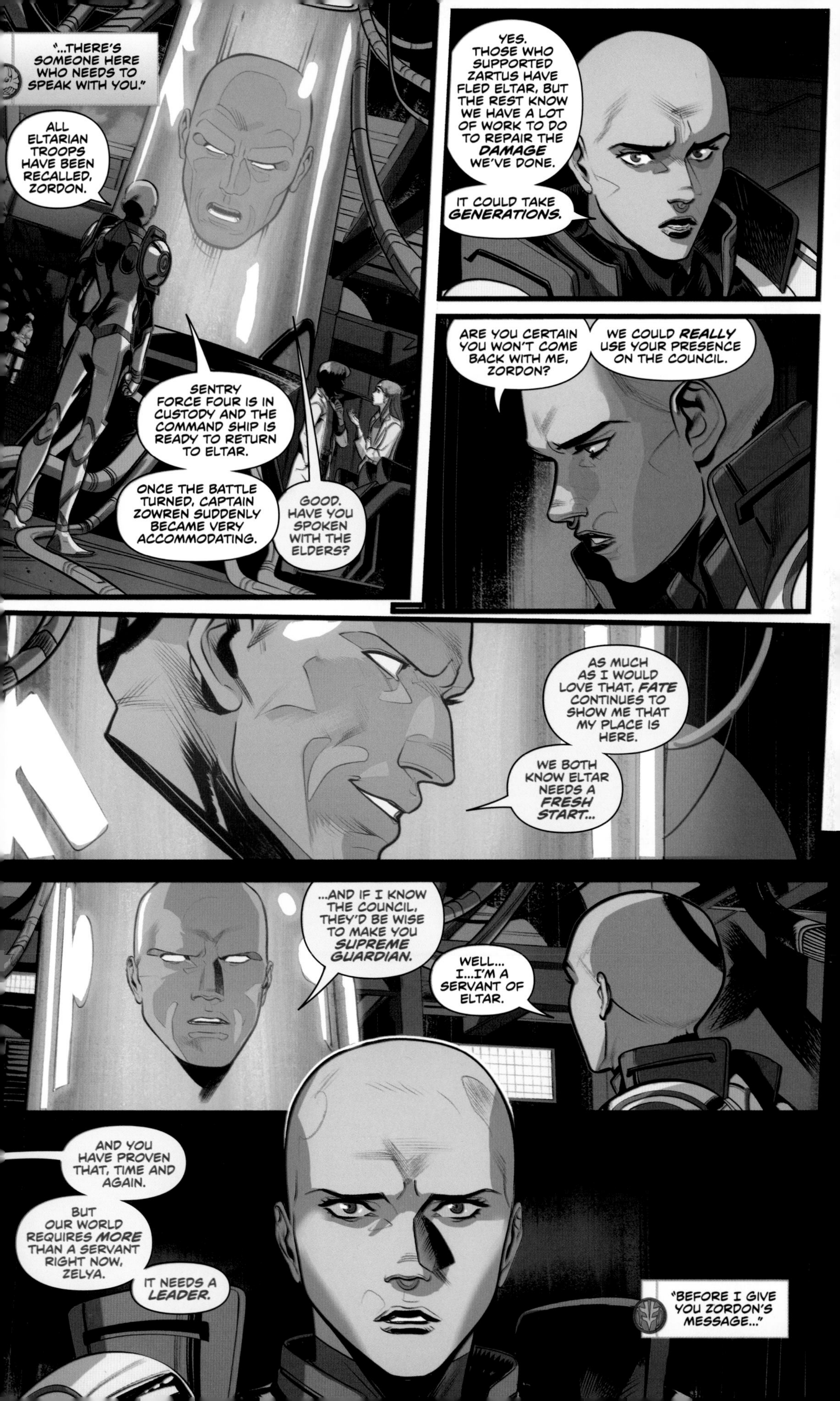

"...THERE'S SOMEONE HERE WHO NEEDS TO SPEAK WITH YOU."
ALL ELTARIAN TROOPS HAVE BEEN RECALLED, ZORDON.
SENTRY FORCE FOUR IS IN CUSTODY AND THE COMMAND SHIP IS READY TO RETURN TO ELTAR.
ONCE THE BATTLE TURNED, CAPTAIN ZOWREN SUDDENLY BECAME VERY ACCOMMODATING.
GOOD. HAVE YOU SPOKEN WITH THE ELDERS?
YES. THOSE WHO SUPPORTED ZARTUS HAVE FLED ELTAR, BUT THE REST KNOW WE HAVE A LOT OF WORK TO DO TO REPAIR THE DAMAGE WE'VE DONE.
IT COULD TAKE GENERATIONS.
ARE YOU CERTAIN YOU WON'T COME BACK WITH ME, ZORDON?
WE COULD REALLY USE YOUR PRESENCE ON THE COUNCIL.
AS MUCH AS I WOULD LOVE THAT, FATE CONTINUES TO SHOW ME THAT MY PLACE IS HERE.
WE BOTH KNOW ELTAR NEEDS A FRESH START...
...AND IF I KNOW THE COUNCIL, THEY'D BE WISE TO MAKE YOU SUPREME GUARDIAN.
WELL... I...I'M A SERVANT OF ELTAR.
AND YOU HAVE PROVEN THAT, TIME AND AGAIN.
BUT OUR WORLD REQUIRES MORE THAN A SERVANT RIGHT NOW, ZELYA.
IT NEEDS A LEADER.
"BEFORE I GIVE YOU ZORDON'S MESSAGE..."

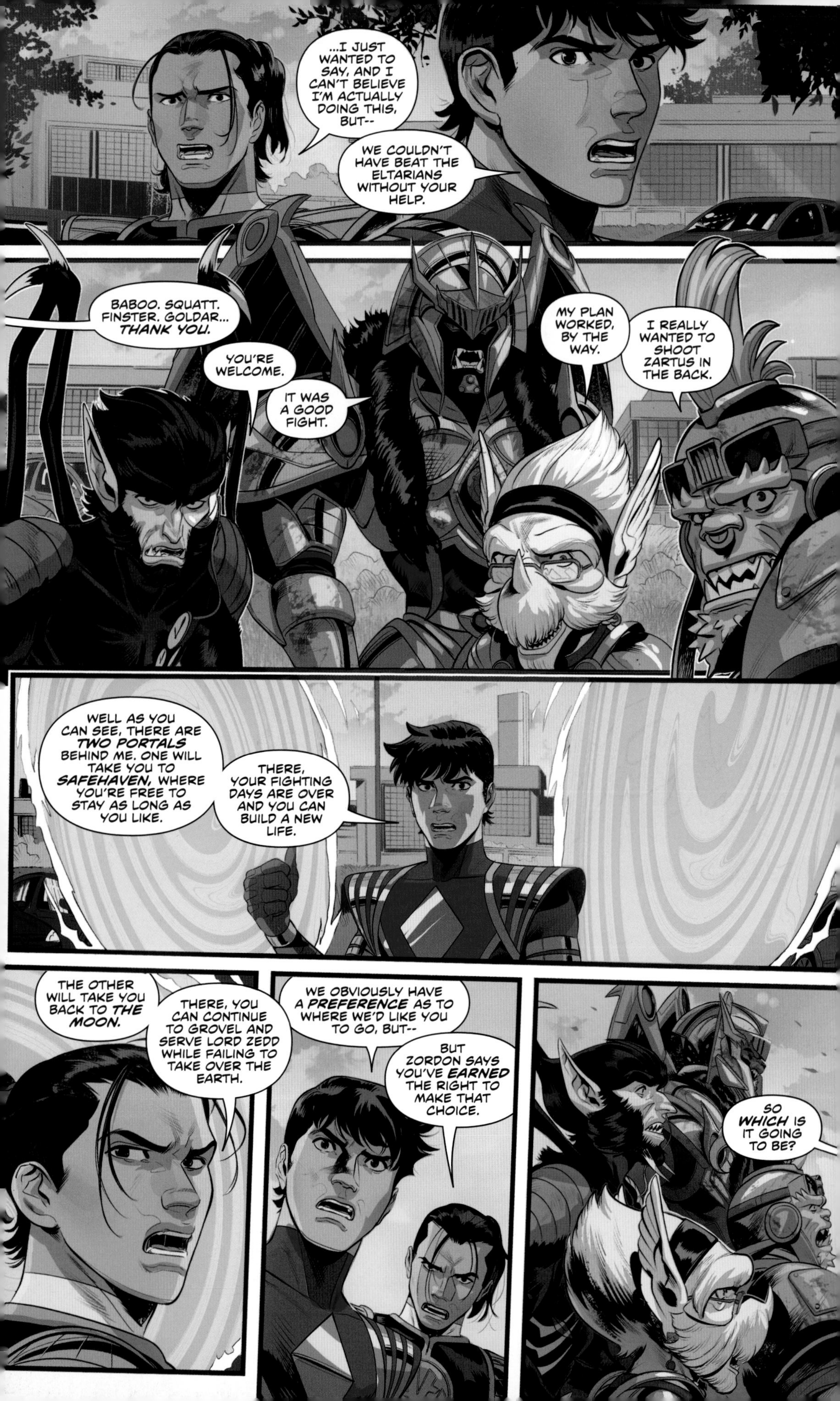

...I JUST WANTED TO SAY, AND I CAN'T BELIEVE I'M ACTUALLY DOING THIS, BUT--
WE COULDN'T HAVE BEAT THE ELTARIANS WITHOUT YOUR HELP.
BABOO. SQUATT. FINSTER. GOLDAR... *THANK YOU.*
YOU'RE WELCOME.
IT WAS A GOOD FIGHT.
MY PLAN WORKED, BY THE WAY.
I REALLY WANTED TO SHOOT ZARTUS IN THE BACK.
WELL AS YOU CAN SEE, THERE ARE ***TWO PORTALS*** BEHIND ME. ONE WILL TAKE YOU TO ***SAFEHAVEN,*** WHERE YOU'RE FREE TO STAY AS LONG AS YOU LIKE.
THERE, YOUR FIGHTING DAYS ARE OVER AND YOU CAN BUILD A NEW LIFE.
THE OTHER WILL TAKE YOU BACK TO ***THE MOON.***
THERE, YOU CAN CONTINUE TO GROVEL AND SERVE LORD ZEDD WHILE FAILING TO TAKE OVER THE EARTH.
WE OBVIOUSLY HAVE A ***PREFERENCE*** AS TO WHERE WE'D LIKE YOU TO GO, BUT--
BUT ZORDON SAYS YOU'VE ***EARNED*** THE RIGHT TO MAKE THAT CHOICE.
SO ***WHICH*** IS IT GOING TO BE?

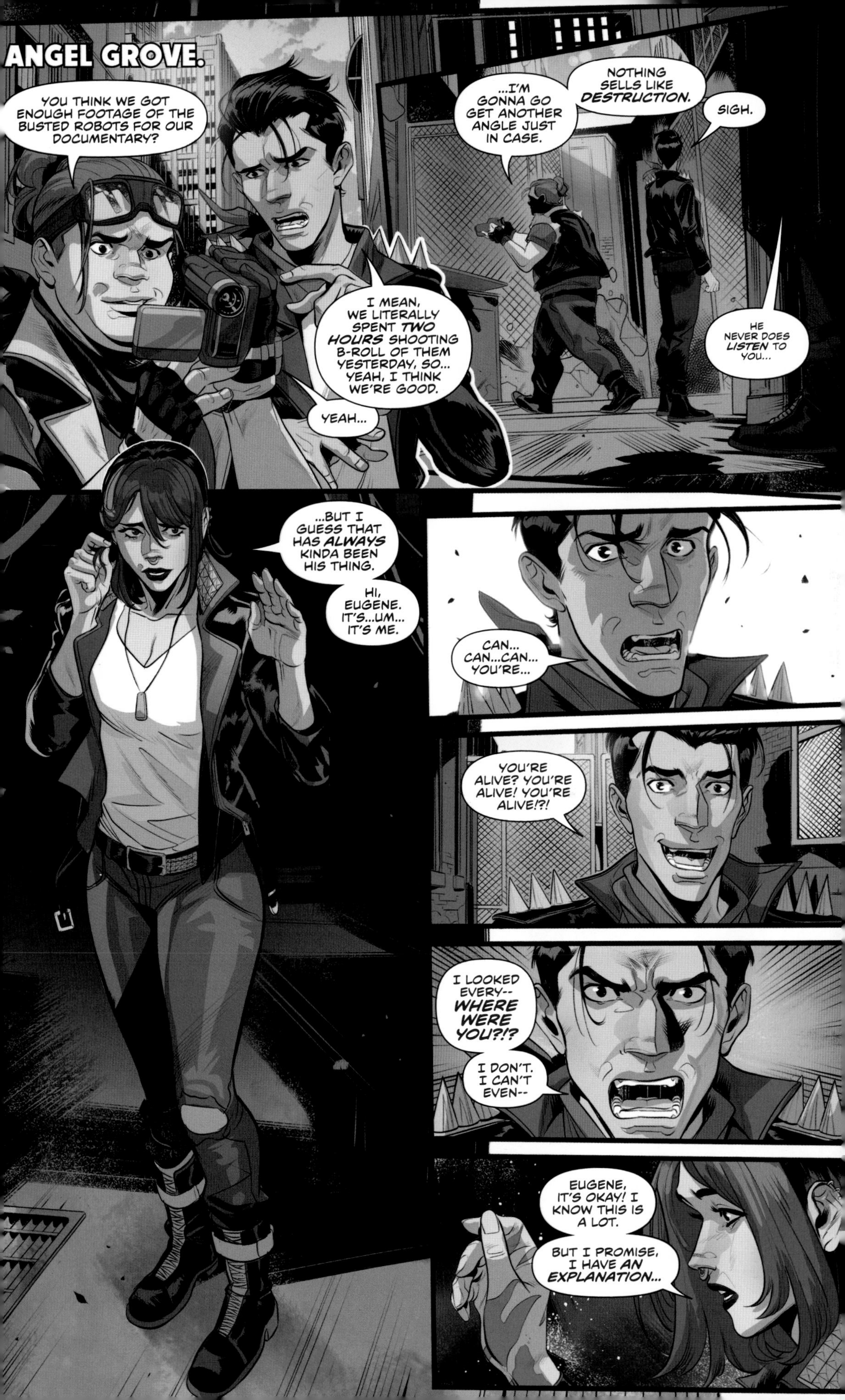
ANGEL GROVE.
YOU THINK WE GOT ENOUGH FOOTAGE OF THE BUSTED ROBOTS FOR OUR DOCUMENTARY?
I MEAN, WE LITERALLY SPENT TWO HOURS SHOOTING B-ROLL OF THEM YESTERDAY, SO... YEAH, I THINK WE'RE GOOD.
YEAH...
NOTHING SELLS LIKE DESTRUCTION.
...I'M GONNA GO GET ANOTHER ANGLE JUST IN CASE.
SIGH.
HE NEVER DOES LISTEN TO YOU...
...BUT I GUESS THAT HAS ALWAYS KINDA BEEN HIS THING.
HI, EUGENE. IT'S...UM... IT'S ME.
CAN... CAN...CAN... YOU'RE...
YOU'RE ALIVE? YOU'RE ALIVE! YOU'RE ALIVE!?!
I LOOKED EVERY-- WHERE WERE YOU?!?
I DON'T. I CAN'T EVEN--
EUGENE, IT'S OKAY! I KNOW THIS IS A LOT.
BUT I PROMISE, I HAVE AN EXPLANATION...

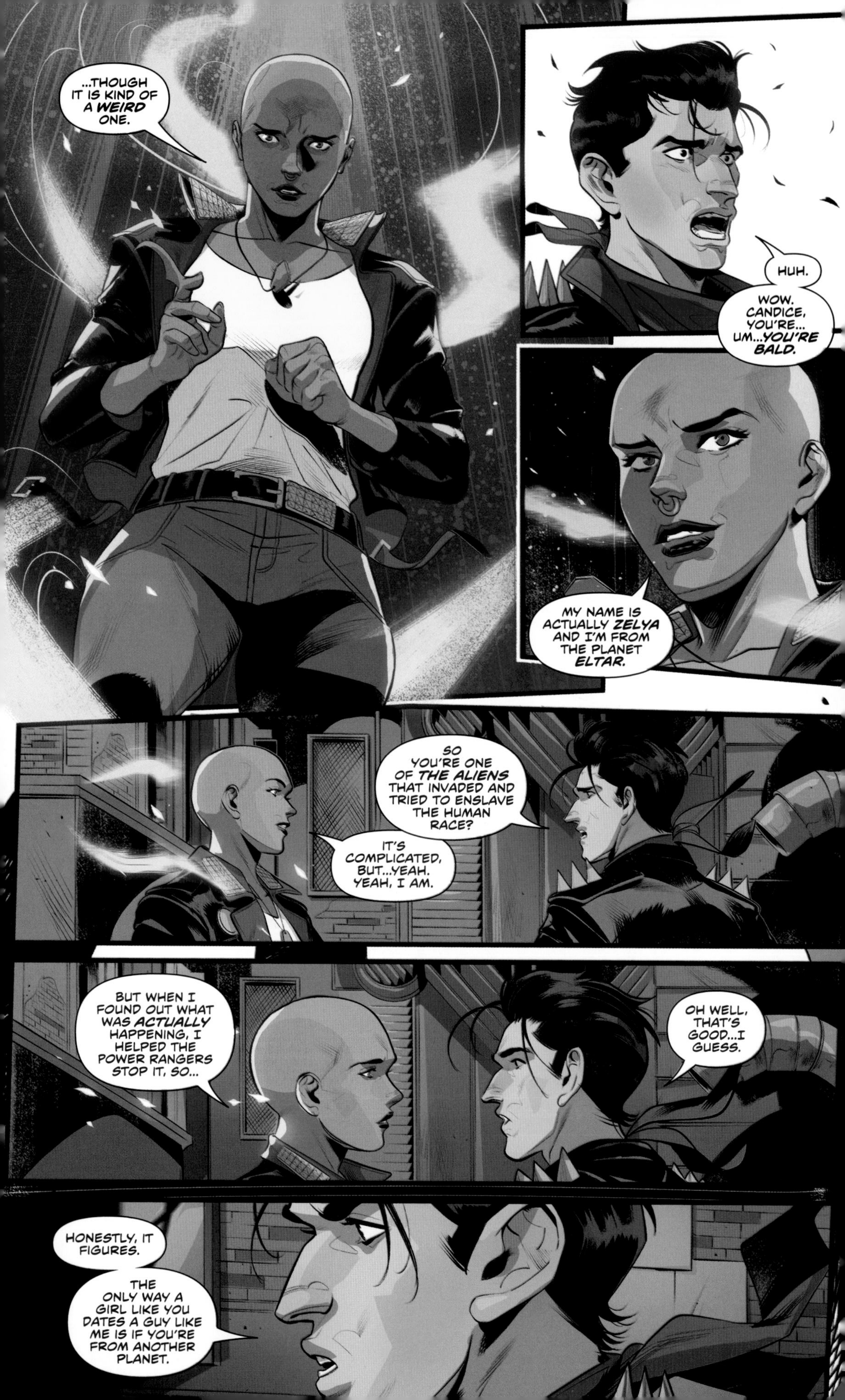
...THOUGH IT IS KIND OF A WEIRD ONE.
HUH.
WOW. CANDICE, YOU'RE... UM...YOU'RE BALD.
MY NAME IS ACTUALLY ZELYA AND I'M FROM THE PLANET ELTAR.
SO YOU'RE ONE OF THE ALIENS THAT INVADED AND TRIED TO ENSLAVE THE HUMAN RACE?
IT'S COMPLICATED, BUT...YEAH. YEAH, I AM.
BUT WHEN I FOUND OUT WHAT WAS ACTUALLY HAPPENING, I HELPED THE POWER RANGERS STOP IT, SO...
OH WELL, THAT'S GOOD...I GUESS.
HONESTLY, IT FIGURES.
THE ONLY WAY A GIRL LIKE YOU DATES A GUY LIKE ME IS IF YOU'RE FROM ANOTHER PLANET.

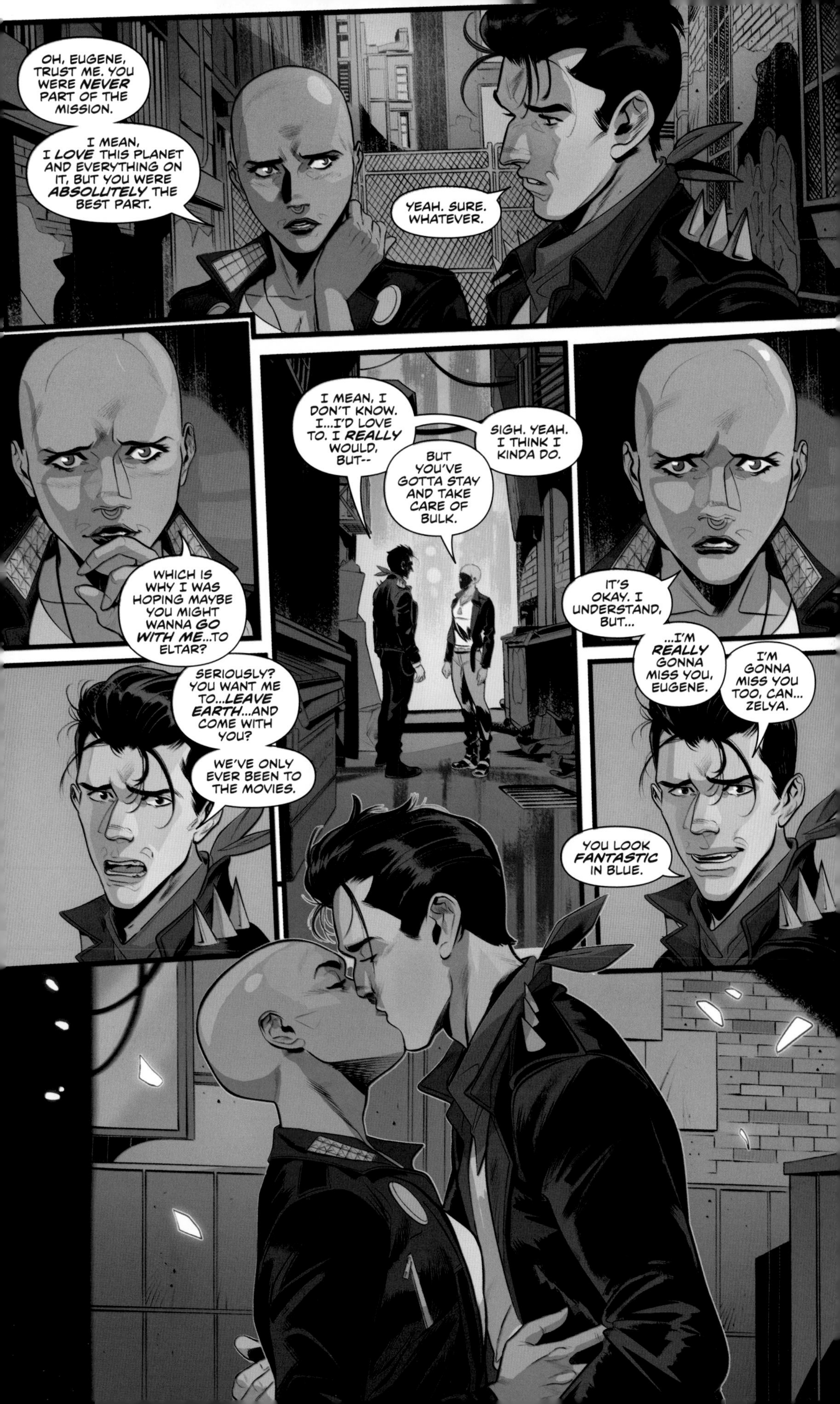

OH, EUGENE, TRUST ME. YOU WERE NEVER PART OF THE MISSION.
I MEAN, I LOVE THIS PLANET AND EVERYTHING ON IT, BUT YOU WERE ABSOLUTELY THE BEST PART.
YEAH. SURE. WHATEVER.
WHICH IS WHY I WAS HOPING MAYBE YOU MIGHT WANNA GO WITH ME...TO ELTAR?
SERIOUSLY? YOU WANT ME TO...LEAVE EARTH...AND COME WITH YOU?
WE'VE ONLY EVER BEEN TO THE MOVIES.
I MEAN, I DON'T KNOW. I...I'D LOVE TO. I REALLY WOULD, BUT--
BUT YOU'VE GOTTA STAY AND TAKE CARE OF BULK.
SIGH. YEAH. I THINK I KINDA DO.
IT'S OKAY. I UNDERSTAND, BUT...
...I'M REALLY GONNA MISS YOU, EUGENE.
I'M GONNA MISS YOU TOO, CAN... ZELYA.
YOU LOOK FANTASTIC IN BLUE.

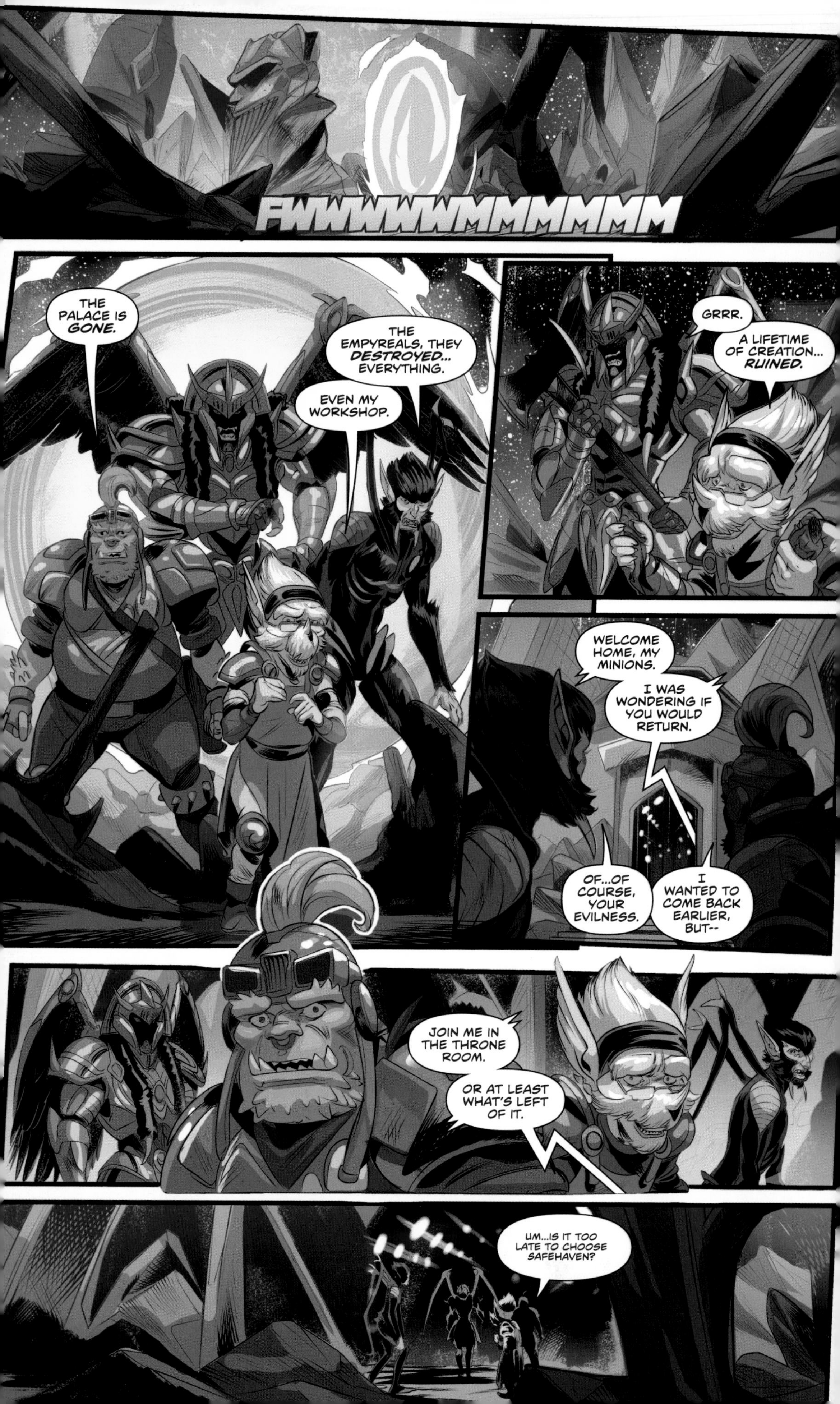
FWWWWWMMMMMMM
THE PALACE IS GONE.
THE EMPYREALS, THEY DESTROYED... EVERYTHING.
EVEN MY WORKSHOP.
GRRR.
A LIFETIME OF CREATION... RUINED.
WELCOME HOME, MY MINIONS.
I WAS WONDERING IF YOU WOULD RETURN.
OF...OF COURSE, YOUR EVILNESS.
I WANTED TO COME BACK EARLIER, BUT--
JOIN ME IN THE THRONE ROOM.
OR AT LEAST WHAT'S LEFT OF IT.
UM...IS IT TOO LATE TO CHOOSE SAFEHAVEN?

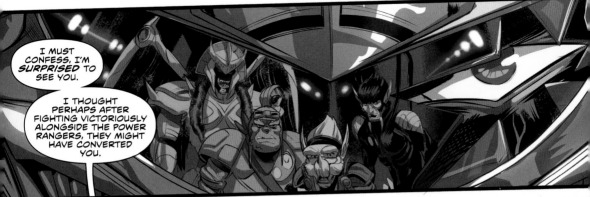

I MUST CONFESS, I'M **SURPRISED** TO SEE YOU.

I THOUGHT PERHAPS AFTER FIGHTING VICTORIOUSLY ALONGSIDE THE POWER RANGERS, THEY MIGHT HAVE CONVERTED YOU.

NEVER.

WE ONLY FOUGHT WITH THEM IN YOUR HONOR.

AND WE RETURNED THE MOMENT WE LEARNED YOU WERE ALIVE, MY LORD.

**LIARS!**

YOU DIDN'T FIGHT TO HONOR ME. YOU FOUGHT TO **SAVE YOURSELVES**... AND YOU DID.

WELL DONE.

I ASSUME THEY OFFERED YOU **A NEW LIFE** AND A CHANCE TO ESCAPE ME, YET...HERE YOU ARE ONCE AGAIN.

WHY?

AND **DO NOT** LIE TO ME.

... YOU'RE RIGHT. WE'RE NOT HERE FOR YOU. BUT IF WE RAN...

...**RITA** WOULD BE ASHAMED OF US.

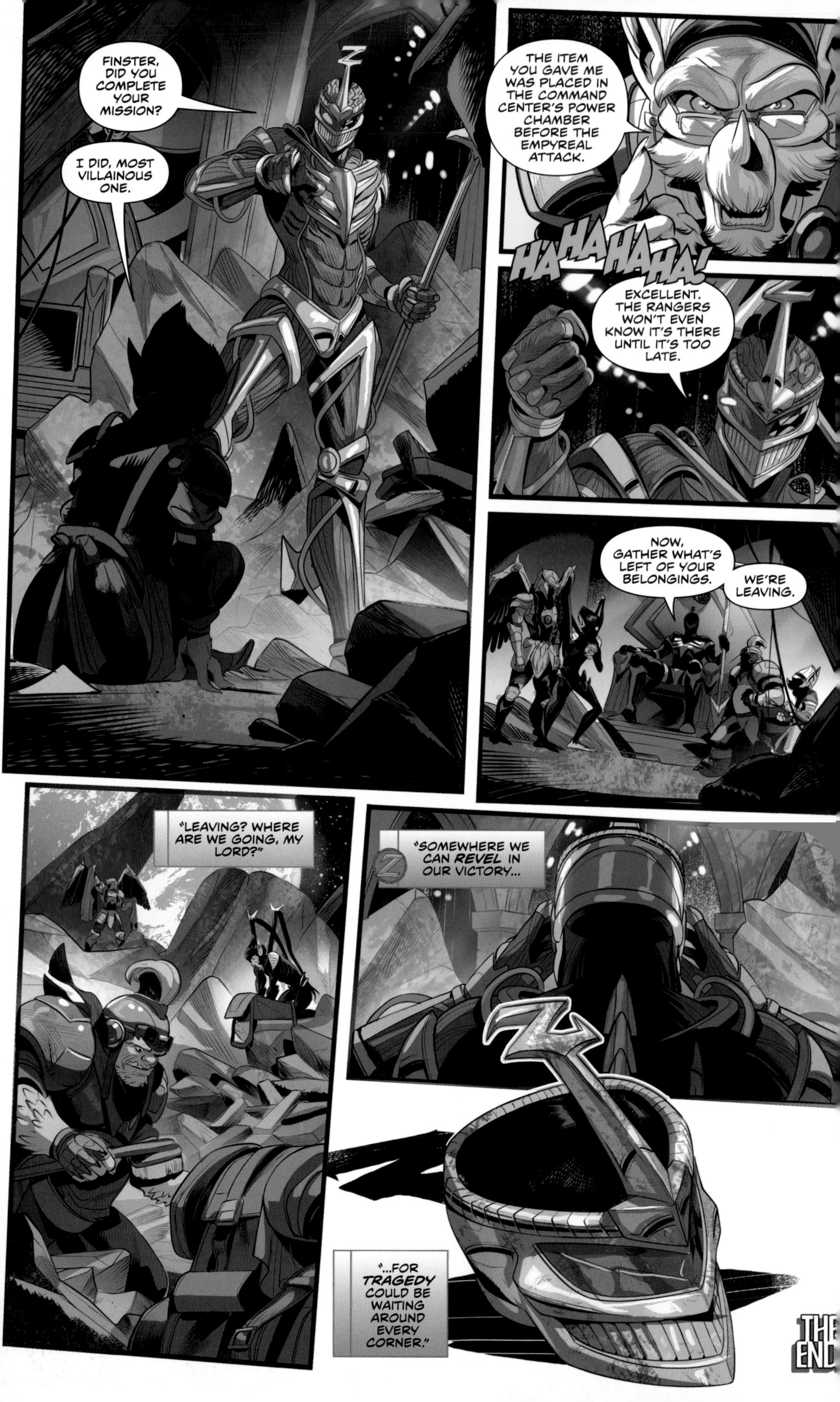
FINSTER, DID YOU COMPLETE YOUR MISSION?
I DID, MOST VILLAINOUS ONE.
THE ITEM YOU GAVE ME WAS PLACED IN THE COMMAND CENTER'S POWER CHAMBER BEFORE THE EMPYREAL ATTACK.
HAHAHAHA!
EXCELLENT. THE RANGERS WON'T EVEN KNOW IT'S THERE UNTIL IT'S TOO LATE.
NOW, GATHER WHAT'S LEFT OF YOUR BELONGINGS.
WE'RE LEAVING.
"LEAVING? WHERE ARE WE GOING, MY LORD?"
"SOMEWHERE WE CAN *REVEL* IN OUR VICTORY...
"...FOR *TRAGEDY* COULD BE WAITING AROUND EVERY CORNER."
THE END

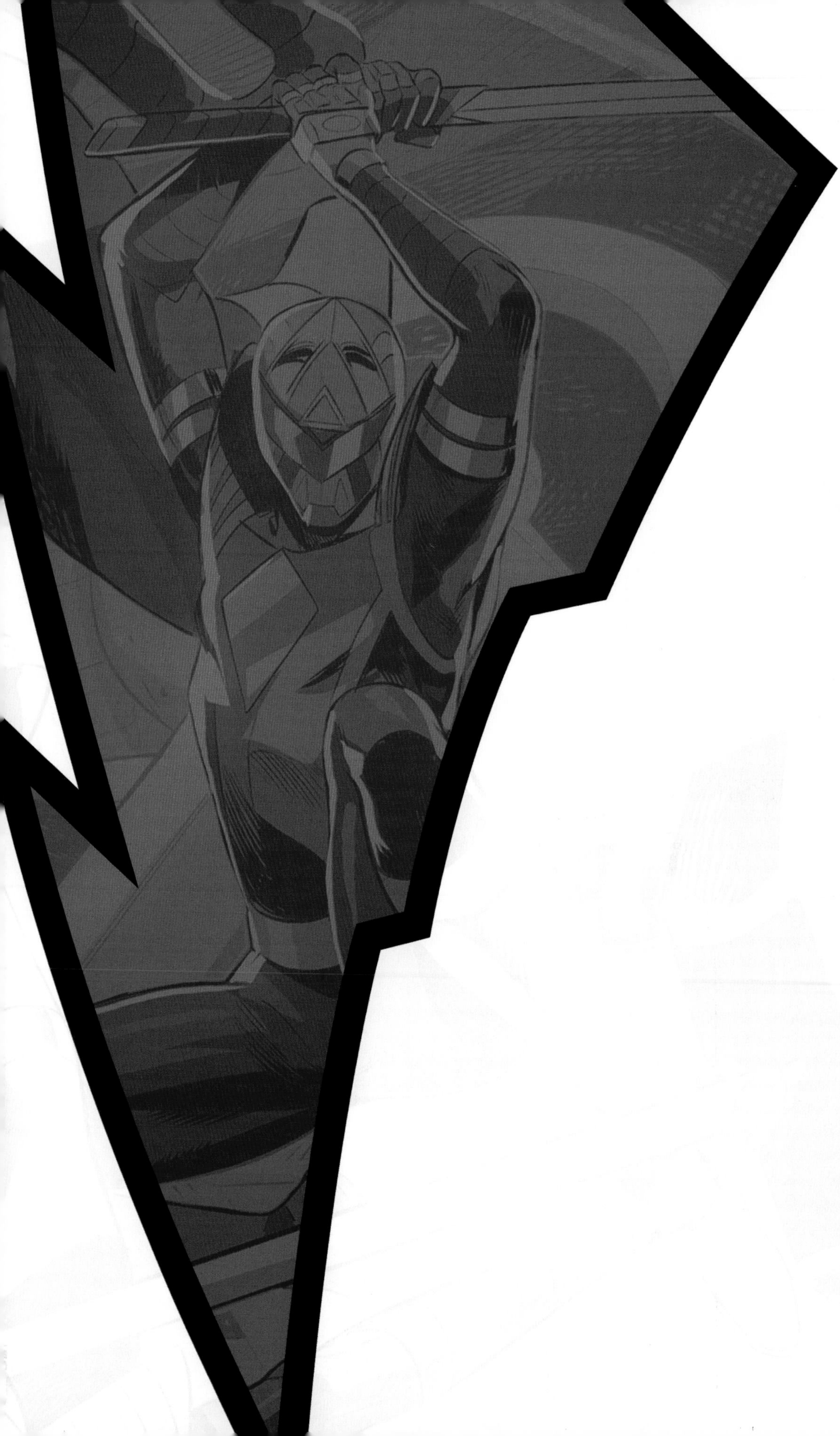

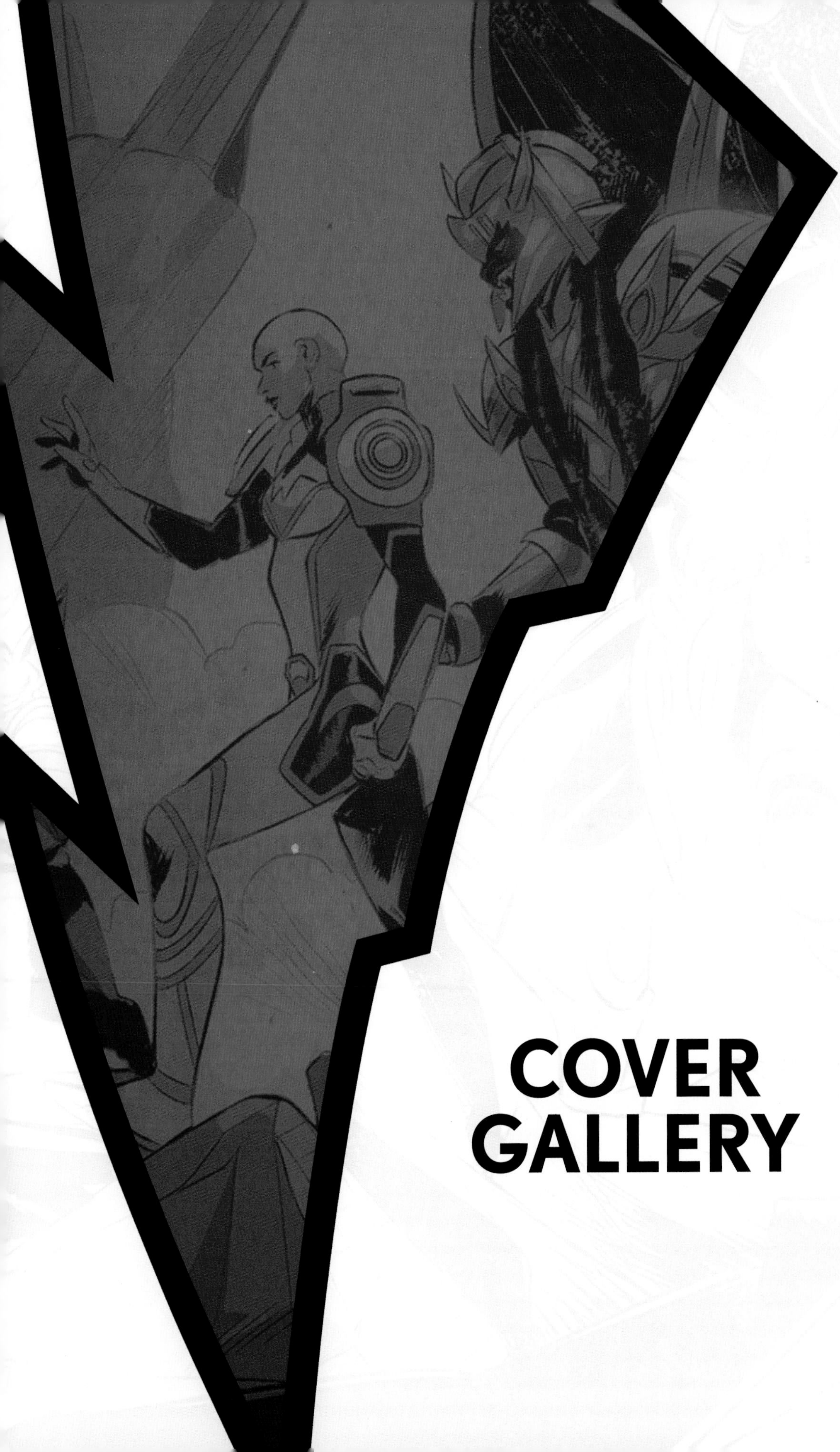

# COVER GALLERY

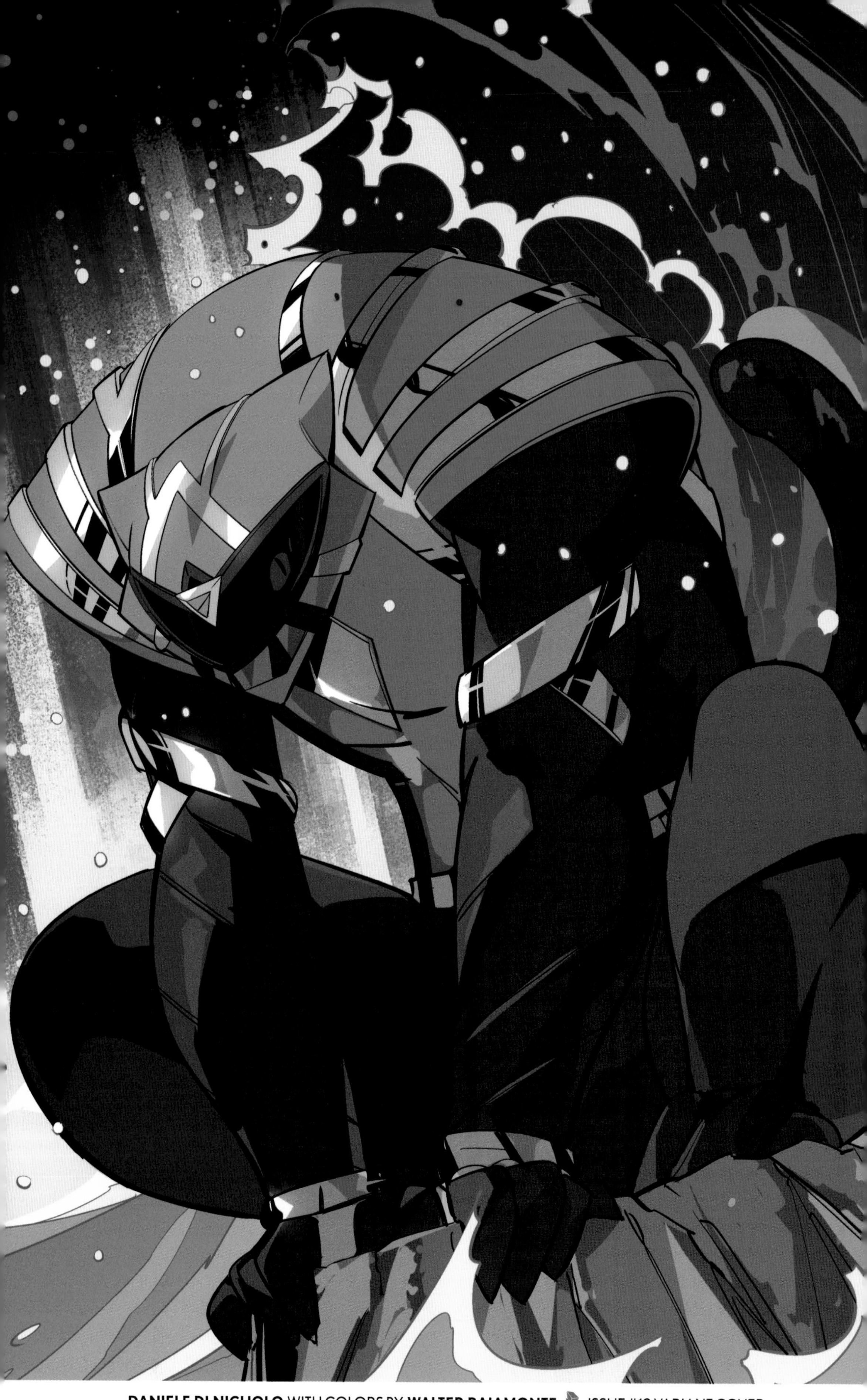

**DANIELE DI NICUOLO** WITH COLORS BY **WALTER BAIAMONTE** ISSUE #13 VARIANT COVER

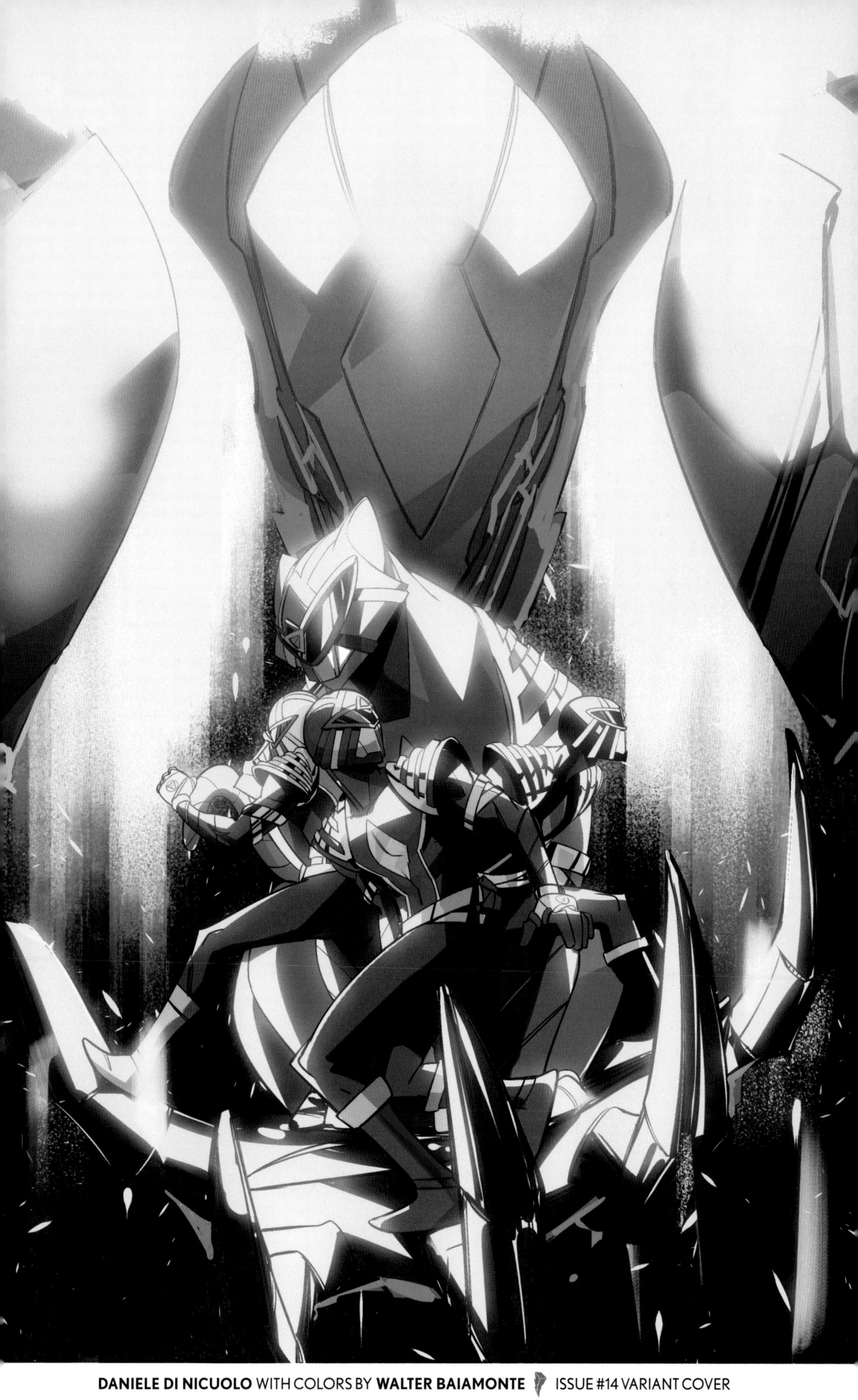

**DANIELE DI NICUOLO** WITH COLORS BY **WALTER BAIAMONTE** ISSUE #14 VARIANT COVER

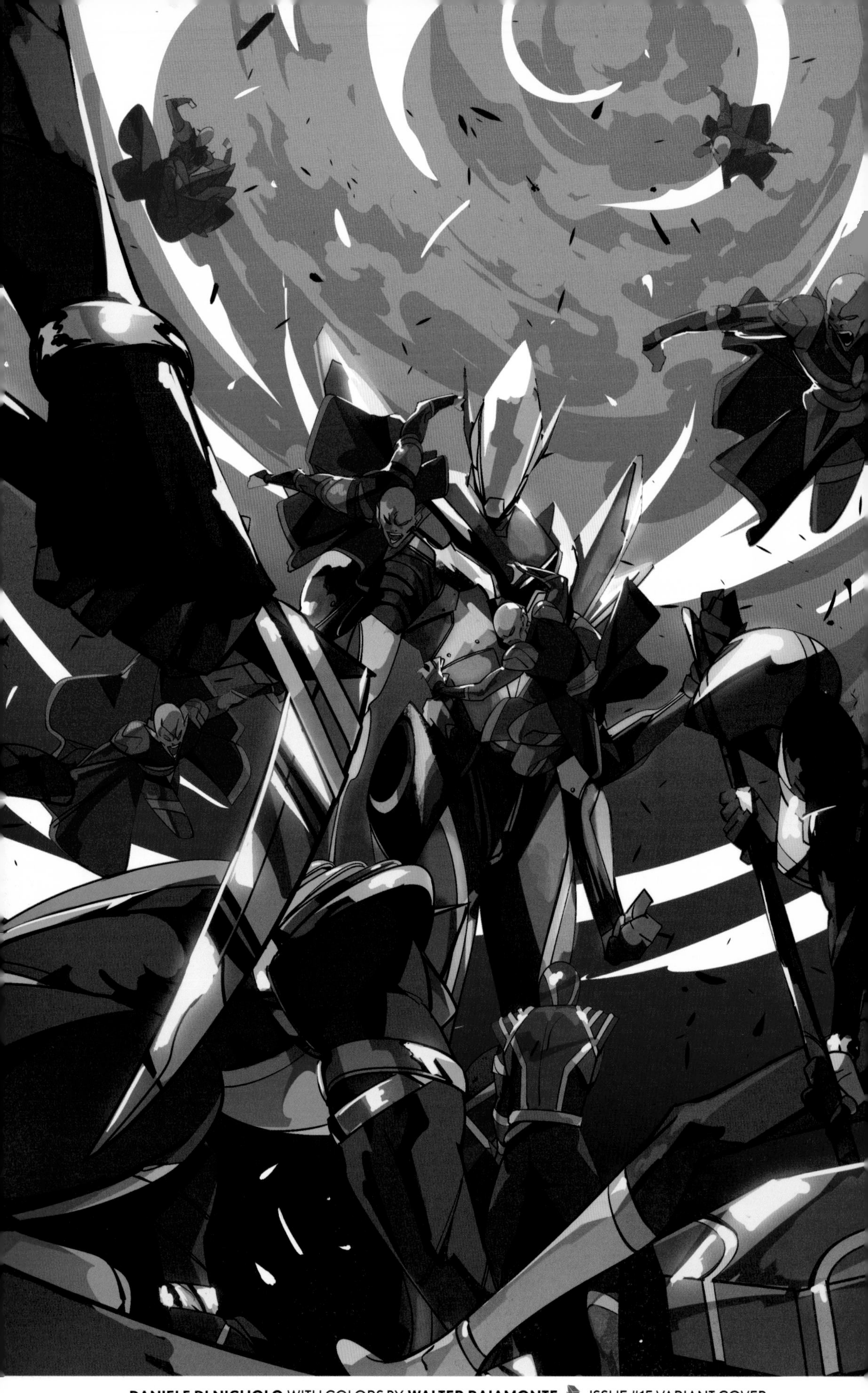

**DANIELE DI NICUOLO** WITH COLORS BY **WALTER BAIAMONTE** ISSUE #15 VARIANT COVER

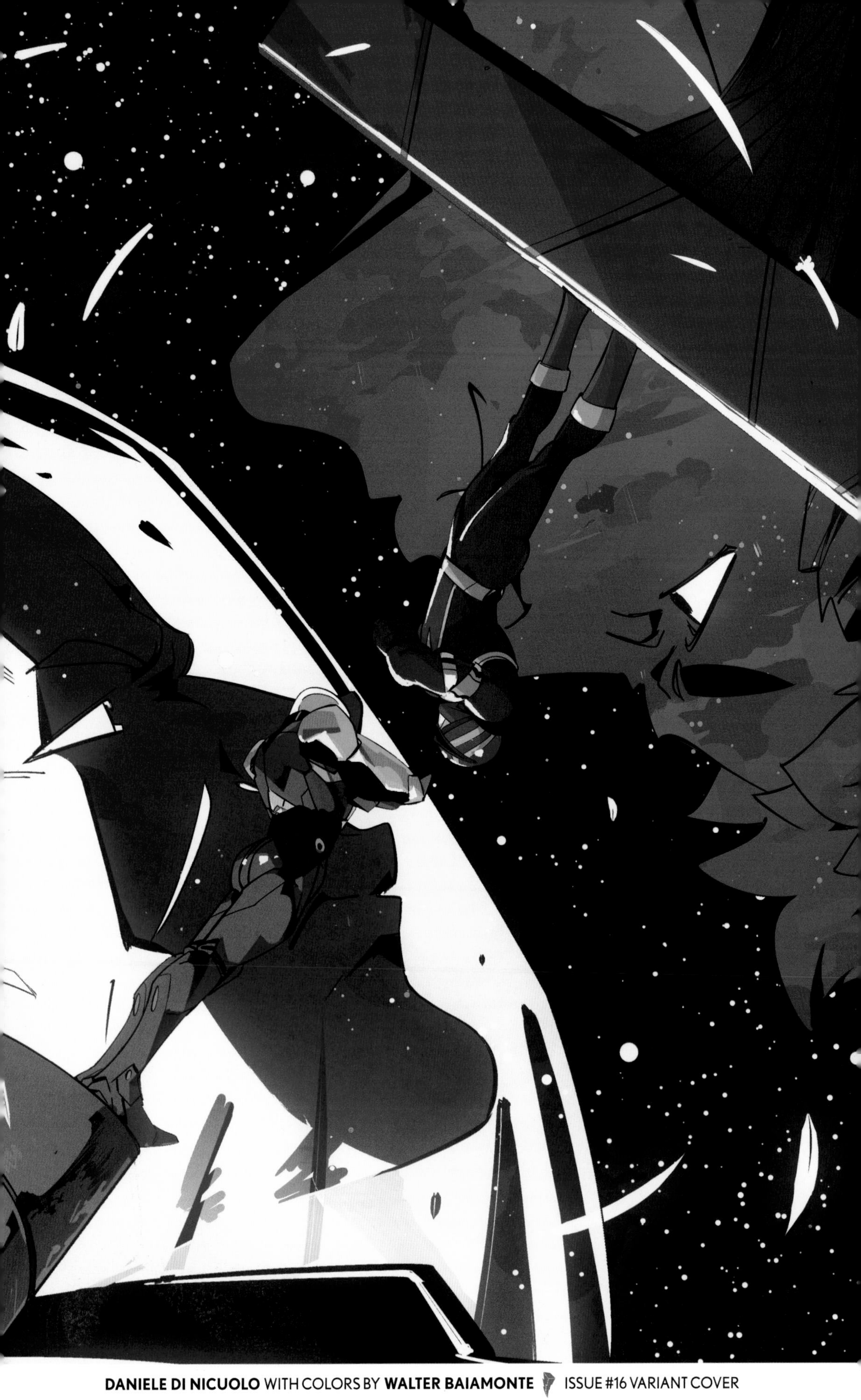

**DANIELE DI NICUOLO** WITH COLORS BY **WALTER BAIAMONTE** ISSUE #16 VARIANT COVER

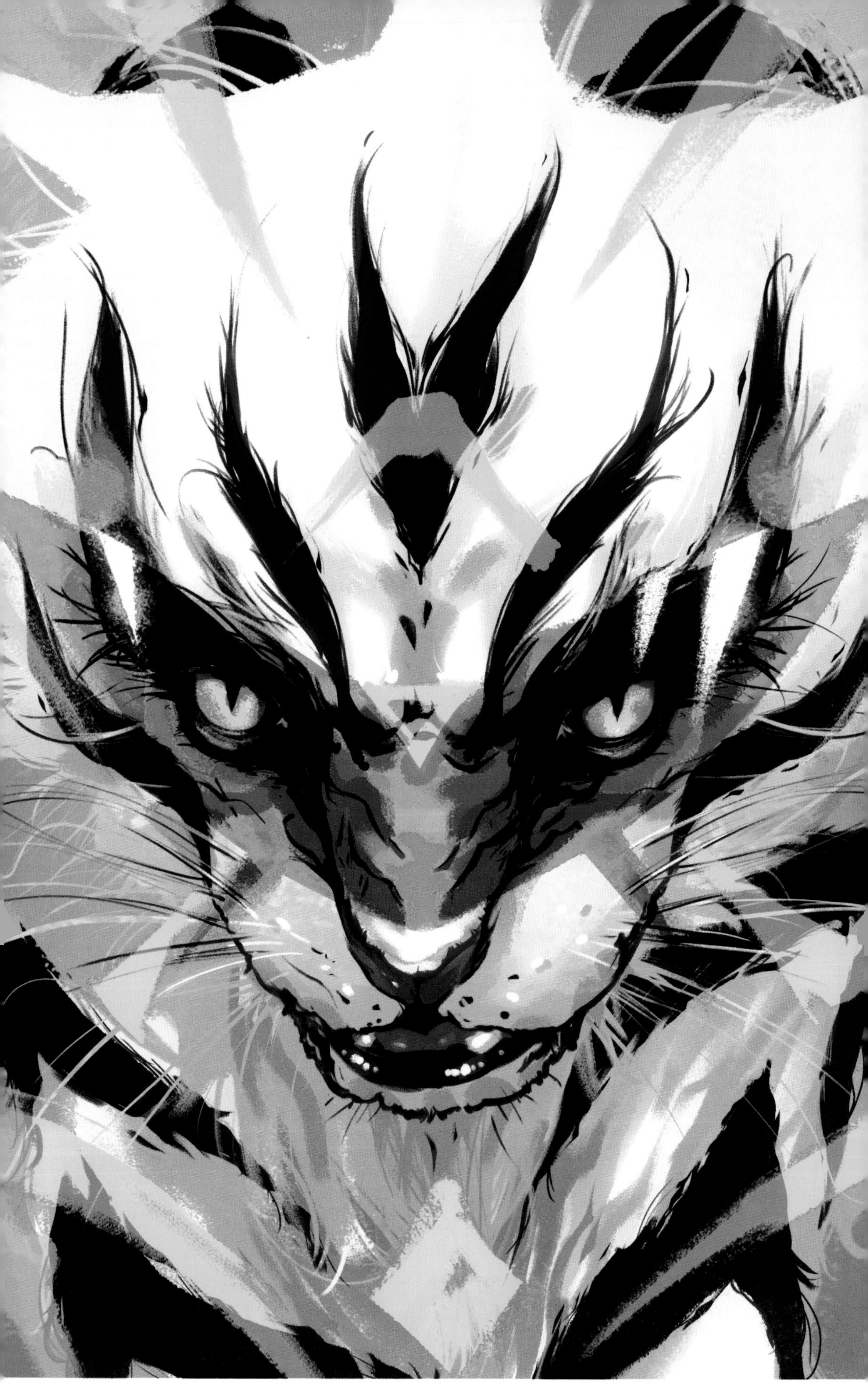

**GOÑI MONTES** ISSUE #14 VARIANT COVER

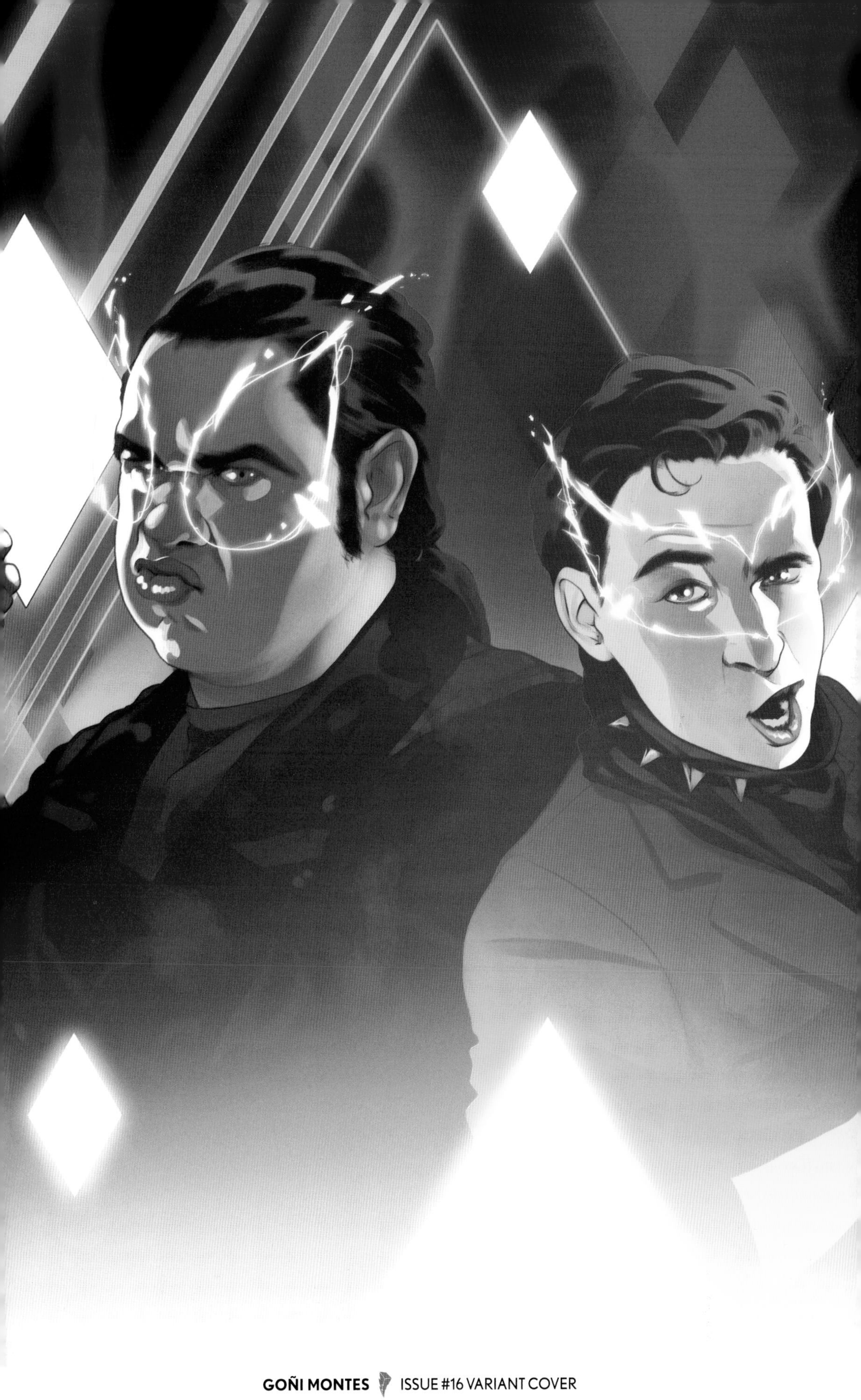

GOÑI MONTES ISSUE #16 VARIANT COVER

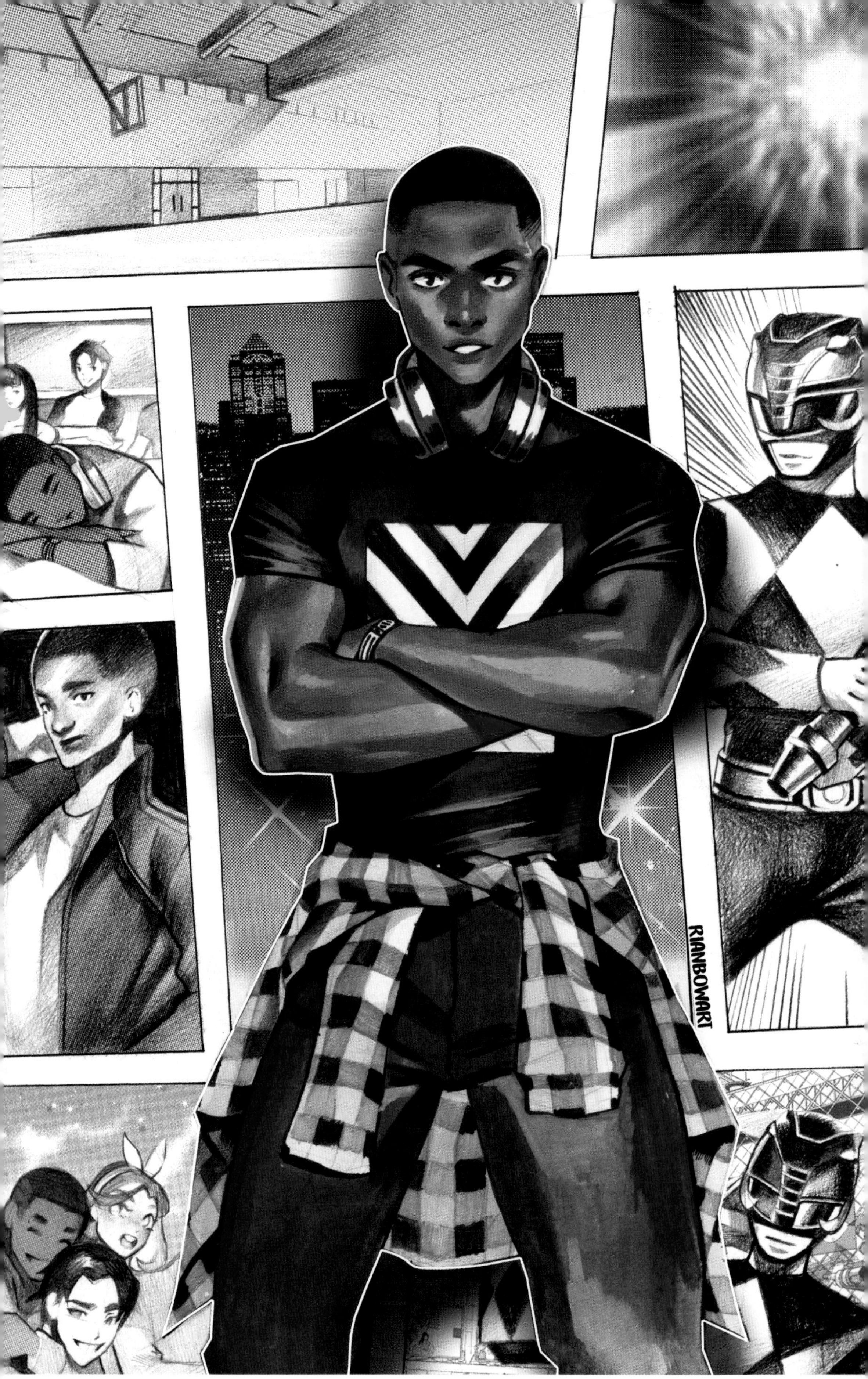
RIANBOWART

**RIAN GONZALES** ISSUE #13 VARIANT COVER

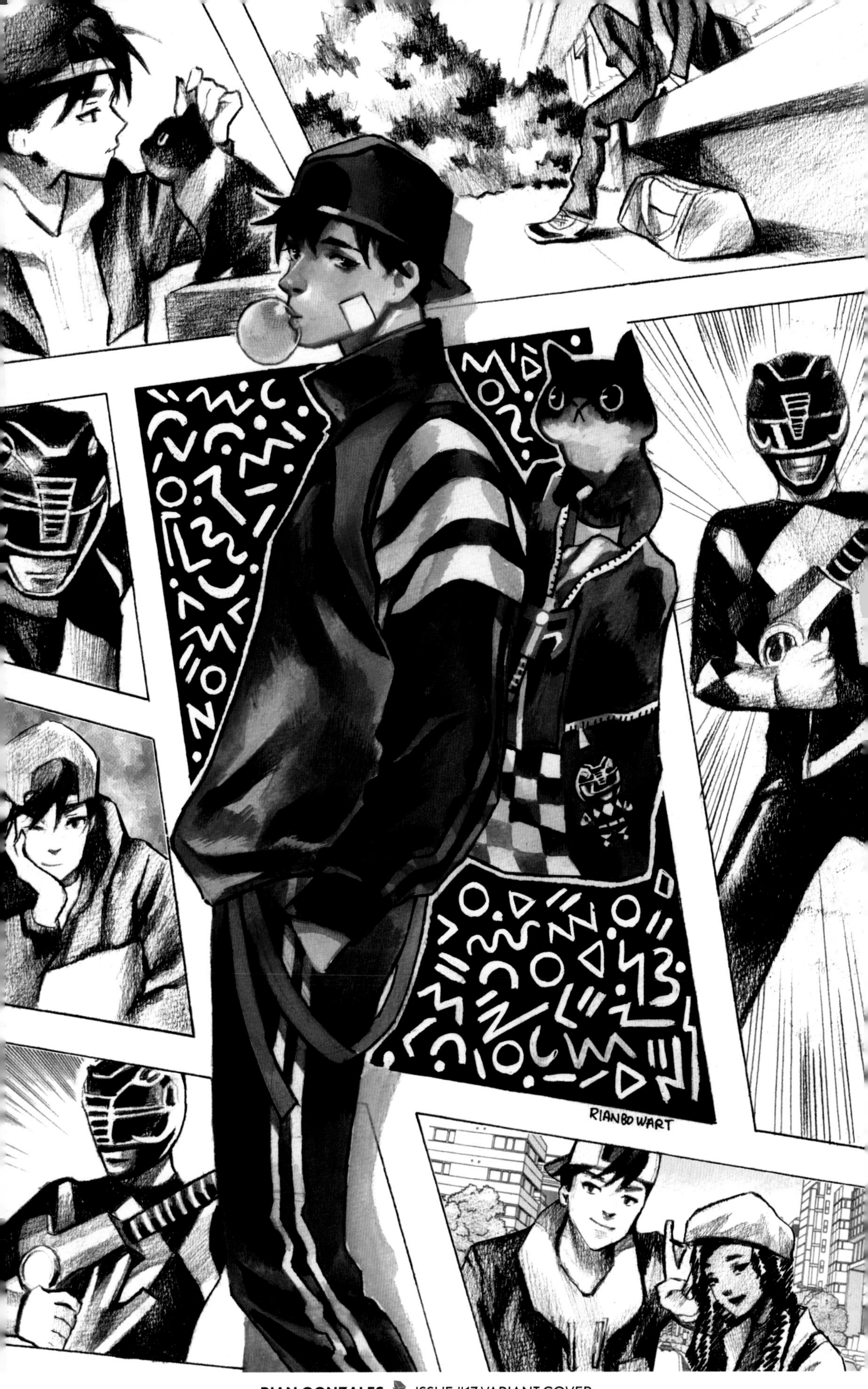
RIANBOWART

**RIAN GONZALES** ISSUE #17 VARIANT COVER

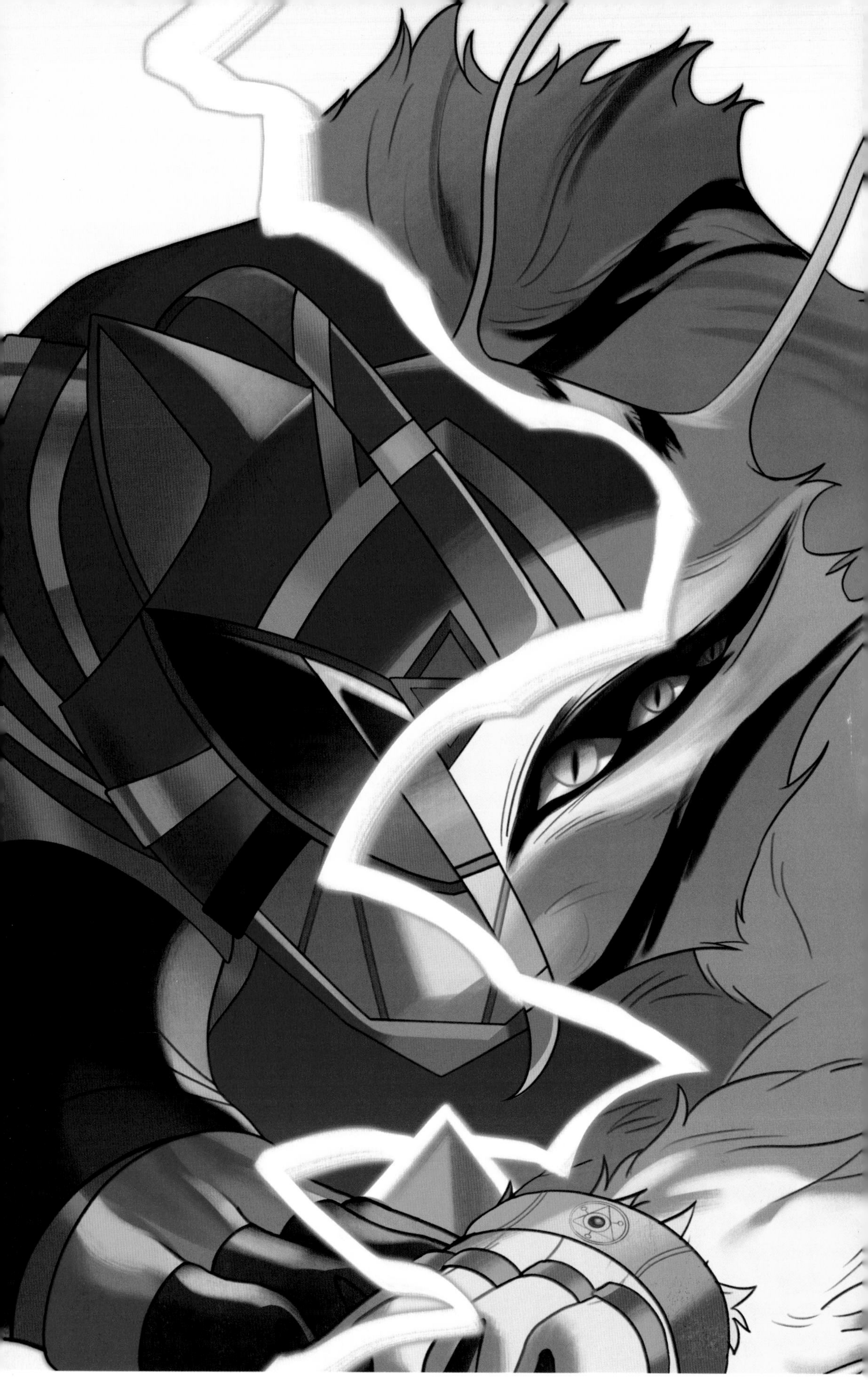

**YEJIN PARK** ISSUE #13 VARIANT COVER

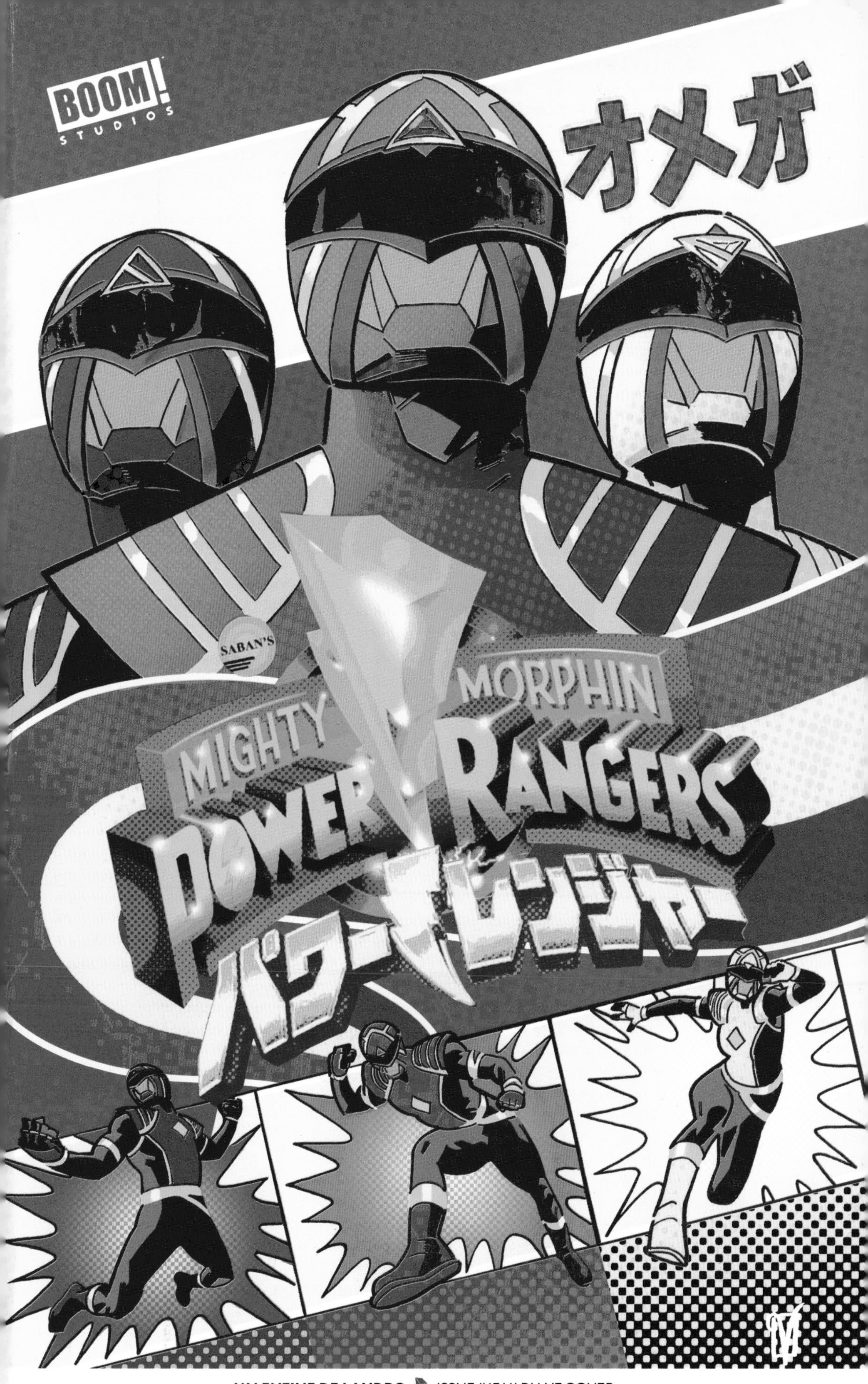
BOOM! STUDIOS
オメガ
SABAN'S
MIGHTY MORPHIN
POWER RANGERS
パワーレンジャー

**VALENTINE DE LANDRO** ISSUE #15 VARIANT COVER